COMICS

READERS' GUIDES TO ESSENTIAL CRITICISM SERIES

CONSULTANT EDITOR: NICOLAS TREDELL

COMICS AND GRAPHIC NOVELS

Julia Round, Rikke Platz Cortsen and Maaheen Ahmed

BLOOMSBURY ACADEMIC
LONDON • NEW YORK • OXFORD • NEW DELHI • SYDNEY

BLOOMSBURY ACADEMIC
Bloomsbury Publishing Plc
50 Bedford Square, London, WC1B 3DP, UK
1385 Broadway, New York, NY 10018, USA
29 Earlsfort Terrace, Dublin 2, Ireland

BLOOMSBURY, BLOOMSBURY ACADEMIC and the Diana logo are
trademarks of Bloomsbury Publishing Plc

First published in Great Britain 2023

A catalogue record for this book is available from the British Library.

Library of Congress Control Number: 2022938913

ISBN: HB: 978-1-3503-3610-0
         PB: 978-1-3503-3609-4
         ePDF: 978-1-3503-3608-7
         eBook: 978-1-3503-3607-0

Typeset by Integra Software Services Pvt. Ltd.
Printed and bound in Great Britain

To find out more about our authors and books visit www.bloomsbury.com
and sign up for our newsletters.

CONTENTS

Contents

ACKNOWLEDGEMENTS

The authors would like to collectively thank Nicolas Tredell for his constant support and advice throughout this project.

Julia Round's thanks must first go to Rikke and Maaheen for being the best collaborators she could have asked for. Also to Professor Roger Sabin for his invaluable advice during one of many panics over this project, and for being an ongoing support and inspiration. And finally, to the comics studies community at large, just for being some of the best people she has ever met – we wish we could have written about all your brilliant work.

Rikke Platz Cortsen would like to thank her co-authors Julia Round and Maaheen Ahmed for great collaboration and many productive, lively discussions on the topic of comics studies. She would also like to thank the many people who have thought, talked, drawn and written about comics, so we can all engage with their ideas and continue the conversation. Finally, she would like to thank her students for their eager participation in discussions of everything comics and the way they continue to challenge and change our understanding of comics and comics scholarship.

Maaheen Ahmed warmly thanks Rikke P. Cortsen and Julia Round. She would also like to thank all comics scholars for making the field what it is.

ABOUT THE AUTHORS

Dr Maaheen Ahmed is Associate Professor of Comparative Literature at Ghent University and principal investigator of COMICS, a multi-researcher project funded by the European Research Council, which pieces together a cultural history of children in European comics. Her previous research has focused on comics and semiotics and the relevance of good monsters in alternative comics. She also has a keen interest on the kinds of memories informing comics. For more on her work, please visit https://www.comics.ugent.be/maaheen-ahmed/.

Dr Rikke Platz Cortsen is an assistant lecturer at University College Copenhagen. Her research focuses on time and space in comics and the way identity is intertwined with place in contemporary Nordic comics. She co-edited the research anthology *Comics and Power* (2015) with Erin La Cour and Anne Magnussen. She shares her work at www.rpcortsen.com.

Dr Julia Round's research examines the intersections of Gothic, comics and children's literature. Her books include the award-winning *Gothic for Girls: Misty and British Comics* (2019), *Gothic in Comics and Graphic Novels: A Critical Approach* (2014) and the co-edited collection *Real Lives, Celebrity Stories* (2014). She is an associate professor at Bournemouth University, co-editor of *Studies in Comics* journal (Intellect) and the book series *Encapsulations* (University of Nebraska Press) and co-organizer of the annual International Graphic Novel and Comics Conference (IGNCC). She shares her work at www.juliaround.com.

CHAPTER 1
INTRODUCTION

While comics and graphic storytelling have been around for many hundreds (if not thousands) of years, critical and academic work in this field has only really developed over the last century. Despite this, comics scholarship has increased exponentially and at the time of writing comics studies is a vibrant and developing field with its own publishing imprints, scholarly journals, degree courses and international conferences. It benefits from the engagement and enthusiasm of both practitioners and researchers, and from the advantages of being a fairly new, very interdisciplinary field with a plethora of theoretical influences. However, the counterpoint to this is a lack of common vocabulary and a potential disconnect between scholarly developments. In particular, the discipline has suffered from a lack of translation, which has frequently kept entire strands of research separated from related areas of scholarship.

Comics studies, then, may already be a daunting place for the new scholar. This Essential Guide is aimed at students and researchers seeking an overview of the current state of the field. We have aimed to flag up the breadth and depth of comics scholarship: giving a selective overview and contextualization of the key research trends, debates and ideas that have emerged over the past decades. While we have sought to be international in scope, and to include a focus on comics beyond the Anglophone, we are simultaneously aware that the sheer quantity of scholarship published and a lack of translated work have made this an impossible task. As such, we make no claims for the exhaustive nature of this content: rather, we have noted those works that we feel give the clearest picture of where comics studies is right now, and that will provide a springboard for future researchers.

The following chapters are based around major clusters of scholarly conversations, but since these often wander across fields, there are necessarily overlaps and cross-references. Much of the theory developed in comics studies disregards what can be considered classic disciplinary borders. For example, any supposedly 'objective' discussion of formal elements in comics is never cleansed of ideological contents or able to be considered apart from the debates surrounding readership, historical development, genres or commercial interests. Any discussion of textbooks must take into account the genres and audiences involved. Analyses of creators are seldom separated from a discussion of their key works or their historiographic context. The arrangement of material in this book is thus intended to flag up shared arguments and also points of dispute, in order to give researchers a road map that signals where these points of interest cohere. For example, disputes continue around how to manage the dynamic relationship between word and image, or the grounding of critical models in particular disciplinary backgrounds; these discussions are heavily influenced by the cultural setting, the period in time, the relationship with legitimacy and the scholar's own attitude to comics, which can be viewed as an art form, a medium, a language, a cultural artefact or a mode of communication.

Our first part offers two complementary ways of 'Approaching Comics', bringing together the mechanics of the medium with its potential for meaning-making. Its opening chapter ('Formalist Approaches') begins by summarizing the critics and practitioners who have analysed the formal properties of the comics page. It covers attempts to define comics and arrive at a working model of 'how comics work' and how to read them, including semiotic, narratological and linguistic approaches. Our intent is not to foreground the definitional debate (which seems doomed to failure); instead this chapter notes the way in which such disputes can emphasize the flexibility of comics and the need for international dialogue. Chapter 3 ('Ideological and Material Approaches') then moves to treat those critics who have considered comics from particular ideological and material perspectives, including a focus on political meanings and propaganda, and their material and sensory aspects. It explores the manipulation of the superhero into a symbol of national identity and heroism, the recasting of comics as graphic novels, and technological advances that challenge our understanding of comics and their materiality.

In Part II, 'Histories and Cultures', we look towards the history of comics, considering some of the early works and the voices of critics, as well as more recent scholars who have written historical surveys of the field. Chapter 4 ('Early Criticism and Legitimation') takes in work from America and Europe, summarizing the early writings on comics from both regions and noting the ways in which these mobilized fears of mass culture or drew justification from folklore or myth. There is a close focus on the 1950s censorship debates around 'American-style' comics and a summary of criticism that has examined global attempts to legislate against comics.

The chapter concludes by comparing the discourses from both regions and reflecting on the different actors, forms and channels that narratives of legitimation have been linked to. Chapter 5 ('Historical Approaches') then surveys critical works that have documented comics history, separating this into particular regions (Europe, America, Asia and Africa) and sections on global histories and transnational works. It demonstrates the comics medium's breath and variety, but notes that historical approaches with a strict national focus often follow the same strategies, while newer approaches instead bring together historical perspectives with shared themes rather than geographies.

Part III ('Production and Reception') is dedicated to work on major creators and the way certain imprints and magazines have shaped comics as well as the way audiences have engaged with the materials through multiple platforms. Chapter 6 ('Creators, Imprints and Titles') begins chronologically with some of the early comics creators and then moves on to artists who have come to the fore in serialized comic form. These early comics artists are often male, and the research tends to focus on their auteur character, but the chapter also offers an overview of existing research on female creators. The term 'graphic novel' gave birth to an interest in the 'graphic novelists' who create them and the auteur debate continues to be at the centre of how individual writers and artists are perceived as essential for the creation of these works. However, as the final section of the chapter shows, magazines and periodicals offer deeper and more holistic insights into the place of comics in cultural history and play an important part in how creators get presented and circulated to audiences. These readers and fans are then the key subjects of study in the works presented in Chapter 7 ('Audiences and Fan Cultures') which reveals that the first forays into studies of comics readers were sceptical and openly dismissive of mass culture. In the early ages of comics criticism, the reception of comics through readers' engagement was considered at best a lazy kind of consumption, at worst a potentially harmful relationship with arguments founded in speculation rather than actual interviews with audiences. This changes in the second part of this chapter which focuses on studies of comics and manga readers using interviews and readings of letter columns: revealing more complex effects and increased agency in the ways that readers relate to the medium. Complex interactions with the medium take centre stage in the discussion of 'fan' as an important label in comics culture that can be empowering and create community. Fan studies in comics look at the distinct practices of collecting, costuming and connecting through discussions about comics.

Studies show how these practices can be influenced by and reflect social and historical contexts or be gendered in very specific ways.

The final part of this book (Part IV, 'Themes and Genres') focuses on different themes that have characterized the comics medium both historically and recently. It also examines how certain genres within comics have dominated the field. These genres have often been conflated with the medium itself just as certain themes have come to signify the graphic novel as it climbed up the Top 20s of literary lists, but other aspects of comics that are less commonly known are also explored as we venture off the beaten path and look at scholarship outside the mainstream. The thematic concerns of Chapter 8 ('Thematic Approaches') run in many directions as the themes of comics have not been consistent, but rather spread across the medium in unpredictable ways that often coincide with the cultural and historical context. The once-novel idea that comics could deal with serious topics has blossomed into a wide variety of solemn themes which have in turn garnered attention from scholars: documentary, trauma, history and memory are all popular examples of the gravity that has marked comics in recent years. These are considered, alongside a focus on ethnicity, childhood, and transmediality, intermediality, and adaptation, which acquire importance as comics migrate into other media and provide new versions of known stories. The multiple character of themes found in comics also applies to the genres discussed in Chapter 9 ('Popular Genres') which begins by noting the way genre has sometimes been equated with medium when it comes to comics. The superhero is a genre born in the medium of comics and has consequently attracted a significant body of scholarship specifically dealing with the particularities of this genre. The chapter also discusses the genres of horror and romance, noting how horror in comics has a special history with censorships and the Comics Code, and exploring the ways that romance has been heavily gendered and thus received less serious and critical attention despite its immense popularity. Chapter 10 ('Outside the Mainstream') covers alternative independent and small press practices, focusing primarily on Anglophone and Francophone productions and interrogating their differences and overlaps. After tracing the rise of underground comix in the United States and the UK, the chapter examines scholarship on autobiographical comics ('autobiographix'). It also explores the discussions surrounding fanzines in the English-speaking world, before turning to the experimentations and market positioning of French and Belgian artists' collectives (L'Association and FRMK), considering material on European fanzines, and themes such as abstraction in comics. Chapter 11

('General Reference Guides and Textbooks') then introduces key 'how to' guides and textbooks. This covers books on teaching comics, making comics and studying comics, and focuses on material that provides accessible and comprehensive introductions into each of these three main aspects of comics studies. Our conclusion wraps up the Guide by delineating the major trends in recent comics scholarship and pointing to persisting gaps.

While an undertaking like this Guide can never be exhaustive, and many excellent publications and whole critical areas have had to be omitted, we hope that our selection gives a useful picture of comics studies in 2020: highlighting key critical developments and signposting areas rich for investigation. Our references have been organized by theme/chapter and we invite readers to consult individual chapters and sections as needed: each chapter functions as a complete text, and connections to other chapters are regularly flagged. This Guide is meant as a road into the field for newcomers and a point of departure for discussion for comics scholars and other interested readers. As comics studies has grown rapidly in recent years, we hope this Guide will offer a useful overview for researchers and readers from diverse areas of interest and encourage them to build on the scholarship already out there. The Guide also aspires to help in the creation of new scholarship by laying out existing paths of inquiry as well as identifying spots where more work is needed.

PART I
APPROACHING COMICS

CHAPTER 2
FORMALIST APPROACHES

This chapter focuses on the various critics and practitioners who have analysed the formal properties of the comics page and comics narratology. It opens by discussing the development of attempts to define comics, and the contributions of practitioners such as Scott McCloud and Will Eisner, who were among the first to attempt to offer theories of 'how comics work' and how to read them. McCloud's theory in particular, although now largely disproved and critiqued, has had great significance as a genuine attempt to cohere and explain the narrative practices and idiosyncrasies of comics. The second section then surveys semiotic approaches to comics, including Charles Hatfield's 'art of tensions' and the groundbreaking work of Belgian theorist Thierry Groensteen, whose 'system of comics' proposes a semiotic analysis in which all elements of the page are interdependent. Formal concerns in comics often tie in with narratology; certain scholars have paid special attention to this as well as to the relationship between comics narratology and a broader cultural perspective concerned with how narratology can be spread across media. The fourth and final section looks at emergent work that approaches comics as a language, covering cognitive and social linguistics.

One of the challenges of global comics studies scholarship is translation and this impacts the development of theories about the formal analysis of comics because the wheel is invented over and over again and groundbreaking points made in one part of the world might not make it to the other side of it. Historically, the three main areas of comics production have been Anglophone, Francophone and Japanophone and they each had their own theorists, but as English has become the *lingua franca* of the research world, not many theoretical works on comics have made it into English from French and Japanese, just as English works are very rarely translated into other languages. This limits the possible interaction between scholars and makes researchers not fluent in these other languages reliant upon other scholars' retelling and re-interpretation of original scholarly work.

Early definitions and approaches

Just like debates about the 'first' comic strip, the attempt to answer the question of 'what is a comic' seems doomed to failure and, more importantly, of questionable value. A central character in both discussions is Swiss artist Rodolphe Töpffer who is not only a contender for the creator of one of the first comics (see Chapter 6 on Kunzle's *Father of the Comics Strip* and Groensteen's *M. Töpffer invente la bande dessinée*), but also one of the first in a long tradition of artists who write poetics of or theoretical musings on their work and thus contribute to the development of a field of comics studies that includes more formal considerations. Though Rodolphe Töpffer is not much help in the discussions of a definition of comics, he has been mentioned as one of the first to consider the mechanics and effects of comics, and he does point to some of the aspects of the comics form that later become staples in the theories of comics.

In his 'Essai de Physiognomonie' ['Essay on Physiognomy'] (1845), Töpffer comes close to pointing at sequentiality as a factor in what the English translation calls 'picture-stories' when he describes how he creates characters by putting them together in a scene and how this scene then initiates a new scene that calls for a previous scene and the picture-story in a series of scenes starts to be created (1965: 14). The sequence of what came before and what comes after an improvised scene is what makes the early stages of a picture-story.

For Töpffer, an essential factor in the creation of picture-stories is line drawing, in that it allows for clarity and a more accessible story because even less experienced readers can clearly understand what is being told to them. This interest in clarity of expression as something central for the picture-stories that will later be classified as comics preoccupies Töpffer for the remainder of the essay where he meticulously examines and classifies the ways subtle changes in the lines drawn in a face can change the expression and the reader's impression of the character and emotional state – a point Will Eisner later also spends much time exploring. Most importantly, Töpffer employs 'graphic examples' to support his claims and uses small variations of a drawing to prove his theses about picture-stories which emphasizes the dynamic relationship between theory and practice that continues to be a central way of analysing comics. By focusing on narrative succession, the effects of line drawing, the importance of microsemiotic variance and the fragment vs. the whole, Töpffer in this early work touches upon ideas that have proven essential in later definitions and discussions of the mechanics of comics.

Töpffer also in his writings mentions another central issue in comics studies: the nature of his publication as inherently mixed. He points out that neither the text nor the images can stand alone because they are meaningless without each other (Grove, 2010: 93). This is something that later plays an important role in definitions of comics discussions.

If we turn our attention back to the question of defining comics, David Kunzle's *History of the Comic Strip* (1973) (discussed in more detail in Chapter 4) epitomizes the central problem of definition when it comes to comics: that the definer will arrive at a culturally specific and self-fulfilling set of criteria which can vary wildly. Kunzle surveys a corpus of early comic strips and arrives at a four-part definition that claims a comic must: (1) consist of a sequence of separate images; (2) deploy images that dominate the text; (3) be intended for mass circulation and reproduction; and (4) tell a story that is both moral and topical. As Thierry Groensteen points out in 'Définitions' (2012) – discussed in detail below – the imprecision and traditional focus (print-dominated) of this definition make it untenable as comics move towards a digital format (2014).

Perhaps the most widely circulated and quoted definition of comics was coined by comics creator Scott McCloud, who in turn derives most of the inspiration for his definition from comics creator Will Eisner. Renowned for his work on the comic strip *The Spirit* (1940–1952) and the popularization of the term 'graphic novel', Will Eisner was also one of the first in English to present a sustained and in-depth discussion of the mechanics of comics as an art form in the seminal *Comics and Sequential Art* (1985). Eisner is an example of the many artist/theorists that populate the field of comics studies, formulating theories about the inner workings of comics developed from their own hands-on experience and as such, his works are peppered with illustrative examples by himself in support of his claims about how comics work. In *Comics and Sequential Art*, Will Eisner proposes the term 'sequential art' as a way to create a distinct discipline preoccupied with how text and images can tell stories and express ideas together. In his later *Graphic Storytelling & Visual Narrative* (1996), sequential art is defined as 'a train of images deployed in sequence', whereas comics are defined as 'the printed arrangement of art and balloons in sequence, particularly as in comic books' (1996: 6). Most importantly, many of the later debates on definitions of comics revolve around these central points: images in sequence, text and image together, and narrative content. In writing about comics, Eisner relies on his experiences of a class taught at the School of Visual Arts in New York, and the focus is on the effects of the individual elements of comics rather than on providing a more rigorous academic analysis. However, in his careful unpacking of how the relationship between text and image works, the visual appearance of text, the storytelling abilities of images and the structuring of page layouts, Will Eisner provides the stepping stones for many formalist discussions in comics studies.

Scott McCloud takes the double role of artist/theorist a step further in *Understanding Comics – The Invisible Art* (1993), where he presents his discussion of comics drawn as a comic with himself as the main protagonist. The book has been immensely important for comics studies as a comprehensive attempt at taking the study of comics seriously and for creating a base of claims that later scholarship has engaged with. Because of its comics form it is approachable and is still widely used in the teaching of comics theory and practice. In the effort to define comics, McCloud builds on Will Eisner's very broad definition (which also includes forms of art other than comics) and develops a definition that to this day is the point of departure for discussions of comics, even if it has been thoroughly criticized: 'Juxtaposed pictorial and other images in deliberate sequence, intended to convey information and/or to produce an aesthetic response in the viewer' (1993: 9). McCloud's definition addresses a need within the study of comics to define what the subject of comics studies is, but runs into some of the problems mentioned above, where the defining of comics becomes a culturally specific and potentially ideological endeavour. At the time when McCloud wrote his book, the need for legitimization of the art form (as discussed in Chapter 4) was a pressing concern and McCloud's discussion of a definition takes great pains to connect contemporary comics to older more established pieces from art history like Egyptian hieroglyphs and the Bayeux Tapestry. As Aaron Meskin notes in his discussion of the problem of definition, McCloud's effort to be precise is simultaneously too broad and too narrow (2007: 370). John Holbo in his comments on McCloud's definition also notes that the process of defining comics very quickly becomes a sorting game where it has to be decided what goes in the definition or not (2012: 5–6). This can result in the reverse, where the works that are thought to be obviously 'comics' might determine how broad the definition becomes. McCloud insists on excluding single panel cartoons from the definition of comics, but Holbo suggests that a gutter within the panel can be implied. Holbo argues that wordless and pictureless graphic novels can be included in the definition, which ends up including literature and pictures in the definition of comics. Both Meskin and Holbo are critical of the need of a definition, certainly one that is founded upon formal criteria.

The understanding of the comics medium as one that is dependent upon the interaction of text and image is present from the very beginning of defining discussions, as we saw with Rodolphe Töpffer. It has been called 'imagetext', a term suggested by W.J.T. Mitchell in his influential essay 'Beyond Comparison' as a moniker for the composite, synthetic mixture of text and image, as opposed to 'image/text' to signal the fissure or gap between text and image in combination, and 'image-text' to designate the relations between the two in mixed media. Mitchell explicitly mentions comic strips as an example of imagetext and underlines that this combination involves a relation between image and text that require a mixing of the two media in a way that designates special functions to each of them. In his re-description of the relationship between image and text, Mitchell is in conversation with the tradition of '*ut pictura poesis*' (as is painting, so is poetry), discussing the similarities between poetry and painting and the 'sister arts' idea that looks at what the two arts have in common and how they can relate to each other. Mitchell very explicitly refuses purist conceptions of the arts within theories of literature and art that is adverse to any kind of mixing and instead argues that all images have some detectable verbal qualities as well as all text has visual aspects – the question is to what degree they are mixed and how that relation works. In an explicit discussion of G.E. Lessing's thesis that poetry and painting have separate domains, Mitchell criticizes this as something that originates in a distinction of value between the two, where text (poetry) is often considered the finer and image (painting) is seen as something that 'pollutes' the pureness of the text (1986: 106–107, 111–112). Lessing's essay poses time and space as the domains that poetry and painting work in, which are then often assigned to text and image as their domains too (1874). Although Mitchell sees this as an ideological attempt to elevate poetry above painting, this distinction is discussed as one that accounts for various aspects of the way comics work as a mixture of text and image.

In 'Definitions', Groensteen's survey of the historical development of definitions in different countries indicates the cultural specificity of what makes a comic: bandes dessinées [literally meaning 'drawn strips'] emerged in the 1940s in France after dalliance with multiple other terms including '*histoires en images*' [stories in pictures] '*films dessinés*' [drawn films] and '*récits illustrés*' [drawn stories]. 'Strips' as used here refers to the rows of images rather than the daily news strips (which are less widespread in the French press). The perception in France is that 'comics' refers to American texts just as 'manga' refers to Japanese. Groensteen also considers Italian '*fumetti*' [literally 'puffs of smoke' to mean speech balloons, although paradoxically, *fumetti* is often used to describe older comics where the text is captioned]. He surveys the Spanish terminology ('*tebeo*' [derived from the magazine title *T.B.O.*] or '*monitos*' [little sketches], the latter also used in Mexico), the German '*bildergeschichten*' [picture stories] and its Dutch counterpart '*beeldverhaalen*' [picture stories] (a more usual modern term is '*stripverhaalen*' [strip stories]). As well as noting the American cultural specificity of the term 'comics' (and its derivations, such as the Japanese '*komikkusu*'), he reflects upon the impact of lexical choice and connotations and is adamant that the choice of words is always meaningful. The different ways different cultures name the medium of comics points to what is considered characteristic. Thus, the French term '*bandes dessinées*' (drawn strips/bands) highlights the composition and arrangement of the images as well their mode of creation, whereas 'funnies' or 'comics' focuses on content and genre and their effect on audiences: to make people laugh. Groensteen also notes how the Chinese '*liánhuánhuà*' [linked images] emphasizes the sequentiality of comics whereas '*historieta*', '*bildergeschichten*' and '*stripverhaalen*' are preoccupied with what they do: namely telling stories, recounting narratives (2014).

Groensteen also notes that adopting a definition implicitly limits a corpus and thus often excludes atypical or experimental work. He draws attention to a number of critics who have done this and the consequences. He cites four key issues that problematize the possibility of an inclusive definition: 'abstract comics' (which do not have a sequential narrative aim); the differences between manga and bande dessinée (such as the breakdown of action, expressivity of characters, mixture of graphic styles, portrayal of movement and sound, layout, and so forth); the emergence of digital platforms; and the demands of different formats such as the graphic novel and artist's book. Ultimately he rejects the 'essentialist approach' and instead argues for a definition of comics that takes account of the 'infinite cycle of rebirths and redefinitions' (2012: 103) and which has been proposed by critics such as Thierry Smolderen and Harry Morgan. These critics denounce the notion of progress and instead argue for a relativist definition that does not view the different comics forms as evolutionary but instead discusses the suitability of each iteration of the medium for its time. Groensteen argues that the disputes are emblematic of an underlying debate between whether comics' strengths are primarily polysemiotic (due to the encounter between text and image) or sequential (based on the juxtaposition of images). This leads him to his hybrid and systemic definition that will be discussed more fully below.

McCloud's focus on sequentiality and images in sequence, which he inherits from Eisner, makes him concentrate on panel transitions rather than the composition of whole pages, as well as on the way the panels as fragments in comics are combined to make a coherent narrative or environment. He grounds this in his understanding of human perception as a process of piecing together bits of visual information to establish our surroundings and assume the existence of parts that are not immediately visible to the observer. This process of noticing individual visual and verbal fragments, and then constructing a narrative from them, is what McCloud calls 'closure' and he considers this mechanism as essential to the way comics work as a medium. As panels fracture the events that they are conveying into unconnected moments, it is closure that allows the human mind to put together these moments and arrange them into a reality that makes sense and seems whole. This leads McCloud to designate the space between panels as an important threshold that signals the gap the reader has to suture in their mind in order to link fragments together and form a coherent narrative or scene.

Panel transitions are categorized by McCloud according to the amount of effort required by the reader to bridge the gap between them and make sense of the sequence. This results in six different categorizations that progress from points in time and space that are fairly close to each other (1: moment-to-moment, 2: action-to-action) through transitions that span a greater gulf in time and/or space (3: subject-to-subject, 4: scene-to-scene) to transitions that either bypass time (5: aspect-to-aspect) or seem to present a nonsensical or opaque logic that makes the reader's effort to understand all the more greater (6: non-sequitur) (1993: 70–73). By using a count of the frequency of the types of panel transitions McCloud claims to be able to spot structural differences between different comics cultures, such as the Japanese manga and American mainstream comics. McCloud proposes that manga differ formally from comics in that they are more expansive and use more images on a scene, but Ingulsrud and Allen in their book *Reading Japan Cool* (2009) express scepticism by noting that McCloud does not go into detail with his research methodologies in this study and that their own attempts to recreate his results have not been successful. This is significant because McCloud's points on manga risk becoming the one truth because of the lack of translated theory on manga. In their presentation of manga, Ingulsrud and Allen provide a short walk-through of Japanese manga research and short summaries of titles written in Japanese, which serve as an overview for the reader who is prevented from accessing these titles in the original language.

Comics theory (like many cultural critical fields) suffers from the lack of translation of research, and in the case of McCloud's panel transitions it is noticeable that the Japanese manga critic and artist Natsume Fusanosuke in his 'manga criticism through manga' pays attention to the formal elements of manga and their impact on the enjoyment that the manga reader experiences. In his 1988 manga criticism *Natsume Fusanosuke manga gaku*, of which a small portion is translated in the journal *Mechademia* vol. 3, (2008), Natsume examines the formal properties of manga through a representation of himself in manga form. In the excerpt from *Mechademia*, the historical development of images, captions and speech balloons is laid out, and Natsume uses this as a stepping stone to discuss the nature of panels, pacing and the function of the frame surrounding panels. Natsume focuses on the way framing constitutes narrative: '[…] in manga, the edge of the frame represents order itself that which sustains the drawings' sense of reality. If the frame should become fluid and unpredictable, the sense of reality gives way to insecurity. And if this technique is pushed to extremes, the narrative completely collapses.' (2008, 70) Just like McCloud, Natsume emphasizes the transition between panels and the framing of them as essential to the way reality is constructed and held up in manga.

A Japanese critic who builds on Natsume's theories is Itō Gō whose important work *Tezuka izu deddo* [*Tezuka is Dead*] from 2005 develops Natsume's focus on reception and reader pleasure as well as attempts to build a theoretical system for analysis of manga. In the excerpt from the introduction to the book, Itō criticizes the dominance of Tezuka Osamu in the history and criticism of manga and insists on building an analytical framework that takes into account more recent and overlooked manga. In Itō's opinion, the risk of neglecting more recent manga is a manga criticism that is perceived as irrelevant to younger audiences and only preoccupied with old manga, potentially making the theorization of manga stale and too dependent upon an icon like Tezuka (2011: 79).

The way both Natsume and Itō identify the reader and their engagement with the material as important factors in the creation of meaning in comics is also at the centre of Scott McCloud's comics theory because closure is created by the reader. McCloud underscores that the reader's imagination is what connects the slivers of information and decides what happened based on the panels laid out by the artists. This emphasis on reader involvement as another remarkable aspect of how comics work in order to make meaning, along with the idea of comics as fragmented, comes from the Canadian media theorist Marshall McLuhan. In his book *Understanding Media – The*

Extensions of Man (1964), he contended that woodcuts like the modern comic strip and comic book do not give much information about the individual moments or things but that it is instead the job of the reader to combine the little information given into a complete story by noticing the elements of meaning provided in the adjoining panels. As the similarity in the titles of their books suggests, McLuhan is a great inspiration for the way McCloud understands comics as a medium and it is from his ideas that McCloud further develops his descriptions of the mechanics of comics.

McCloud's attention to the way time and space play a significant role in the reader's experience of comics and to the way comics are structured leads him to yet another formal point that has become a central issue for comics scholars. McCloud notices how the combination of images in sequence and text in speech balloons, captions and sound effects allows for a complication of temporality in comics that is grounded in the way time is organized spatially on a comics page. Once again, McCloud places the reader at the centre of comics mechanics, when he explains that the reader of comics has been trained to think of time as spatial, claiming that in comics 'time and space are one and the same'. (100) According to McCloud, this means that the spatial proportions of panels and pages in comics can affect the temporality of a story when the reader fills in the blanks and perceives this spatio-temporal correlation. In this idea, McCloud is once again following Will Eisner who noted that: 'Once established and set in sequence the box or panel becomes the criterion by which to judge the illusion of time' (1985: 26); but the emphasis on illusion is less pronounced in McCloud's account.

Understanding Comics has served as a point of departure for many discussions of how comics work and although McCloud's thoughts on comics are often discussed as a theoretical framework that can be easily accessed and one that is taught in many beginners' classes of comics, many scholars have challenged McCloud's ideas and some of the criticisms highlight important differences in how comics are perceived to work. Neil Cohn, whose work will later be discussed specifically in relation to theories of comics as language, criticizes the concept of closure that makes the space between the panels the main place where mental processing happens; he points out that the process of making sense of the panel transition happens in a backwards direction, when the reader reaches the second panel (2010: 135). In this same article, Cohn also disputes McCloud's time=space thesis by arguing that this idea of 'temporal mapping' rests on a false proposition that panels are the same as moments and that this in turn makes McCloud suppose that the physical space of the page is the same as the temporality the reader transverses in their reading process which then in turn becomes the same as the fictive time in the story which is being read. This notion does not account for the ways time can be prolonged in panels or for non-linear reading patterns.

In his step-by-step criticism of *Understanding Comics*, 'Inventing Comics' (2001), comics artist Dylan Horrocks begins by underlining that part of the problem with McCloud's work is that his theory should be contested, but that too many readers have accepted both his definition and key concepts as indisputable truths. He then discusses how the rhetoric of McCloud helps shape his arguments and ends by suggesting that many of the essentialist definitions of comics are policing borders in a way that ends up determining what qualifies as a comic. Horrocks sees the logophobia of comics theorists that emphasize image over text in comics as a way of making a clear distinction between comics and illustrated texts (like children's books) and notes how McCloud places himself directly in a very old 'war between words and pictures' (2001: 37). This discussion (or 'war') of text and image is an important ground for a criticism of McCloud's definition that often surfaces and is expressed by comics artist R.C. Harvey, who throughout the years has continued to object to the lack of attention paid to verbal content in comics. Harvey insists that text as speech is an essential and unavoidable part of any definition of comics, because speech balloons are something unique to the form.

Semiotic approaches

Defining comics has proven a seemingly impossible and enervating task, but plenty of energy has been poured into thinking about how comics work and how they make meaning. Formal approaches give the impression of making universalist points, but due to their cumulative advances on existing models and points drawn from certain local examples of material, they can often seem very culturally specific. When looking at the formal elements in comics, it can be difficult to draw a clear-cut line between semiotics and linguistics because the approaches are often mixed when analysing comics or used as metaphors or in imprecise ways that do not have the same specific meanings in the original disciplines. In this section, the development of theoretical models from Francophone and Anglophone thinkers will be considered, as these have dominated the subfield of formal comics studies – but one of the earliest semioticians who studied comics is Italian.

With Umberto Eco's writings on comic strips, the medium gets a serious treatment by a curious reader who is interested in it because of its power to communicate and influence readers emotionally, but who insists on close reading the elements of comics to look at their meaning-making and the significance of myth in comics. Eco's work demonstrates how difficult it can be to draw a clear line between scholarship that is 'semiotic', 'linguistic' or 'narratological' in that these approaches often influence each other in the study of comics. Eco's essay 'Il mito di "Superman"' (1962) ['The Myth of Superman'] (1972) (discussed in Chapter 4) has a prominent place in comics scholarship because it offers a reading of Superman as myth in the interpretative semiotic tradition and addresses the double nature of superhero comics stories in that the hero has to navigate the continued progression of a serialized narrative but is also influenced by his mythic quality which keeps repeating over and over again.

As Marc Singer has argued, Eco's reading has been interpreted, re-interpreted and misunderstood in a number of ways, especially in superhero scholarship (2019: 36–58). Eco's interest in studying comic strips and comic books from Superman through Peanuts to Batman and his fascination with understanding how they work and their relevance at a relatively early stage in the theoretical canon has proved an important point of departure for the study of comics.

The French Comics Theory Reader dedicates a section to 'Formal Approaches' and its introduction to the selection of texts reproduced in this volume offers a clear narrative of the development of specific models for comics analysis in Francophone scholarship. It begins by mentioning how Gérard Genette's landmark text *Figures III* [*Narrative Discourse*] (1972) proposes an initial brief model that the photo story or comics page invites a 'dual reading process, both successive and global' (Miller and Beaty, 2014: 116).

Pierre Fresnault-Deruelle in 'From Linear to Tabular' (1976) extends this to consider the ways in which the reader's awareness of (two-dimensional) patterns on the page can affect their understanding of the (three-dimensional) panel content and notes that meanings can thus be generated by the overall composition. He draws attention to the specific practices of the strip (the sequential row of panels) and the page, pointing out that each has its own domain, where the strip is temporal (linear) and the page is spatial (tabular) (121). Fresnault-Deruelle proceeds to inventory various types of strips according to their genre, noting that, within these, specific narrative techniques emerge that are led not by content but by form. For example, the hope-followed-by-failure plot in Peanuts strips: whereby Charles Schulz has made the formal construction of his portrayed world match the day-to-day production of the strip and made what might be considered a limitation into an advantage. Charles Schulz has perfected the repetition in his strip to make small variations of a theme in a way that makes these variations the centre of the excitement. This contrasts with the continuing strips that, in the interests of protracting the story, use what Fresnault-Deruelle names the 'point switching technique': halting the narrative and instead exploring different aspects of the same story. When this occurs, the 'stripological' syntagm is hiding an iconic sequence of what is deemed a 'paradigmatic type' so that the comics artist has greater freedom to show aspects of a scene and showcase different points of view.

As comics progressed, the composition of the page became a tool to integrate visual aspects such as form, surface, value and colour. Thus, Fresnault-Deruelle suggests that a tension arises (a term also employed by Charles Hatfield, see below) due to an 'ambiguity between the codes of representation (across the surface of the page) and those of the events represented (the three-dimensional fictional world). The page functions both as system (signifier) and matter (signified)' (130). Thus, the grid emerges as an arbitrary set of signifiers that guarantees discursive iconic potential: the artist's style has to work within a code that allows variations of format within and can also operate at the level of the book. In this way comics can break with a one-directional narrative mode by changing the set pattern of panels and making the most of the visual aspects of the medium. Fresnault-Deruelle draws attention to the different usages of this dichotomy in various comics and concludes that this dynamic function of 'iconographic intertextuality' evidences the beginnings of a new art form.

In a 1988 article, 'La Narration comme supplement: archéologie des fondations infra-narratives de la bande dessinée', Thierry Groensteen contributes heavily to the devising of a narrative model that will be specific to comics. Groensteen performs an experiment to explore the potential dominance of the visual in comics and expose the assumptions critics and scholars often make about the primacy of narration. Groensteen puts six unrelated panels from different artists onto a 'protopage' and establishes four interpretive effects that the reader performs to create association. These are (1) the citation effect (attached to each panel as it seems to refer to an implicit source); (2) the repertoire effect (produced by gathering disparate images together); (3) the configuration effect (global visual qualities of the page that create harmonies or oppositions between panels and allow them to produce meaning not just separately but as a group); and (4) the effect of stylistic uniformity (as regularity insinuates that the images are linked). Drawing on Balthazar Kaplan and Gilles Deleuze, Groensteen explores the variety of ways in which images can confront each other, identifying five primary distributive functions (principles that motivate the arrangement of images). These are (1) amalgam (simple juxtaposition); (2) inventory (sharing a thematic repertoire); (3) variation (sharing a paradigmatic class); (4) inflection (repetition of a motif with different treatment); and (5) decomposition (juxtaposing details from the same motif). He then notes two additional factors that combine with the five primary distributive functions to organize the page. The first is the presence of a key: a textual element that justifies the selection, and which can be internal (appears on the page) or external (found outside the page, e.g. in the title or in another text). The second factor is *mise en série*, which results from the intersection of two distributive functions and produces a recurrence of the same motif. Groensteen uses these categories to conclude that there are different stages of 'narrative crystallization' and to produce his definitions of a string ('a linear or tabular succession of disparate images, whose ordering is neither externally nor internally determined; it is the product of an amalgam'); a series ('a continuous or discontinuous succession of images linked by a system of iconic, visual or semantic correspondences' as produced by his primary distributive functions); and a sequence ('a succession of images whose syntagmatic linkage is determined by a narrative project') (1988: 176). He concludes that this theoretical framework will open up new analytical models that can be truly specific to comics, and indeed the impact of his subsequent monograph *Système de la Bande Dessinée* (1999) [*The System of Comics* (2007)] (see below) would seem to bear this out.

Benoît Peeters' typology of layout types in *Case, Planche, Récit* (1991) builds on this approach as well as Fresnault-Deruelle's concept of the comics page as structured as both linear and tabular, demonstrating how different types of layouts depend on whether the demands of narrative (linear) or composition (tabular) are privileged. Peeters designates four different kinds of layout: conventional, decorative, rhetorical and productive (translation online, 1). In the conventional layout, the regular grid of the 'waffle iron' is completely independent of the narrative of the story, which is reminiscent of the way the pages had to be divisible into strips in early comics publishing. In the decorative layout, the page is arranged in a way that looks interesting from the perspective of the page, but it is not dictated by the story, whereas the rhetorical layout shapes the panels to support the narrative, and the productive layout arranges the spatial disposition of the page in a way that makes new narratives possible. The latter two layouts have the composition of the page and the narrative working together and supporting each other in different ways, as opposed to the conventional layout that makes space for the narrative and the decorative layout where the aesthetics of the page layout dominates the narrative.

These experiments and critical models addressing the semiotics of layout have sparked new conversations. In his comment on the translation of Peeters' work in the journal *ImageText*, Jesse Cohn comments on the criticisms that have been put forward of Peeters' classification of page layout and points out the way the categories are not necessarily clearly distinguishable (2007: 2–6)[1]. Further, Cohn discusses how Peeters' conception of page layout confuses the description of an objective structure of narrative with the experience of the reader who engages with it. Pointing to the gap between Anglophone and Francophone comics scholarship, Cohn also notes that the problem of translation of French terms for the structure of the page is a challenge which can influence the cross-cultural understanding of theories of page layout.

As Cohn notes in his comment, Peeters' classification has been influential in Francophone scholarship, and Thierry Groensteen's *Systéme de la Bande Dessinée* builds on Peeters' concepts and seeks to classify the comics layout in terms of regularity or irregularity, and ostentation versus discreteness. Renaud Chavanne (2010) then develops and problematizes the concept of regularity by introducing a model that considers degrees of semi-regularity and using this to analyse the effect of page composition.

Groensteen's *The System of Comics* is one of the works most clearly working with semiotics and before its translation into English in 2007 it had already had a profound impact on comics scholarship because of its very systematic walk-through of the specific elements of comics, and its combination of a range of theories with special attention to how these theories work in comics as well as analysis of material that was not solely picked from a Francophone canon. Groensteen begins by calling comics 'a language' but uses this to distinguish his approach from sociological or historical studies of comics. He describes his approach as 'neo-semiotic', in opposition to a semiotics concerned with ideas of finding the smallest possible unit of meaning within panels by categorizing drawing styles or specific types of marks. Rather than breaking down panels into even smaller units, Groensteen is interested in comics as a system in which panels (which he designates as the smallest unit of meaning) relate to each other – a principle he calls 'iconic solidarity'. The description of how iconic solidarity works is central in Groensteen's theory of comics because he sees the co-existence of panels in the space of the page as an important factor in how meaning is created in the art form. He focuses first on what he calls the 'spatio-topical' system – the positioning of panels on a page and the importance of site, form and area – to describe how these aspects of the panels help create meaning. This emphasis on the space of comics also underlines the importance of margins, different functions of frames, page layout and placement of speech balloons as aspects that all can intentionally manipulate the content of the narrative in specific ways.

Groensteen's other central concept is 'arthrology' which indicates the way panels can articulate meaning in their relation to each other, either across a sequence ('restricted arthrology'), or across an entire work ('general arthrology'). In looking at sequences and the processes of restricted arthrology, Groensteen notes how narrative is determined by 'pluri-vectoriality', in which the combination of panels to make meaning happens in several directions, not just moving forward sequentially.

This pluri-vectoriality also extends to how Groensteen understands the relations between panels across a work. Here, it is central to understand that Groensteen makes a distinction in the formal construction of comics: between 'hyperframe' [*hypercadre*] – the structure of the page – and 'multiframe' [*multicadre*] – panels in a broader network. The hyperframe is the structural organization of a single page whereas multiframe is a broader term that considers the way panels and pages are connected throughout a work. Thus, a hyperframe is an example of a simple multiframe where panels are connected across a page, but there are multiple ways semiotic elements can be connected in groups (a half page, a strip, a spread, several pages in a sequence or the whole book).

This distinction underlines the scalable quality of comics as a network, a system of units (panels, strips, sequences) that can connect, disconnect and reconnect with each other across smaller segments as well as across the entire comics network. Following this line of thinking, one of the most impactful concepts from *The System of Comics* is 'braiding' [*tressage*] which examines the potential connection of any panel to any other in the work. Groensteen describes braiding as the way panels can connect across the work, taking into account a larger frame of reference that is established in many directions within the work and not necessarily in the direction of the narrative progression.

When discussing the formal elements of comics, this approach emphasizes the narrative movement from panel to panel and the connection of a panel to its neighbouring panels, but also points out that additional meaning can be added to the work from the connections that can be made between panels spanning pages and in any direction. Groensteen makes a point of noting that braiding is a surplus effect on the narrative and that these extra effects are not central to how the narrative develops, but that the potential for a networked relation between all panels in the comic can be explored in different ways to add meaning and layer the possible interpretations provided to the reader.

Along similar lines, other approaches to comics within French criticism have taken a pictorial or diagrammatic perspective. After reviewing the work of various classic artists, Pierre Sterckx (1986) describes painting as a 'diagram', made up of layers of images, pigments, geometrical shapes, lines and so forth. The interweaving of these different strata means we should never comment on one in isolation; that the force of the painting comes only from 'the quality of the diagrammatic interactions that it demonstrates, and the play of the infinite reciprocity of its levels' (142). He proceeds to look closely at Hergé's work in this way, demonstrating the movement from past to future in *Le Secret de la Licorne* [*The Secret of the Unicorn*] in a scene where Captain Haddock runs through a canvas of his ancestor: an act that forms the basis of the structure of this book, as he bursts from past to future, and also comments on its production, as his figure can be seen as a tracing (Hergé's known style of working) that produces the 'clear line'.

Jan Baetens and Pascal Lefèvre (1993a) explore the interrelationship between text and image, seeking to establish differences between the different orders of text that feature in a comic (of various types, which previous scholars have treated in an *ad hoc* way). They set out 'three types of correspondences: the material relation between two types of signs; the quantitative balance or imbalance of the two domains and the modalities of inclusion of text within the image; and finally, the semantic links between the legible and the visible' (185). Drawing on diverse examples from *Watchmen* (1986–87) to *The Cage* (1975) as justification for the sheer range of possibilities in comics, they do not seek to categorize every conceivable link, but instead set out four rules that cover text–image relationships. These are: the subordination of the text to the image; the avoidance of redundancy; the goal of transparency (the goal of a smooth read that is not disrupted by either the omission or an excess of information); and the 'now-read-on' function which incites the reader to continue to the next panel. They also pay attention to the margins of the work (1993b) considering how the main body of the text relates to the 'secondary' units of the paratext. Paratext means all the elements of the book that are not part of the main text, such as author name, back text, foreword, notes, etc. Discarding the loaded term of paratext itself (in favour of margin, periphery, surround and frame), they explore a number of false oppositions relating to the way the text and its margins are habitually handled. These include the hierarchy assigned to the text–image relationship; the space afforded to the text versus its periphery; the homogeneity of the work versus the heterogeneity of its margins; the ordering of the two units; and the different ontological status assigned to the two. They also consider the one-way relationship between the two and the circumstances that have led to the prioritizing of the commercial (rather than the critical or explanatory) function of the marginalia, arguing that this function rests on three pillars: the enigma, seduction and identification/recognition effects. These work to trigger narrative expectations in different ways. They also consider those comics that go against this formula, instead 'unfurling' information within the book-as-network that includes its margins, and offer examples of this in action.

In her 2013 book *Narrative Structure in Comics*, Barbara Postema collects many of the previous thoughts on formalist notions in comics scholarship into what she describes as a 'loosely semiotic [...] methodology' (2013: xvi) that very significantly carries the subtitle 'Making Sense of Fragments'. Furthering the thought of people like Groensteen, McCloud and Peeters, Postema argues that the gap is a central concept in how comics work to make meaning and that various types of bridging the gaps are at play in this process of making sense of fragments. Following Scott McCloud, Postema begins by noting the iconicity of comics and how the reader fills in the gaps when looking at highly iconic drawings, like for instance Charles Schulz' *Peanuts*, in a discussion of the relationship between realism and iconicity. This then moves on to an analysis of the way narratives work when it comes to images, which looks specifically at how time can be added in comics and how temporality works. Temporality is often added through sequence, and Postema returns to the bridging of gaps that is needed in between panels to add action to sequences, after discussing the importance of layouts for the structuring of narrative. Postema criticizes Groensteen and Peeters in their categorization for saying little about how the layout functions in relation to story and for not accounting for layouts that fall outside their categories. Instead, she proposes her own taxonomy of page layouts based on the number of panels on the page and the nature of the gutters or lack thereof. Another gap that Postema considers central is the gap between text and image, which she analyses through a slew of examples with different relationships between the two. Although images appear in succession like words, and text is also visual, Postema insists that the gap between text and images has to be traversed by the reader and that theories of comics as a hybrid where the verbal and the visual blend seamlessly do not account for the two very different types of sign systems.

The semiotic strain is strongest in the Francophone tradition, but Anglophone scholarship has also taken an interest in the mechanics of comics that have ties with semiotic readings. A micro-semiotic approach to the comics strip is found in the 1988 essay 'How to read Nancy' by Mark Newgarten and Paul Karasik, who in 2017 expanded this reading to a book-length study in *How to Read Nancy*. In this, Karasik and Newgarten use the supposed simplicity of Ernie Bushmiller's *Nancy* to point meticulously to the many types of signs that can produce meaning in a comics strip by carefully taking the strip apart down to the smallest lines and inked scratches. Their method is to some degree creator-inspired because in their analysis of the strip, they rely heavily on interviews with Bushmiller to determine exactly how the strip is constructed. As art historian James Elkins notes in the introduction, formalist studies and close-readings in general have historically been considered 'ideologically suspect' because some formalist readings used their narrow focus on form and formal elements to disregard identity issues pertaining to race, gender, sexuality, disability and class which conveniently did not have to be addressed in a search for the pure version of art and the essence of an art form. However, Newgarden and Karasik insist that this very careful micro-semiotic study of all the ink traces in one comic strip can disclose important things about how comics work. Their choice of Bushmiller's strip has to do with its degree of readability in that the primary purpose of the construction is to make the joke come across to the reader. They are picking apart the strip to show how a message can be delivered to an audience in the most effective way through the mechanics of the comic strip – panels, speech balloons, lines and shapes. This dismantling *tour de force* begins with the idea, how to get the gag, and then carefully moves through points that have been discussed previously: the primacy of image in comics' narratives, the interaction of text and image, and the special quality of speech balloons as simultaneously objects in the space of the page and spoken dialogue that has to be imagined as part of the diegesis. Karasik and Newgarden's meticulous unpacking and deconstruction of the elements of comics which reaches inside the panels to discuss the semantics of single lines, inked blots and placement inside panels is at a level where few formalist readings have ventured without attempting to construct a semiotic ledger that can 'translate' certain micro-signs into specific meanings. Karasik and Newgarden's analysis is not a carefully developed theory and it does not pretend to be, but in their microscopic attention to detail they survey the signs at play in comics and illustrate the way the mechanics of comics can support content in ways that might not be immediately clear to the naked eye.

Charles Hatfield draws upon many of the aforementioned theories in a theory of comics that unites many levels of comics analysis in his book *Alternative Comics: An Emerging Literature* (2005). As the title suggests, Hatfield analyses 'alternative comics' and spends a great deal of time emphasizing the ways in which comics can be considered literature. Embedded in Hatfield's notion of alternative comics is the way comics have become culturally more acceptable and the term emphasizes comics as a personal literary expression which has experienced a revolution in terms of how it is perceived as well as in the artistic ambition and formal experiments of its creators. Through this discussion a concept of comics emerges as 'an art of tensions' that works at different levels of the comics form. The tension between word and image that has been discussed earlier is one tension, and Hatfield relies heavily on W.J.T. Mitchell's understanding of the way image and word can supplement each other or work against each other in comics. Hatfield's second tension is between single image and image in sequence, which resembles the discussions Groensteen also points to in his comments on how the panel works in a sequence. Hatfield connects this to McCloud's concept of closure and discusses how the tension between single image and image-in-series can differ depending on how easy it is for the reader to connect the panel to its surrounding panels. Hatfield's third tension is between sequence and surface, in regard to which he references Fresnault-Deruelle's understanding of the structuring principles of a page as both tabular and linear. He then connects this to McCloud's points on temporality in comics and underlines how the tension between sequence and surface can conjure temporally ambiguous panels and create synchronism which needs to be deciphered by the reader on the back of an experience with the other tensions. In de-coding panels that depict several moments in time or panels that stretch across the same background (polyptychs), Hatfield states that the reader needs to have an understanding of how the first two tensions work.

Hatfield extends the discussions of the formal qualities of comics in that his fourth tension connects the materiality of the page with the expression of the content, designating a tension between text-as-experience and

27

text-as-object. Hatfield discusses how aspects such as lines and style can work with and against the physical appearance of the text and how various artists have explored that to extend the possibilities of expression and the generation of meaning in comics.

Hatfield's focus on the importance of examining the materiality of comics in line with formal characteristics highlights how a lot of formal comics theory takes its point of departure from print comics and, although many of the formalistic points made in the field can be employed in discussions of comics published in a digital format, there are also certain qualities of this mode of production and publishing that not only influence the channels of circulation, but also add to formalistic descriptions of and debates on how comics work.

Once again, Scott McCloud has taken some of the initial steps in exploring this area, when in 2000 he published a follow-up to *Understanding Comics* called *Reinventing Comics*, which addressed many aspects of the comics industry but was particularly interested in the uses of technology and its potential to create digital comics that might alter the way comics were understood as a medium. McCloud is famed for coining the term 'infinite canvas' to describe the way digital comics can potentially organize their panels in other ways than the linear panel transitions described by McCloud himself. The expansion of comics from physical to digital form makes it possible to connect panels in new ways, allowing for scrollable panels and a much larger number of panels being stored as part of the narrative. Semiotic approaches have developed into systemic models for analysis of the special visual/verbal qualities of comics narratives, even looking beyond the text itself into the means and modes of its production.

As the title of Barbara Postema's book suggests, semiotic and formal concerns are tightly interwoven with narratological discussion and breaking down the mechanics of comics often has the specific purpose of understanding how comics tell stories. In *Contemporary Comics Storytelling* (2013), Karin Kukkonen moves away from the semiotic approach and insists on a cognitive model of analysis in the study of comics which emphasizes the embodied cognition of comics readers: the way readers cognitively make meaning happens through inference from intertextual references, the way storyworlds relate to the experienced world, and how readers infer the fictional minds of characters in the stories. In examining these three aspects of the cognitive approach, Kukkonen uses the series *Fables* to discuss the intertextuality involved in the postmodern re-imagining of well-known fairytales, just as the series *Tom Strong* serves as a fictional world to explore for an instance of how imagination helps build worlds. The series *100 Bullets* is the example Kukkonen uses to examine how fictional minds work in comics and she ends by noting that a comics narratology has to take into account the way in which the medium poses specific challenges to key concepts in narrative theory, such as the distinction between story and discourse and the role of the narrator, as well as how the dominant seriality of comics often poses further questions to the field of narratology.

Comics as language

When discussing definitions of comics and how to approach them theoretically, a common phrase circulating is 'comics as language'. Several books on comics use this connection as part of their titles (Bongco, 2000; Frahm, 2010; Saraceni, 2003; Varnum and Gibbons, 2002), but as linguist Frank Bramlett has argued, this labelling is less a definition than a metaphor which does not actually treat comics as a language in a linguistic sense (2012: 1). The discussion of comics as a language sometimes shares common ground with some of the theories from Saussurean semiotics, but this branch of comics studies has developed in directions that also take into account other aspects of language and work with cognitive and social linguistics.

A theorist who has been trying to nuance this discussion of comics as language specifically from the point of cognitive linguistics is Neil Cohn. In his writings, he has discussed many of the instances of equating comics with language. Going against the metaphorical use of language, Cohn argues that '[…] comics are written in visual languages the same way that novels or magazines are written in English' (2013: 2). To Cohn, the sociocultural context should be separated from the structural aspects and as such his study of comics is a linguistic and cognitive analysis of how visual language works. Cohn does discuss comics as a visual language, but he is mainly preoccupied with the visual elements of the visual language, not paying particular attention to the verbal and verbal-visual parts of comics. Cohn describes his understanding of visual language as referring to how a 'visual lexicon' can be detected in comics. From the lines within panels to the patterns of panels, Cohn argues that there are certain repetitions and structures that can fix themselves in the memory and be reactivated by readers or artists, often without either realizing the repeated use of certain figures or panel patterns. Parallel to language, Cohn identifies a visual grammar, a structural way that panels are organized which depends on narrative structure. He argues against McCloud's panel transitions, pointing out that they do not take into account global narrative structures; he dismisses Groensteen's networked panel as offering too many possibilities of connection between panels; and he finds fault with the theory of predetermined narrative scripts, arguing that there are narratives in visual languages that do not rely on scripts. Cohn's identification of a grammar is a categorization of the functions of panels within a narrative sequence, which he also expands to include the way page layout is organized. Because these functions construct meaning in certain ways, there are combinations that are more likely or obvious and some that disrupt the reading. In comics research, Cohn's theories are somewhat unusual in the way that he has worked with his colleagues to test his ideas by making experiments with readers, monitoring their brainwaves and using eye-tracking to discern reading patterns. This kind of experimental comics research is becoming more popular and adds new data to theories about how people read comics. One of Cohn's claims is that experience and exposure to comics reading enhance your ability to read comics. As a final point, Neil Cohn also discusses visual styles as 'dialects' or 'accents' to show how different national and international drawing styles might differ slightly but are all still written in 'visual language'.

One scholar who has very explicitly dealt with the notion of comics as language is Hannah Miodrag with *Comics and Language* (2013) where she in three sections takes apart a line of arguments in this crossover, looking at 'Language in Comics', 'Comics as Language' and 'Images as Language'. She argues that the anxiety surrounding comics and their legitimacy hitherto has influenced theories of how comics work and what they are and has resulted in both an idea that comics can be considered a type of language because it fuses text and image and an idea that favours the visual content and looks at comics as a visual language. Working from Ferdinand de Saussure's semiotics, Miodrag strives to separate text and image and insists that the two have to be looked at separately; she points to how sequentiality has been a key factor in the emergence of the concept of 'comics as language'. Miodrag notes that the presentation of a story is more closely related to narrative theory than to linguistics and instead she supports Groensteen's description of comics as a system of signs. She argues that the focus on images in definitions of comics has led to an inattention to the written language in comics that makes presumptions about how words work compared to images – that words are signs that have precise meanings, whereas images have multiple interpretative possibilities. Miodrag challenges this and asserts that, even if certain elements of the comics medium resemble language, this does not make it into a language. In her final section she argues against thinking of images as a language because it is not possible to assign specific meanings to elements like style, composition, colour, etc. Though some signs in comics are conventionalized, images are 'radically heterogenous', which makes it difficult to identify the 'pictemes' of a visual language.

Unflattening by Nick Sousanis (2015) bridges the gap between cultural and linguistic interpretations of comics communication. Using the comics medium, Sousanis explores different ways of seeing drawn from biology, philosophy, art, literature and mythology and reflects on the potential the medium has to open our minds to new ways of seeing, thinking and communicating. Beautifully drawn in black and white, it opens with a series of bleak images of factory line humanoids alongside the suggestion that we have limited our perceptions over time. In the first three chapters, Sousanis examines the qualities of visual and verbal communication. He suggests that we have boxed ourselves in, both externally and internally, with the systems we use: creating conceptual limitations to our understanding of the world around us. He considers examples from both linguistics and philosophy and draws attention to their construction of boundaries and Others. He then moves to a discussion of the physiology of human sight, using this as a metaphor for the same self-imposed limitations. Sousanis argues that we need to undo these boundaries. His argument rests on the premise that 'The medium we think in defines what we can see' (52) and he proceeds to explore the syntagmatic nature of language against the paradigmatic nature of image. By bringing together the hierarchical and the rhizomatic, the descriptive and the incarnate, comics' communication allows us to connect two different modes of attention simultaneously. His following chapters consider the way in which perception underpins thought; for example, sight literally allows us to visualize and stitch together new ideas. In Chapter 5 Sousanis likens our imagination to filling a gap or opening a door. He notes that the 'door' is a metaphor that cuts both ways: it can operate as both a bridge and a barrier. He then highlights the tendency to rely on habits and assumptions and how certain types of knowledge can become unquestioningly accepted. Sousanis suggests that by flipping our perception or disrupting our routine we can reveal the connections and gain awareness – for example of the ways in which all the factors in our life (no matter how trivial) have influenced our thinking and shaped our identity. Drawing on the thoughts of the American philosopher John Dewey, he points out that capacity is something that can be used actively and expanded upon in a relationship with the world rather than a tabula rasa on which others write. Arguing poetically for an 'unflattening' that will empower us to change our way of thinking, Sousanis uses the comics medium to demonstrate how our patterns of thinking can be disrupted and our eyes opened.

Conclusion

Whether you are interested in comics and semiotics, comics as/and language, or culturally specific connections or definitions, there is a general divide between those who consider comics a mode of communication and those who examine their aesthetic aspects. Both groups are concerned with how meaning is constructed in comics, but there is a distinction between whether they investigate how that meaning can be conveyed as efficiently and clearly as possible, or whether their interest is in the murkiness that might arise in the clash between signs, the way language can be obfuscating and images allude to multiple interpretations. Early landmark texts have given way to more complicated theories that have sought to establish critical models grown from comics' own unique qualities.

Many of the semiotic theoreticians of comics are part of a French language tradition and naturally their primary material for analysis often comes from *bandes dessinées*. This sometimes shows in the way their arguments concerning, for instance, page layouts are influenced by the traditional European album tradition. It can be argued that the cultural context and the formal specifics of a national comics tradition might influence arguments that base their formal discussion of the structure and composition of a certain kind of comics.

The formal concerns of comics inform questions of materiality as the meaning making discussed in distinctions between paper and digital often leads to new ways of understanding the medium just as the ideological aspects of comics often influence, and are influenced by, formal deliberations. Our next chapter looks up from the specifics of debates on form and connects these materials to a broader field of societal topics.

Note

1. See also Ahmed, Maaheen (2016) *Openness of Comics*. Jackson, MS: University Press of Mississippi: 18–19 for a reworking of Peeters' schema that allows for a sliding scale between the categories of the layout.

Works cited

Baetens, Jan and Lefèvre, Pascal. 'Texts and Images'. In Ann Miller and Bart Beaty (eds), *The French Comics Theory Reader*. Leuven: Leuven University Press, 1993a, pp. 183–190.

Baetens, Jan and Lefèvre, Pascal. 'The Work and Its Surround'. In Ann Miller and Bart Beaty (eds), *The French Comics Theory Reader*. Leuven: Leuven University Press, 1993b, pp. 191–202.

Bongco, Mila. *Reading Comics: Language, Culture, and the Concept of the Superhero in Comic Books*. New York and London: Routledge, 2000.

Bramlett, Frank (ed.) *Linguistics and the Study of Comics*. Houndmills, Basingstoke, Hampshire and New York: Palgrave Macmillan, 2012.

Chavanne, Renaud. *Composition de la Bande Dessinée*. Montrouge: Editions PLG, 2010.

Cohn, Jesse. 'Translator's Comments on Benoît Peeters "Four Conceptions of the Page."' *Imagetext* 3:3, 2007. https://imagetextjournal.com/translators-comments-on-benoit-peeters-four-conceptions-of-the-page/

Cohn, Neil. 'The Limits of Time and Transitions: Challenges to Theories of Sequential Image Comprehension'. *Studies in Comics* 1:1, 2010: 127–147.

Cohn, Neil. 'Comics, Linguistics and Visual Language: The Past and Future of a Field'. In Frank Bramlett (ed.), *Linguistics and the Study of Comics*. Houndmills, Basingstoke, Hampshire and New York: Palgrave Macmillan, 2012, pp. 92–118.

Cohn, Neil. *The Visual Language of Comics: Introduction to the Structure and Cognition of Sequential Images*. London: Bloomsbury Academic, 2013.

Eco, Umberto and Chilton, Natalie (trans.). 'The Myth of Superman'. *Diacritics* 2:1, 1972: 14–22.

Eisner, Will. *Comics and Sequential Art*. Tamarac, FL: Poorhouse Press, 1985.

Eisner, Will. *Graphic Storytelling*. Tamarac, FL: Poorhouse Press, 1996.

Frahm, Ole. *Die Sprache des Comics*. Hamburg: Philo Fine Arts, 2010.

Groensteen, Thierry. 'La narration comme supplement: archéologie des fondations infra-narratives de la bande dessinée'. In Thierry Groensteen (ed.), *Bande dessinée, récit et modernité*. Paris: Futuropolis, 1988, pp. 45–83.

Groensteen, Thierry. *The System of Comics*. Jackson: University Press of Mississippi, 2007.

Groensteen, Thierry. 'Definitions'. In Ann Miller and Bart Beaty (eds), *The French Comics Theory Reader*. Leuven: Leuven University Press, 2012, pp. 93–114.

Grove, Laurence. *Comics in French – the European Bande Dessinée in Context*. New York: Berghahn Books, 2010.

Harvey, R. C. 'It's Not My Fault: Confessions of a Comics Junkie. Or, How I Became a Crazed Fanatic about Cartooning, Its History and Lore'. *International Journal of Comic Art* 7, 2005: 3–42.

Harvey, R. C. 'Defining Comics Again: Another in the Long List of Unnecessarily Complicated Definitions'. *Comics Journal*, 2010.

Hatfield, Charles. *Alternative Comics: An Emerging Literature*. Jackson: University Press of Mississippi, 2005.

Holbo, John. 'Redefining Comics'. In Aaron Meskin and Roy T. Cook (eds), *The Art of Comics*. Chichester: John Wiley & Sons, 2012, pp. 1–30. https://doi.org/10.1002/9781444354843.ch1

Horrocks, Dylan. 'Inventing Comics: Scott McCloud's Definition of Comics'. *The Comics Journal* 234, 2001: 29–39.

Ingulsrud, John E. and Allen, Kate. *Reading Japan Cool: Patterns of Manga Literacy and Discourse*. Lanham: Lexington Books, 2009.

Itō, Gō. 'Tezuka Is Dead: Manga in Transformation and Its Dysfunctional Discourse'. *Mechademia: Second Arc* 6, 2011: 69–82.

Karasik, Paul and Newgarden, Mark. *How to Read Nancy: The Elements of Comics in Three Easy Panels*. Seattle, WA: Fantagraphics Books, 2017.

Kukkonen, Karin. *Contemporary Comics Storytelling*. Lincoln: University of Nebraska Press, 2013.

Kunzle, David. *History of the Comic Strip, Volume 1, The Early Comic Strip: Narrative Strips and Picture Stories in the European Broadsheet from c. 1450 to 1825*. Berkeley: University of California Press, 1973.

Lessing, Gottfried Ephraim. *Laocoön: An Essay upon the Limits of Painting and Poetry. With Remarks Illustrative of Various Points in the History of Ancient Art*. Boston: Roberts Brothers, 1874.

McCloud, Scott. *Understanding Comics: The Invisible Art*. Northampton, MA: Kitchen Sink Press, 1993.

McCloud, Scott. *Reinventing Comics: How Imagination and Technology Are Revolutionizing an Art Form*. New York: Perennial, 2000.

McLuhan, Marshall. *Understanding Media: The Extensions of Man*. New York: New American Library, 1964.

Meskin, Aaron. 'Defining Comics?'. *The Journal of Aesthetics and Art Criticism* 65, 2007: 369–379.

Miller, Ann and Beaty, Bart (eds). *The French Comics Theory Reader*. Leuven: Leuven University Press, 2014.

Miodrag, Hannah. *Comics and Language: Reimagining Critical Discourse on the Form*. Jackson: University Press of Mississippi, 2013.

Mitchell, W. J. T. *Iconology: Image, Text, Ideology*. Chicago: University of Chicago Press, 1986.

Mitchell, W. J. T. *Picture Theory: Essays on Verbal and Visual Representation*. Chicago: University of Chicago Press, 1994.

Natsume, Fusanosuke. 'Komatopia'. *Mechademia: Second Arc* 3, 2008: 65–72.

Postema, Barbara. *Narrative Structure in Comics: Making Sense of Fragments*. Rochester, New York: RIT Press, 2013.

Saraceni, Mario. *The Language of Comics*. London and New York: Routledge, 2003.

Singer, Marc. *Breaking the Frames: Populism and Prestige in Comics Studies*. Austin, TX: University of Texas Press, 2019.

Sousanis, Nick. *Unflattening*. Cambridge, MA: Harvard University Press, 2015.

Sterckx, Pierre. 'La loupe ou l'éponge'. *Les Cahiers de la bande dessinée* 69, May–June 1986: 77–80.

Töpffer, Rodolphe and Wiese, Ellen (trans.) *Enter the Comics*. Lincoln: University of Nebraska Press, 1965.

Varnum, Robin and Gibbons, Christina T. *The Language of Comics: Where Word and Image Intersect*. Jackson: University Press of Mississippi, 2002.

CHAPTER 3
IDEOLOGICAL AND MATERIAL APPROACHES

This chapter reviews critical works that have analysed comics from a particular ideological or cultural stance. The first section discusses ideological and political readings, focusing on those critics who have looked at specific cultural moments and how comics can be read politically, as propaganda or as potentially subversive of power dynamics. One of the ways ideology shows in comics is in colonialist history and the depiction in comics of the colonizing activities of states which has also received scholarly attention.

A general discussion of how ideology connects to comics includes an ongoing debate about the cultural legitimacy of comics and how it plays into comics scholarship. The chapter also considers the term 'graphic novel' and the way it connects aspects of cultural legitimacy, marketing strategies, physical format and formal innovation. The graphic novel's physical form and format as a distinguishing characteristic point to the second segment in this chapter that explores theories about the materiality of comics and the many ways in which reading conditions play a role in thinking about comics as a medium. This segment considers critics who have discussed the sensory qualities that inform our reading of the medium and the ways in which materiality and sensory information are referenced on the page, as this can be intertwined with discussions of ideological influence.

Political and ideological perspectives

An important early contribution to scholarship on the ideological influences of comics is found in Ariel Dorfman and Armand Mattelart's *Para Leer al Pato Donald* (1971) [*How to Read Donald Duck – Imperialist Ideology in the Disney Comic* (1975)], which examines Disney comics from an anti-imperialist perspective and argues that the supposed naiveté of these children's comics hides an ideological influence which promotes American capitalism. The authors analyse some of the comics' travel stories and point out how the majority of the duck family's encounters with indigenous people rely on an imperialist intention of exploiting the natives for gold or profits and that other peoples are portrayed through a stereotypical lens that infantilizes the native populations of the areas of the world Donald and his family visit. In their criticism of Disney, Mattelart and Dorfman insist that the apparently innocent entertainment has dire consequences and exploits an imperialist system to further its consumerist appeal. 'Power to the Duck means the promotion of underdevelopment. The daily agony of Third World peoples is served up as a spectacle for permanent enjoyment in the utopia of bourgeois liberty' (98). This Marxist-inspired reading draws on ideas about the power of the cultural industry put forth by the Frankfurt School and follows the concern voiced in debates surrounding comics generally about the way comics can exercise a seemingly unnoticed ideological influence on their readers under the guise of mere entertainment. *How to Read Donald Duck* cautions against being uncritical of popular media like Disney comics and its readings provide a model of how ideological critical interpretations of comics might be carried out.

Mattelart and Dorfman's work is revisited in another landmark text in the analysis of ideology in comics: Martin Barker's *Comics, Power, Ideology and the Critics* (1989). This responds to previous critical works that have analysed comics outside of their cultural context and in a critical vacuum – thus ignoring audience-centric approaches to the medium. Taking to task 'arbitrary' approaches to comics study and the arguments about the subjectivity of media, Barker's aim is to reconsider claims about media effects by looking closely at the ideas of previous scholars alongside their methods of investigation and analysis. Barker bases his book around a series of case studies of British comics from *Action* to *Jackie*. His approach is to survey and cite the existing critical response to various titles, including both scholarship and popular knowledge, sustained by creator interviews, press releases and other sources. He then attacks these assumptions using close analysis of the texts and audience survey data and responses. First, Barker reviews a number of classic readings of *Jackie*, pointing out that these are 'almost all hostile' (139) and make the critical error of assuming that these comics form a unity. This error takes two forms: the presumption that the comic's various parts (e.g. the various stories, editorial, letters page) deliver a singular message, and that different titles form a unity (i.e. they all carry the same message regardless of genre, intended audience or time of publication). He cites a range of critical viewpoints, including Connie Alderson's argument in *Magazines Teenagers Read* (1968) that comics are commodities offering amorality, anti-intellectualism, rejection of complexity, daydreamy escapism and a 'debased' usage of the word and concept of love. He also discusses the work of Sharpe (1976), who critiques comics' use of stereotypes within her wider study of the role models and stereotypes available to girls through media and lifestyle, and McRobbie (1978a, 2007 [1987b], 1981), whose semiological analysis identifies four codes (romance, fashion and beauty, pop, and personal and domestic life) in the content of *Jackie*. One by one Barker dismisses their arguments: concluding that the analyses they are based on all 'start from unsatisfactory theories of influence and ideology' (159) and that these critics have approached the comics with a particular goal in mind and have thus been enabled to prove it. His discursive strategy also involves the reader by inviting them to guess the end of particular stories based on the theories that previous critics have established. This enables readers to feel an active part of disproving the ideas put forward.

How comics can support certain ideologies and their potential effects on audiences is also central to an essay collection that looks at the historiographical impact of Japanese manga dealing with historical topics. *Rewriting History in Manga* (Otmazgin and Suter, 2016) addresses the discussion of how manga might influence readers in terms of historical content and specifically how different types of manga might shape historical memory. As Nissim Otmazgin explains in the Introduction, the concern about the potential of manga to influence historical memory has developed alongside a growing revisionist historiography in Japan that emphasizes a more nationalistic approach to Japanese history, complaining about Japan's 'masochistic' behaviour and promoting a strong pride in Japan as a nation. Well-known 'God of Manga' Osamu Tezuka has created manga which argued that war is generally bad and because of his great popularity, a more pacifist version of Japanese history is prevalent in Tezuka's works, whereas many scholars and critics point to Kobakashi Yoshinori's manga as one that glorifies Japan's war victories and actively suppresses evidence of massacres committed by Japanese soldiers with the explicit intention of changing the hearts and minds of Japanese people in a more nationalist direction. Several chapters in this collection examine the way manga can potentially change the minds of readers and reshape historical memory, but an important chapter in this discussion is a study of what Japanese students reading revisionist manga take from it and to what degree they change their minds. In Chapter 7: 'Decoding "Hate the Korean Wave" and "Introduction to China" A Case Study of Japanese University Students', Alexander Bukh presents results from a survey which polls students after their reading of controversial manga and concludes that these readers seem perfectly able to navigate the material and pose critical questions to it. Very few of the students changed their minds about historical events from reading the manga, and quite a few also commented on the visual manipulation these manga used, showing their manga reading skills play a role in their interpretation of historical material. Despite the small scale of the study and the complexities involved in interpreting the results, Bukh suggests that students are not taking in revisionist propaganda just because it is in manga form. In the Conclusion, Rebecca Suter notes that the results of this collection are both a rewriting of the history of manga (that manga did not begin in the 1950s with Osamu Tezuka) and a problematization of the big national focus on 'Japan Cool' and national branding strategy of manga as the best Japanese export. Finally, this book underlines the importance of audience studies when dealing with popular cultural products in general but also emphatically states the difficulty of doing such audience studies. How manga's shaping Japan's historical memory is not a causal, linear and unified process; audience interaction and the co-production of manga across multimedia platforms complicate the notion of using it to impact directly upon people's understanding of history and as a means of ideological imprinting.[1]

Colonialism and comics

The relationship between comics and ideology is explored in a different part of the world in Mark McKinney's *The Colonial Heritage of French Comics* (2011), which deliberately looks at both older and more recent French language comics to uncover racist and colonial bias and determine the degree to which French language comics have been decolonized since 1962, when the majority of the countries colonized by France had gained independence. The introduction explains the book's close readings of especially the works of Alain Saint-Ogan with the great impact his works have had on other comics creators including *Tintin*'s creator Hergé who then in turn inspired many artists in the years to follow. McKinney criticizes the way older comics like Saint-Ogan's *Zig et Puce* have recently been republished without any critical discussion of their colonial and racist contents.

In the treatment of these comics as classics re-published in high-quality editions, McKinney contends that the comics publishers and critics are contributing to a colonial nostalgia which reproduces racist and colonial ideas and notions of France's colonial past as benign: feeding a nostalgic longing for a past when France as a nation was more powerful and conquered the world. McKinney focuses his inquiry around two key types of events that have shaped the representation of colonial subjects and the colonial imaginary in France: colonial exhibitions and colonial expeditions. Colonial exhibitions were an international phenomenon that brought together goods, technological inventions, and people from the colonies to be exhibited for the colonizing countries' citizens in an effort to boost colonial efforts and sway public opinion in a positive way regarding the colonial expansion. The 1931 *Exposition Internationale* in Paris sold more than 33 million tickets and featured people from the colonies showing their cooking, crafts and performances in huts built to mimic their native homes. The colonial expeditions had the same purpose of showcasing the greatness of the French empire in trans-African car rides which served as both commercial expansion and entertainment as an imperialist extravaganza heavily documented and reported by the media. As McKinney shows, these types of events pop up in comics in several versions but many of the past and contemporary varieties spring from the *Exposition Internationale* and the trans-African *Crosière noire* 1924–1926, an expedition to cross African which was a mix of government and corporate interests, promoting French imperialism and advertising commercially for car manufacturers. By analysing some of the many comics that have the colonial exhibitions as a setting or central theme, McKinney shows how the early days of French comics incorporated and exploited racial stereotypes and contributed to the French government's intention to encourage French citizens to move to the colonies and aid the colonial endeavours. McKinney's stated goal is to produce a genealogy of colonial representation in French comics because this allows for a mapping of how colonial ideology is transmitted, modified and reproduced in both the time of colonization and the following historical period. McKinney finds that more recent comics have taken post-colonial critical research and changed attitudes into account and has found a few comics that use the human zoos and trans-African expedition to criticize racist and colonial tropes, but still sees these ideologies lingering in contemporary comics and especially in the uncritical re-publication of comics from the colonial French past. McKinney's book has a rather narrow focus but begins the discussion of how colonial ideology is present and reproduced in comics and readily admits that much further work needs to be done in this area.

Mark McKinney proceeds with this project in *Redrawing French Empire in Comics* (2013), which offers another example of writing history with comics by turning to disciplines such as memory studies and post-colonial critique. Examining a variety of French-language graphic novels – ranging from well-known alternative comics such as David B. [Beauchard]'s *Epileptic* (2009; originally *L'Ascension du haut mal* [1996–2003]) and Yvan Alagbé's [*Yellow Black People*] (1997) to more mainstream productions such as the *Carnets d'Orient* – McKinney shows how comics artists interrogate France's colonial legacy, especially in Algeria and in Vietnam. Suggesting that former colonies often figure as *lieux de mémoire* [sites of memory] for many French people (35), McKinney first turns to nineteenth-century orientalist and colonialist representations of Algeria in prints and satirical cartoons to highlight how recent French and Algerian 'are […] to some extent *trabendistes* [smugglers], and their comics a form of *contre-bande-dessinée* [contraband/counter-comics]: ones that traffic in counter memories and archival material (forms of colonial loot […]) and disrupt other memorial constructions and identities' (79).[2]

Jennifer Howell picks up McKinney's call for further study of colonialism and comics in her book on the way comics work in a colonial and postcolonial context, specifically with regard to the French–Algerian war (1954–1962): *The Algerian War in French-Language Comics* (2015). Howell discusses the way we understand history and memory and how they relate and uses Marianne Hirsch's concept of 'postmemory' (developed in a reading of Art Spiegelman's *Maus*) to open the debates about the Algerian war in recent years. She examines the representations of this war in the French public sphere by analysing school textbooks on the topic and then considering comics that contest the colonial narrative of official France which was the dominant historical account in the post-war years.

Howell notes how comics as a source material for the teaching of history are challenged by students who do not consider them valid historical evidence, and points to the way comics artists work with historians, for example when highly acclaimed historians who specialize in the war write prefaces to the comics to legitimize their historical significance. The comics Howell analyses are all created by the generation after the one that experienced the war, which is why the concept of postmemory is helpful to understand the impact of the war on both the first and second generation. In their treatment of the subject, the comics challenge the dominant narratives and dare to let difficult questions linger without trying to provide definite answers. Howell insists that the comics do important work in the way they prioritize the personal narrative rather than the supposedly objective, distanced overview the school textbooks favour.

Because of their visuality, comics are able to recycle, reproduce and recontextualize iconic historical images and question their use in the solidification of French history on the war. By reconfiguring classic photos in a text/image narrative, these comics highlight other possible interpretations and challenge the way these photographs have become fixed in their meaning throughout the writing of history. Howell also foregrounds how these comics emphasize the perspective of the *frontalier* – a term Howell borrows from Homi Bhabha to designate the liminal status of people 'in-between' French and Algerian identity. Many of the comics creators are *frontaliers* themselves and their focus on the experiences of some of the in-between destinies of the war reorients the discussion of memory, history and postmemory. Jennifer Howell regards these comics as essential in the telling of national history and in questioning dominant narratives about the colonial and post-colonial past in Algeria and France.

Superheroes and ideology

The preoccupation with comics as a possible vehicle for certain ideological or political views is one that continues to shape comics scholarship, and Barker's caution against grouping comics and judging them as one thing is a key concern in studies of comics and politics. Because superheroes have been such a dominant and popular genre in America, their ideology and political agendas have been discussed widely in the field.

In *Champions of the Oppressed* (2011), Christopher Murray examines the connections between propaganda, superheroes and American politics. He focuses on the role superheroes played in American propaganda before, during and (to a lesser degree) after the Second World War, flagging up the processes of mythmaking and national identity that lay behind this. He begins by noting how the superhero as a character was perfectly fitted to carry the hopes and dreams of Americans because it embodies transformation. The superhero is grounded in the idea of transformation which taps into the American Dream of becoming someone else, moving up the ladder and changing your fate; just as the superhero's split personality resonated with the many immigrants who came to America hoping to take part in the American Dream and experience this transformation. Murray explains how the superhero from its very inception became a political metaphor that was inspired by President Roosevelt's New Deal as a symbol of reform and hope. By casting Superman as a 'champion of the oppressed',

Siegel and Shuster used him as a metaphor for American strength fighting against oppression. In linking propaganda and the superhero, Murray reveals that both are closely connected to myth, in that propaganda works as myth in supposedly presenting truths and the superhero presents a version of national identity in opposition to the enemy – both superhero and propaganda purport to convey what is right and wrong. In his second chapter, Murray connects myth, the superhero and the all-American hero and argues that myths are always ideological and that although they might appear to be telling eternal truths, myths can change over time, according to context and can help create value. Superheroes became part of the war effort before America entered the war and the fusion of advertising, popular culture and propaganda worked to influence American attitudes towards the war. Murray coins the term 'The Super-everyman' to designate the way the superhero tied in with the concept of the all-American hero. Although superheroes fought evil, it was important especially after the United States entered the war, to emphasize the courage and contributions of everyday heroes, both at home and in the war. Superheroes participated in the war effort by fighting alongside brave, US soldiers and by fighting spies and sabotage at home in the states. Superhero comics showed how what Murray calls 'The Other Americas' (women, children and people of colour) could participate in the war effort but concludes by saying that as soon as the war was over, the promises of greater equality for these groups were forgotten. Murray's study shows how superhero comics before and during the war were entangled in the various propaganda strategies of the United States and that this was very much because of the superhero's mythic qualities and ability to play off already existing ideas about American heroism.

The pre-existence of ideas about American heroism and American identity is also at the centre of Matthew J. Costello's *Secret Identity Crisis: Comic Books and the Unmasking of Cold War America* (2009), which takes as its starting point the 'liberal consensus' which formed after the Second World War and looks at how superheroes were influenced by the Cold War and vice versa. The liberal consensus is a myth of American unity of identity which is part of post-war reality that made Americans think that they were living in the best possible country with the best free market economy. In an effort to protect this society, enemies had to be fought and Costello uses Marvel superheroes to explore how this fight played out. Though initially the superheroes fought communists the same way they had gone up against Nazis during the war, the liberal consensus began to crumble and the superheroes began to struggle with its unifying message. Costello notes how the heroes come into conflict with the government and the moral certainty becomes ambiguous. This undermining of the national identity consensus develops further in the 1970s where superheroes reflect the political turmoil in American society and the identity crisis of the nation affects the superheroes with Captain America turning into Nomad and Tony Stark questioning himself in critiques that go against the Vietnam War. In this analysis of superheroes and the Cold War, Costello shows how superheroes and politics are closely intertwined and demonstrates how the many transformations of superheroes like Iron Man, Captain America and Hulk are shaped by and react to their political contemporary culture and reflect general moods of a nation.

The intimate relationship between superheroes and the nation has been part of the genre since its very inception, but geographer Jason Dittmer takes this idea one step further in his examination of nationalist superheroes in *Captain America and the Nationalist Superhero: Metaphor, Narrative and Geopolitics* (2013). Dittmer defines the term 'nationalist superhero' as a superhero who identifies themself with a nation-state, and he examines how this specific subgenre of superheroes not only represents certain foreign policies but also influences audiences' understanding of the nation-state. Although Dittmer also looks at nationalist superheroes from Canada (like Nevala of the Northern Lights and Captain Canuck) and Great Britain (Captain Britain), the study pays most attention to Captain America and shows how the nationalist superhero that was created under certain historical circumstances in the United States as a non-ironic character meant to embody America was less successful in its versions in other countries. Through his analysis, Dittmer shows how the body of the nationalist superhero is white, male and heteronormative and that this reflects on the body of the nation-state so that it is perceived as sharing the superhero's qualities as 'a man of action'. Dittmer sees a similarity between the nation-state and superheroes in that both are sequential narratives that are developed at certain historical moments, maintain the status quo and connect to current events, and notes that a key feature of Captain America is the way Americans of all political attitudes can see their version of America reflected in him. In looking at the space of the nationalist superhero, Dittmer notes the close relationship between geographical territory and the hero, and he ends by looking at what he calls 'anomaly' – the cases where the nationalist superhero stories break with genre conventions. These breaks are rarely actual breaks and do not challenge the status quo of the genre.

This specific reading of a subgenre of the superhero highlights the way in which the main genre is connected to the nation-state and emphasizes how the superhero genre is thoroughly entangled with especially the American nation-state and is both impacted by and in turn impacts audiences' perception of international relationships.

Cultural legitimacy as ideology

The relationship between comics and art has been framed as problematic and inscribed by the assumptions and stereotypes around high and low culture. Bart Beaty's *Comics versus Art* (2012) surveys the medium's struggle for legitimacy. It opens by surveying the institutional history of comics and proceeds to explain and evaluate the cultural assumptions and strategies that have been used to applaud certain writers and titles, while simultaneously holding the rest of the medium at bay. He argues that comics have been feminized, sidelined and consistently positioned at odds with masculinized definitions of auteur-based commercial art and high art.

Beaty looks at the different ways in which critics and practitioners have defined comics. He notes that these definitions fall into two main types, social and formalist, and that neither type coheres well with definitions of 'art'. Beaty looks closely at the use of comics in the pop art world, demonstrating how the selection, alteration and isolation of images by artists such as Lichtenstein reduce comics artwork to the state of Warhol's soup cans, he further argues that comics' adoption by camp went against the requirements of masculinized high art. He then examines the ways in which other media depict comics, noting that, even at the height of Hollywood cinema, comics artists make only limited appearances. Beaty pays particular attention to the role of fandom in creating/restoring an author function to comics but demonstrates that this process necessarily excludes much of the collaborative work that goes into the creation of a title. He considers comics' aesthetic as a type of 'maximalism' and puts this type of work into context alongside the emergence of cultural objects such as the 'art toy'. One of his key arguments is that much of comics' value is based on nostalgia: comics collections have both affective and economic value but in both instances the object's relative worth comes from its nostalgic value. This is reinforced by the rhetoric and contents of established auction houses and price guides, which privilege age and condition: creating a notion of 'blue chip' comic stocks that come exclusively from the golden and silver ages. He concludes by considering the uses of comics in gallery spaces, drawing attention to the masculinist discourses that underline their selection and display, and offering an extended case study of the work and prestige of Chris Ware. According to Beaty, Ware

> perfectly occupies the space allotted to a cartoonist in the art world at this particular moment in time – innovatively cutting edge in formal terms, technically brilliant as a designer and draftsman, but viciously self-deprecating in his willingness to occupy a diminished position in the field, strongly masculinist in his thematic concerns and aesthetic interests, and wilfully ironic about the relationship between comics and art in a way that serves to mockingly reinforce, rather than challenge, existing power inequalities.

(226)

Beaty and Woo (2016) pick up this idea with a shorter collection provocatively entitled *The Greatest Comic Book of All Time*, in which they propose a series of contenders for this title and reflect on what circumstances/measures of value would be needed for each to win it. It is an intriguing strategy and produces fascinating results. As in Beaty's previous work, the underlying argument is that comics lack their own prestige-making institutions and have thus borrowed heavily from traditions in literary studies. The book opens by plotting the citations of comics creators within the popular press and the Academy, using a trend line to demonstrate that there are a handful of creators who pull away from the pack and around whom today's scholars have built a canon of British-American comics. The rest of the book explores these different archetypes as representative of larger structures: the most important cartoonist (Art Spiegelman); the critically ignored bestseller (Rob Liefeld); the mostly unread but critically acclaimed (Martin Vaughn-James); and other structuring devices ('Not by a white man'; a Kirby superhero story; an *Archie* comic[3]). The book is an exploration of 'how the structure of the field of comics influences the development of the canon, making some works more "plausible" than others' (14).

Beginning with a discussion of *Maus*, Beaty and Woo point to the limitations (and invisibility) of the rest of Spiegelman's *oeuvre*, his own outward-facing roles as a teacher and as 'the face of comics to the cultural establishment' (23), and his reappropriation of terms such as 'comix'. The critiques of his work from competitors are evaluated as 'part of a struggle [...] to unsettle the rapidly coalescing consensus around what makes a comic book great' (25), which is further evidenced by the similar nature of competitors such as Alison Bechdel's *Fun Home: A Family Tragicomic* (2006). Their opening discussion concludes that *Maus* remains the most canonical comic book because reputable cultural gatekeepers keep choosing it as a classic.

The subsequent chapters consider the importance of institutions that are not high-culture; imagining what would be the case if these were the dominant discourses. The chapter on R. Crumb is juxtaposed with Spiegelman and draws attention to the ways in which novelistic tropes and academic models from literature departments have privileged a certain type of comics creator, forcing Crumb out of the Academy and limiting critical attention to his book-length works (which are few and often adaptations). David Bordwell's model of interpretative frameworks is applied to Crumb's work to demonstrate the difficulties of claiming his greatness at the higher (scholarly) levels of implicit and symptomatic readings. Essentially, Crumb's misogynistic caricatures expose the cracks in comics scholarship and the Academy largely ignores them. Subsequent discussions of Jack Kirby demonstrate difficulties in applying the auteur model to a collaborative artist ruling over an ever-shrinking domain (superhero comics of a particular era) as the field of comics production continues to expand in ever more literary directions. Beaty and Woo also consider Alan Moore's work and highlight to the disproportionate attention paid to British writers working within (and elevating) popular or generic traditions.

In exploring the *avant-garde* writer Martin Vaughn-James' work, Beaty and Woo ask:

> What if instead of arguing that comics should be understood as a kind of novel (even when it is nonfiction), we had said "comics is capable of lyricism and harmony, just like any other form of music," or, "comics rigorously structures space and movement, just like any other form of architecture"?
>
> (67)

Commercial success (Rob Liefeld); popularity and childish appeal (*Archie* comics); racial and gendered bias (Gene Luen Yang, Jillian and Mariko Tamaki, and Raina Telgemeir); foreign-language context and recasting (Marjane Satrapi); and temporal changes (Dave Sim's *Cerebus*) are also explored. The book ends with an evaluation of Dylan Horrocks' *Hicksville* that looks to its self-referential qualities. Beaty and Woo's conclusions (taken from their chapters on Horrocks and Sim, respectively) can be summarized firstly as 'Comics has forsaken the autonomy it once held as a maligned subculture with its own codes and practices and become dominated by fields external to it and by their corresponding regimes of value' (139). Secondly, their competing analyses draw attention to how 'Prestige is not a function of the work itself, but a reflection of what people are able, or willing, to do with the work' (131).

Christopher Pizzino's *Arresting Development* (2016) explores comics' tendency to be self-reflexive and interrogate and enact their own status struggles. Pizzino argues that comics (and their scholarship) has constructed a simplistic 'coming of age' narrative that (rather than actually progressing past this) has simply been repeated in countless news stories over the past thirty years: holding the field in stasis. He claims that the signs of this struggle can be read on the comics page, through what he calls 'autoclasm' or self-breaking: a split energy that addresses comics' status problems on the page itself. Pizzino draws attention to the contradictions and doublethink that underlies much comics criticism and scholarship: using as an example Charles McGrath's article 'Not Funnies' from the *New York Times Magazine* (2004), which pits 'comics' and 'so-called graphic novels' against '"real" books' and in so doing throws up numerous contradictions. Pizzino demonstrates these paradoxes through analysis of McGrath's qualifiers and scare quotes, and his description of Alan Moore and others as 'literary' creators while ignoring the fact that their work has mostly appeared in the 'slender series installments' from mainstream publishers that he recommends avoiding. Alongside journalistic sources, Pizzino looks at scholars such as Roger Sabin (1993), Jean-Paul Gabilliet (2005) and Paul Lopes (2009) who have commented on the medium's history and status (see Chapter 5). He does seem to put words in Sabin's mouth (attempting to demonstrate that he uses the word 'adult' as an evaluative term to mean a comic that is 'better' than those written for children, e.g. by carrying aesthetic or political value); but he acknowledges that Sabin avoids repeating the same false 'coming-of-age' narrative, even if he may have internalized some of its concepts. He then evaluates Gabilliet's and Lopes' model of legitimation: pointing out that their claim that legitimation 'begins within the medium, and the culture devoted to it, and then spreads into wider cultural fields' (42) ignores the degree to which internal legitimation means applying external standards. Having established that the simplistic development narrative attached to comics is a myth and that the medium is still very much engaged in a status struggle, the main body of Pizzino's book then looks at four key case studies, arguing that each articulates a different aspect of comics' difficulties in relation to the discussion of legitimacy.

In *Breaking the Frames* (2019), Marc Singer contends that the anxiety surrounding the cultural legitimacy of comics has resulted in comics scholarship that does a disservice to the field and falls in two groups: one that is anti-intellectual and insists on lauding comics and its popular origins, and one that tries to move comics away from the popular into the realm of a more easily identifiable legitimized cultural product. He says of the former group that, although they laud comics as a medium, they know little about the industry or comics criticism. According to Singer, comics scholarship needs critical readings that register the complexities of the medium rather than celebratory readings that put comics on a pedestal regardless of their content and context, in an explicit move away from the perceived intellectualization of comics by academics. The opposite side of this coin is the move to make comics more culturally legitimate by dissociating the works from the term 'comics' and renaming them. Singer notes how some scholars have gone to great lengths to invent terms like 'graphia', 'graphica', 'sequential art', 'graphic narrative' and 'graphic novel' to avoid referring to 'comics', which signals their discomfort with the latter term comics and risks ignoring the already considerable body of work in the field of comics studies. Of the alternative terms, 'graphic novel' is one that has caught on and become a commonly used term, for example in bookstores and libraries to denote a certain type of comics.

'Graphic novel' is a contested term that, just like the definition of comics, has been discussed in detail throughout its relatively short history. The main divide runs between those scholars who say 'graphic novel' is simply another term for comics and those who use the term to distinguish a certain type of comics from other comics.

In their thorough analysis of the term in *The Graphic Novel – an Introduction* (2015), Jan Baetens and Hugo Frey come down on the side of 'graphic novel' as a meaningful term to describe the characteristics of certain comics. They begin by quoting some of the most famous phrases from the other side of the argument: Art Spiegelman, in a 1988 issue of *Sprint* magazine, noted that his own *Maus* and Frank Miller's *Batman: The Dark Knight Returns* 'were dubbed graphic novels in a bid for social acceptability'; and Alan Moore, the creator of *Watchmen*, one of the frequently mentioned graphic novels of 1986, said: '[t]he problem is that "graphic novel" just came to mean "expensive comic book"' (1–2). The quotes point to two aspects of the criticism of the term 'graphic novel': that it is a publishing or marketing ploy invented to sell more expensive comics; and that it was intended to play into the legitimacy discussion by separating some comics from their counterparts (often designated as genre fiction: superheroes, humour, fantasy, horror). Frey and Baetens acknowledge the scepticism, especially from creators of comics, towards the term but they are adamant that there is such a thing as the graphic novel.

They propose four areas in which these graphic novels can be set apart from other kinds of comics:

1. Form: In pointing to the formal qualities of comics, Baetens and Frey flag experimentation with panel composition and page layout, stylistic choices and the role of the narrator, as key elements that might differentiate graphic novels from other comics.

2. Content: The content of graphic novels is 'adult' which, contrary to many assumptions, does not necessarily mean pornographic or violent, but of a nature that children might not find interesting. This could be in the genres of autobiography, memoir and history, but Frey and Baetens underline that the graphic novel can just as easily contain fictional and fantastical content. The diversity of topics is a point in question and 'adult' here is a matter of expanding the possible substance of these comics beyond traditional content aimed at children.

3. Publication format: Baetens and Frey point to the straightforward nature of using the difference between a comic book (pamphlet, a stapled floppy with fewer pages) and a book (bound with different dimensions, more pages) to make a clear distinction between graphic novels and other kinds of comic; but they immediately complicate this idea by emphasizing the role of serialization both in comic books and the initial publication of many graphic novels. The physical format is one of the levels at which the graphic novel can be set apart from other comics, but this criterion, like the others, must be treated with caution in view of the complexities involved in comics publishing and the problem, on the creator's side, of producing the many pages of a graphic novel before seeing it in print.

4. Production and distribution: As opposed to the funny books and comic books published by mainstream comics publisher and distributed through special comics shops and newsagents, the graphic novel began being published by renowned publishing

companies and is frequently distributed through bookstores, and publishers like Drawn & Quarterly and Fantagraphics have grown and established themselves alongside the two traditional major companies DC and Marvel.

In their argument for the development of the graphic novel as not just a fancy word for longer, more expensive comics, Baetens and Frey provide three sections in their book, each of which addresses the main elements of their description of the graphic novel phenomenon. The first section frames the discussion in a historical context by looking at the predecessors of the graphic novel in key events in comics history which have made the graphic novel possible. The moral panic of the 1950s (see Chapter 4) is described as an important event in the idea that comics are not for children and the authors note the paradox that Fredric Wertham's crusade against comics is in fact an example of taking comics seriously in a way that resembles the intentions of the proponents of the term 'graphic novel' to indicate a kind of comic that tackles more adult themes and wants to be taken seriously. They then note how the underground comics movement of the late 1950s and early 1960s was also a landmark in the development of comics with adult themes and with an intent to experiment within the medium.

While the English-speaking world is the predominant source of the term 'graphic novel', it has made an impact across the globe and is debated just as eagerly outside Anglophone contexts. In the foreword to the English translation of his book *On the Graphic Novel* (2015), Santiago García notes how the discussion of the term 'graphic novel' is more evident in Spanish comics because of the way this market developed. Following a crash in the comics market in Spain in the mid-1980s, the majority of comics in Spain were Japanese or American imports, so the recent emphasis on 'graphic novel' as a terminology has helped rejuvenate Spanish comics. García's examination of the term focuses mainly on the history and current discussions of graphic novel as a heavily debated term but includes discussions from Spanish comics scholars and the Spanish conversation on the topic.

Material and sensory issues

The many perspectives on the term 'graphic novel' point to another theoretical theme that has recently risen within comics scholarship that also refers to the ideological aspects of legitimization and to hierarchies of print vs. digital. Many scholars mention the format of the book-like publication as key to the differentiation of the graphic novel from other comics like newspaper strips and comic books with fewer pages and a stapled back. An attentiveness to physical format and materiality has developed as a scholarly angle on comics that insists on the importance of the format in which comics appear and their interaction with readers and distribution through various platforms.

Aaron Kashtan takes this approach in *Between Pen and Pixel: Comics, Materiality, and the Book of the Future* (2018), which proposes that comics can be a test case to discuss the future of the book by looking at the intersections between digital and paper versions of comics. Kashtan encourages comics scholars to focus more on the materiality of comics and points to Katherine Hayles' concept of 'media-specific analysis' as 'a mode of analysis that pays attention both to the physical and material parameters of a text and the ways in which these parameters are involved in the creation of meaning' (24). While most scholars use 'medium' as an abstract term for comics, 'a generalized, Platonic form, which is independent of the technologies used to display comics' (24), Hayles suggests an understanding of 'medium' as overlapping with materiality. Kashtan insists that various versions of a comic in different formats are not the same work and that scholars need to take physical format and the reader's interaction with it into account in determining how comics make meaning. In his framing of this discussion Kashtan compares digital and print versions of comics and points to how digital comics also have material qualities and notes that the discussion surrounding digital and print modes often moves into an unproductive opposition that is dominated by either 'biblionecrophiliac' (a term from Ben Ehrenreich) tendencies or digital proponents who have doomed the paper book. Kashtan argues that digital and print modes are always intertwined in comics and the ways in which the two inform each other should be the object of study for comics scholars. Although Alison Bechdel's *Fun Home* uses books as objects with which to show affection, Kashtan also demonstrates a criticism of the fetishization of the printed book as object and takes apart a superficial reading of handwriting as personal and typewriting as impersonal in *Fun Home* by turning towards production aspects and pointing to the digitally created font modelled on Bechdel's handwriting and the digital reproduction involved in the publication of print comics.

Many new developments in technology have influenced the way readers encounter comics and Kashtan devotes a chapter to the discussion of the digital distribution platform *Comixology*, and how comics flow from print to digital and back via this platform. *Comixology* has had significant impact on the accessibility of comics but also impacts how comics are presented to readers. One important feature is the function 'Guided View' which allows readers to study panels in a predetermined sequence. Readers also have the option of looking at the entire page outside of 'Guided View' and the tension between these two modes parallels the tension between 'tabular' and 'linear' (116) described by Fresnault-Deruelle (see Chapter 1). 'Guided View' can be more or less fruitful in digital adaptations of print. In his examples, Kashtan demonstrates how comics can successfully be 'remediated' from one medium to the other (print to digital or digital to print) but underlines that this success depends on an understanding of how each medium operates and allows for the differences in media to exploit fully the affordances of each one.

Kashtan develops his complication of preconceived notions of what is digital and print through a reading of Chris Ware's *Building Stories* (2012), which is seen by many as the epitome of the 'Kindle proof' book: it celebrates the paper form and relishes the possibilities of print, and thematically criticizes the advent of digital technology. Kashtan, however, illuminates how Ware's work is deeply intertwined with digital technologies in that the book's aesthetic appearance is heavily informed by the digital colouring its production entails. This affinity with the digital goes beyond production circumstances and, according to Kashtan, dominates the structural organization of the work, which resembles hypertext and relies on some of the same logics involved in reading digitally. Kashtan ends with the emphasis on materiality that comes from making your own comics[4] and underlines how the teaching of comics should always include practice because making comics enables students to develop a 'sensitivity to material rhetoric', which is important for twenty-first-century writing.

Kashtan also discusses in the importance of touch in connection with comics, which is a key element in Ian Hague's *Comics and the Senses* (2014). Hague examines comics through a multisensorial lens and challenges the predominance of the visual in comics scholarship; instead he encompasses all the senses in an effort to study the *object* of comics in its material conditions.[5] Hague's focus on materiality begins by refuting the idea that comics is a visual medium, noting that: 'The overall effect of the ocularcentric and synaesthetic approach to comics is to render the comic as an object immaterial and transparent' (21). Hague instead insists that comics are material and have a materiality that matters for their meaning and that comics cannot just be understood through the visual sense or through a synaesthetic approach that considers the visual sense the one through which all other senses are mediated. Going through one sense in each chapter, Hague discusses first the importance of sight, not just as a conceptual understanding but as a physical process, emphasizing the way comics are read as an embodied experience that is shaped by the eye and its physiological design. Hague then looks at all the other senses and picks apart the reading experience of comics as one that is explicitly embodied and influenced by the smell, sound, touch and taste of comics. The tactile experience of comics reading has been overlooked, and Hague argues that this material aspect of comics needs to be considered when analysing or making them. There are many as yet unexplored multisensorial possibilities in how audiences might experience comics. By highlighting the importance of understanding comics consumption as a performance, Hague lays the ground for the important question: How do comics work? Hague's analysis opens an important path to answering this question that traverses the multisensorial aspects of comics, acknowledges that visuality is not the only sensory feature of comics and stresses that this visuality in itself is very physical and complicit in producing effects in readers' bodies.

Conclusion

Comics' ideological and cultural perspectives can be interpreted very broadly.[6] In *Comics and Ideology* (2001), the anthology edited by Matthew P. McAllister, Edward H. Sewell Jr and Ian Gordon, the subjects range from the ideology of ownership in the American comics book industry through feminist readings, the ideology of superheroes and the analysis of queer characters and readership. However we define it, the capacity of comics to carry ideological content that can potentially impact readers has been discussed since the very start of comics scholarship. Comics can be a powerful tool for conveying points, whether in the service of a colonial power, in time of war, or in the interests of legitimizing a whole medium. Conversely, many scholars have shown that comics can do important work in criticizing dominant ideologies and complicating the most commonly accepted cultural tropes. Scholarship on the term 'graphic novel' shows that there are ideological nuances at play within the medium of comics itself, and work on the material qualities of comics highlights how comics' visuality has perhaps been overplayed and can instead be understood within wider physical and cultural contexts.

In the next chapter, we will go back in history and look at how the early criticism of comics has shaped some of these current debates and look closely at the origins of comics scholarship.

Notes

1. For an anthology of research manga and history, see Rosenbaum, Roman (ed.) (2013) *Manga and the Representation of Japanese History*. New York: Routledge. The connections between comics and history very often offer a space that is fertile for discussion of ideology and political ideas from very different avenues that can then be collected under this broader title. See for instance Iadonisi, Richard (ed.) (2012) *Graphic History: Essays on Graphic Novels and/or History*. Newcastle upon Tyne: Cambridge Scholars Publishing.

2. For further reading on colonialism in French comics see Delisle, Philippe (2008) *Bande dessinée et imaginaire colonial: Des années 1930 aux années 1980*. Paris: Karthala.

3. See Chapter 5 for a fuller discussion of Bart Beaty's *Twelve-Cent Archie*.

4. For guidance on making zines and comics, please see Todd, Mark and Watson, Esther Pearl (2006) *Whatcha Mean, What's a Zine?: The Art of Making Zines and Mini Comics*. Non Basic Stock Line; and Biel, Joe (2018) *Make a Zine! Start Your Own Underground Publishing Revolution*. Portland, OR: Microcosm.

5. See Chapter 1 for a discussion of Charles Hatfield's *Alternative Comics*, which notes the materiality of comics as one of the central tensions of the comics medium, the one between comics as object and comics as story.

6. One way of thinking about ideology and how it can play a role in media is to think about the ways in which power is implicit or enacted in relations between reader and work or within the comics. One such volume is Cortsen, Rikke Platz, La Cour, Erin and Magnussen, Anne (eds) (2015) *Comics and Power*. Newcastle: Cambridge Scholars Publishing, which contains analyses of comics across cultures and with very different approaches to how comics, ideology and culture interrelate.

Works cited

Alderson, Connie. *Magazines Teenagers Read: With Special Reference to Trend, Jackie, and Valentine*. Oxford and New York: Pergamon Press, 1968.

Baetens, Jan and Frey, Hugo. *The Graphic Novel: An Introduction*. New York, NY: Cambridge University Press, 2015.

Barker, Martin. *Comics: Ideology, Power and the Critics*. Manchester and New York: Manchester University Press, 1989.

Beaty, Bart. *Comics versus Art*. Toronto: University of Toronto Press, 2012.

Beaty, Bart and Woo, Benjamin. *The Greatest Comic Book of All Time*. London: Palgrave Pivot, 2016.

Biel, Joe. *Make a Zine! Start Your Own Underground Publishing Revolution*. Portland, OR: Microcosm, 2018.

Cortsen, Rikke Platz, La Cour, Erin and Magnussen, Anne. *Comics and Power – Representing and Questioning Culture, Subjects and Communities*. Cambridge: Cambridge Scholar Publishing, 2015.

Costello, Matthew J. *Secret Identity Crisis: Comic Books and the Unmasking of Cold War America*. New York: Continuum, 2009.

Dittmer, Jason. *Captain America and the Nationalist Superhero: Metaphors, Narratives, and Geopolitics*. Philadelphia: Temple University Press, 2013.

Dorfman, Ariel and Mattelart, Armand. *How to Read Donald Duck: Imperialist Ideology in the Disney Comic*. New York: International General, 1976.

Gabilliet, Jean-Paul. *Of Comics and Men: A Cultural History of American Comic Books*. Beaty, Bart and Nguyen, Nick (trans.). Jackson: University of Mississippi Press, 2005.

García, Santiago and Campbell, Bruce (trans.) *On the Graphic Novel*. Jackson: University Press of Mississippi, 2015.

Hague, Ian. *Comics and the Senses: A Multisensory Approach to Comics and Graphic Novels*. New York and London: Routledge Taylor & Francis Group, 2014.

Howell, Jennifer. *The Algerian War in French-Language Comics – Postcolonial Memory, History, and Subjectivity*. London: Lexington Books, 2015.

Iadonisi, Richard (ed.) *Graphic History: Essays on Graphic Novels and/or History*. Newcastle upon Tyne: Cambridge Scholar Publishing, 2012.

Jenkins, Henry. *Convergence Culture*. New York: New York University Press, 2006.

Jenkins, Henry. 'Transmedia Storytelling'. *MIT Technology Review*, 2003. https://www.technologyreview.com/s/401760/transmedia-storytelling/ Accessed 20 February 2020.

Kashtan, Aaron. *Between Pen and Pixel: Comics, Materiality, and the Book of the Future*. Columbus: Ohio State University Press, 2018.

Lopes, Paul. *Demanding Respect: The Evolution of the American Comic Book*. Philadelphia: Temple University Press, 2009.

McAllister, Matthew, Sewell, Edward H. Jr and Ian Gordon, Ian (eds). *Comics & Ideology*. New York: Peter Lang Publishing, 2001.

McKinney, Mark. *The Colonial Heritage of French Comics*. Liverpool: Liverpool University Press, 2011.

McKinney, Mark. *Redrawing French Empire in Comics*. Columbus, OH: Ohio State University Press, 2013.

McRobbie, Angela. *Jackie: An Ideology of Adolescent Femininity*. Birmingham: Centre for Cultural Studies. University of Birmingham, 1978a.

McRobbie, Angela. 'Working Class Girls and the Culture of Femininity'. In *Women Take Issue; Aspects of Woman's Subordination*. University of Birmingham Centre for Contemporary Cultural Studies: Women's Studies Group. London: Routledge, 2007 [1978b], pp. 96–108.

McRobbie, Angela. 'Just like a *Jackie* story'. In Angela McRobbie and Trisha McCabe (eds), *Feminism for Girls: An Adventure Story*. London: Routledge, 2013 [1981], pp. 113–128.

McRobbie, Angela. *Feminism and Youth Culture: From Jackie to Just Seventeen*. London: Macmillan, 1991.

Murray, Christopher. *Champions of the Oppressed?: Superhero Comics, Popular Culture, and Propaganda in America during World War II*. Cresskill, NJ: Hampton Press, 2011.

Otmazgin, Nissim and Suter, Rebecca. *Rewriting History in Manga: Stories for the Nation*. New York: Palgrave Macmillan, 2016.

Pizzino, Christopher. *Arresting Development: Comics at the Boundaries of Literature*. Austin, TX: University of Texas Press, 2016.

Rajewsky, Irina O. *Intermedialität*. Tübingen: A. Francke, 2000.

Rosenbaum, Roman (ed.) *Manga and the Representation of Japanese History*. New York: Routledge, 2013.

Sabin, Roger. *Adult Comics*. London: Routledge, 1993.

Sharpe, Sue. *Just Like a Girl: How Girls Learn to be Women*. Harmondsworth: Penguin, 1976.

Singer, Marc. *Breaking the Frames: Populism and Prestige in Comics Studies*. Austin: University of Texas Press, 2019.

Todd, Mark and Pearl, Watson Esther. *Whatcha Mean, What's a Zine?: The Art of Making Zines and Mini Comics*. New York: Clarion Books, 2006.

PART II
HISTORIES AND CULTURES

CHAPTER 4
EARLY CRITICISM AND LEGITIMATION

This chapter examines the earliest writings on comics in Europe and America. It begins by exploring the first writings about American comics in the early twentieth century, giving a snapshot of the debates about the medium's literary worth and potential dangers. It then focuses on censorship: first considering the debates and fears around comics in America and Britain in the 1950s and then summarizing scholarship that has examined legislation and censorship around comics worldwide. The chapter's last three sections focus on the rise of Francophone comics criticism, the legitimization debate around bande dessinée that started in the mid-1960s, and offer summaries of the key scholarly publications in both French and in English.

Early comics criticism in America

American comics grew out of the 'funny pages' of national newspapers in the (late) nineteenth century. These evolved into Sunday colour supplements that were collected and reprinted, leading to a demand for original material around the 1930s. Comics' popularity came hand in hand with criticism, however, and Hajdu notes that in 1909 the *Ladies Home Journal* published an article titled 'A Crime Against Children', claiming the Sunday supplements undermined literacy and glorified lawlessness.[1] Vassallo (2011: npag) also notes that in 1911 the *New York Times* reported on a meeting of the League for the Improvement of the Children's Comic Supplement, which accused the Sunday supplements of being 'vulgar', 'offensive and harmful' and claimed they 'affect [the] minds of children'.

A clear debate emerges in early comics criticism in the United States, which situates comics within more general discussions on the visual arts and popular culture. This pits genteel literary tradition against emergent modernism and new, mass-produced forms of creativity. Two good sources, both edited by Jeet Heer and Kent Worcester, which collect many early articles are *Arguing Comics* (2004), which collects work from literary authors and thinkers, mostly from the first half of the twentieth century, and *A Comics Studies Reader* (2009), which continues this trend by reprinting key critical essays from critics and scholars dating from the 1920s onwards.

Perhaps the earliest American writer to defend comics was Gilbert Seldes in *The Seven Lively Arts* (1924), which reverses many of the tropes often used to criticize popular culture as inherently lowbrow and seeks to reveal the literary potential and artistic value of comics and other media. Seldes' book is divided into sections focusing on comic strips, movies, musical comedy, vaudeville, radio, popular music and dance; each section contains a general essay and then a focus on a famous creator. His chapter 'The "Vulgar" Comic Strip' can be read in full online (Seldes, 1924). It traces a brief history of forerunners and influences (beginning with Jimmy Swinnerton's *Little Bears and Tigers* for the San Francisco *Examiner c.*1892 and noting Wilhelm Busch's *Max und Moritz* (first published 1865) as the 'originals' of the *Katzenjammer Kids*) and describes the path of syndication that Seldes claims has made comics the most popular mass art form. He acknowledges that there can be bad art, but argues that comics are not all about violence and notes examples of 'good strips [...] [that] are self-contained, seldom crack jokes, and have each a significant touch of satire' (224). Seldes then proceeds to a close analysis of George Herriman's comic strip *Krazy Kat*, considering its aesthetics alongside its structure and themes. He draws attention to the ways in which this comic strip plays with the space of the page and other storytelling conventions, and discusses Krazy's idiom. Overall, Seldes considers Krazy as a modern incarnation of eternal folklore based on fantasy, irony, delicacy, sensitivity and beauty.

The poet e e cummings also writes about Krazy Kat in 'A Foreword to Krazy' (*Sewanee Review* [1946]; reprinted in *Arguing Comics*). This refers back to Seldes' celebration of the strip. cummings explores many of the same areas as Seldes, identifying overarching themes in the strip (such as 'love conquers all'), and drawing attention to the completely opposing personalities and worldviews of the three main characters. He argues that interpretation of the strip depends entirely on the reader's own politics and point of view: they may interpret Ignatz Mouse as an anarchic fiend and Offissa Pupp as a safeguarding hero, but can just as easily see Ignatz as a plucky little guy fighting Offissa Pupp's institutional bullying. Neither character understands Krazy, but again they view her quite differently: 'To our softhearted altruist [Pupp], she is the adorably helpless incarnation of saintliness. To our hardhearted egoist [Ignatz], she is the puzzlingly indestructible embodiment of idiocy' (2004: 31). For cummings, *Krazy Kat* is therefore a strip in which an eternal conflict of perspective is acted out and opposite points of view clash and are mediated. cummings goes on to relate this eternal melodrama to the contemporary political situation, demonstrating how its perpetual conflict and chaotic framing combine to create something eternally fascinating. He argues that *Krazy Kat* is politics as perpetual motion, and by defining Krazy as a 'spiritual force' and a 'living ideal' he shows how comics can represent eternal themes (such as the clash between David and Goliath) in new ways.

Robert Warshow revisits *Krazy Kat* in a short article titled 'Woofed with Dreams' (*Partisan Review* [1946]; reprinted in *Arguing Comics*). He argues that the strip format encourages 'lumpen culture' (culture for the dispossessed and uneducated) and that the anonymity of comics production, where writers and artists are replaceable, and the endless nature of the stories support this. Yet Warshow also claims that these texts can offer a freshness that might not be possible higher up the cultural scale. He therefore rejects cummings' reading as an attempt to elevate the format, saying 'We do best, I think, to leave *Krazy Kat* alone. [...] *Krazy Kat* is about a cat who gets hit on the head with bricks'. Ultimately, for Warshow, even if *Krazy Kat* has much to offer as wild fantasy and escapism, it can never be raised to the levels of 'respectable' art.

Irving Howe's 'Notes on Mass Culture' (*Politics* [Spring 1948]; reprinted in *Arguing Comics*) takes an aggressive stance towards mass culture and focuses on the possible effects it might have on audiences, criticizing 'pseudo-cultural amusements' such as music, movies, comics and so forth. The tone resembles the criticism of mass culture by Frankfurt School theorists such as Theodor Adorno and Max Horkheimer who feared that the main aim of carefully standardized culture was to render the masses passive and, ultimately, incapable of independent thinking or resistance. Howe's article speculates about effects on audiences whilst acknowledging that the continued existence of mass culture texts is unavoidable. His argument is not wholly negative (he says that rejecting mass culture would not be preferable), but his language is revealing; words like 'contamination' litter the page. He also seems less concerned with unpicking the relationship between culture and consumer than theorizing about the effects of mass-cultural texts on society. He suggests that these work in three main ways: by the unconscious urge to obliteration (seeking entertainment over work), by the dissociation of personality (through stereotyping and conformity), and by the unpunished violation of law (content that violates tradition and convention).[2]

In these early debates about comics, there is a sense that critics and authors are seeking to protect a literary tradition that is under threat from popular culture and new media. It is notable that many of the strips that are closely discussed, such as *Krazy Kat*, attracted more highbrow readers than regular comics readers. Regardless of whether these early critics were for or against comics, their arguments hold canonized literature and art quite far apart from new media and popular culture. In general, any value they find in comics relies on finding literary or symbolic value in the medium or aligning it with established traditions such as folklore and myth.

Heer and Worcester (2004) argue that a 'third wave' of early American comics criticism takes place after 1950 and diverges from the high-low culture debates that preceded it by starting to try to understand comics on their own terms. In *The Mechanical Bride: Folklore of Industrial Man* (1951; extracts reprinted in *Arguing Comics*), Marshal McLuhan contends that many comics titles are a new form of folk myth. For example, he reads *Little Orphan Annie* as an exemplar of the American dream and individualism; and offers a psychoanalytic reading of *Superman* as a symbol of totalitarian might whose enhanced abilities signify the contemporary drive towards immediacy. In his subsequent book *Understanding Media* (1964) McLuhan devotes a chapter ('The Print') to comics, arguing that they are a highly participatory medium and thus resituating the medium as a challenge to consumer culture rather than its embodiment (see Chapter 2 for further discussion).

Other writers, such as the Italian semiotician Umberto Eco, also consider comics characters as new folkloric figures, with a more positive slant. In 'The Myth of Superman' (a 1962 review of *The Amazing Adventures of Superman*, translated 1972, and reprinted in *Arguing Comics*), Eco argues that Superman and his stories carry mythic and oneiric (dreamlike) overtones, which results in a double function. Superman is a hero archetype with mythic and religious qualities (and thus immobile), but his stories exist in a sphere that must attract readers and keep them reading. Eco argues that contradictions like this create a 'temporal paradox' that characterizes the superhero genre. Story time exists and is played out within each individual narrative but is not carried forward to the next instalment. Eco notes that comics use many narrative strategies to negotiate these hazards, such as backstories, deception, dreams, disguises, repetition of key gestures and moments, and so forth. He therefore argues that Superman can only function as a myth if the reader renounces the need for temporality, which has consequences for 'the existence of freedom, the possibility of planning, the necessity of carrying plans out, the sorrow that such planning entails, the responsibility that it implies, and, finally, the existence of an entire human community whose progressiveness is based on making plans' (19). The ideological consequences of this loss, for Eco, are profound; popular narrative becomes a 'narrative of redundance' whose appeal lies in 'an indulgent invitation to repose, the only occasion of true relaxation offered to the consumer' (21). Eco concludes by considering the contradictions between Superman's civic and political ideologies from this perspective – he cannot change his world, despite his potential omnipotence. Both plot and character are frozen in mutually dependent stasis. While McLuhan and Eco both approach these characters as folklore, they claim this based on comics' unique qualities and popular culture status. However, their arguments differ on whether the medium invites active participation and anti-consumerism, or passive consumption and stasis.

Although it is not exclusively about comics, John Shelton Lawrence and Robert Jewett's *The American Monomyth* (1977) also brings a folkloric lens to bear on American culture and its narratives, including comics. Lawrence and Jewett argue that these stories adapt Joseph Campbell's model of the hero's journey (in *The Hero with a Thousand Faces* [1949]) into a uniquely American form, whereby a threatened community is saved not by its established institutions or governance, but instead by a selfless superhero, who then retires back into obscurity. Lawrence and Jewett identify this pattern across a wide range of cultural artefacts and make a case for the value of these narratives as informing the national character.[3]

In 1979 the *Journal of Popular Culture* 12(4) drew together many of the above ideas in a special section titled 'The Comics as Culture', edited by M. Thomas Inge. This assembles essays that argue for comics' value regardless of their popular culture status, drawing on the legitimizing qualities of literature and folklore to do so. For example, Inge's introduction concludes by pointing out that Shakespeare was once considered mere popular entertainment, and subsequent essays explore the works of notable creators such as Milton Caniff and Walt Kelly, alongside an interview with underground cartoonist Trina Robbins, and wider critical analyses including Western comics, fantasy, aesthetics and the hero archetype. Overall, then, these early arguments primarily evaluate the potential of comics based on their politics, formal experimentation and links to literary tradition and myth. Throughout these decades, however, the medium was also decried and vilified until the increasing moral panic around comics resulted in the American Comics Code (1954).

The American Comics Code

The American Comics Code was introduced in 1954 after a decade of intense moral panic and publicity focusing on the damage that crime and horror comic books were supposedly inflicting on children. This culminated in a Senate investigation in which senator Estes Kefauver attempted to hold comics publishers accountable for the unsuitable material being sold to children via crime and horror comic books (for fuller details of the court proceedings and the Comics Code, please see critics such as Hajdu and Nyberg, below). In the lead-up to the Code, numerous critics, of which the following are only a small sample, both celebrated and attacked the medium. Other responses and participants in this debate can be found at the *Seduction of the Innocent* website (O'Day, 2012), which collects information on the comics cited by the critics discussed below, and includes links to additional articles of the same period discussing the issue from all angles.

The initial debate around American comics is characterized by four key texts spanning 1947–1954: Coulton Waugh's *The Comics* (1947), Gershon Legman's *Love and Death: A Study in Censorship* (1949), Fredric Wertham's *Seduction of the Innocent* (1953) and Geoffrey Wagner's *Parade of Pleasure* (1954). These books explore the development of the medium with respect to its history and relevant legislation, and foreground concerns such as sensationalism, violence, fascism, racism, sexuality and other social issues. In *The Comics*, Waugh celebrates the medium, tracing the development of the American comic strip against a backdrop of corporate and social history in the first half of the 1900s. He opens by looking closely at the work of 'the three Grand Old Men' (16), the American creators James Swinnerton, Richard Outcault and Rudolph Dirks, although he also acknowledges the significant input of predecessors such as Wilhelm Busch (*Max und Moritz*). He considers their various contributions and uses these to provide an early three-part definition of qualities that comics 'usually' have: a recurring character, a sequence of pictures, and speech in the drawing (14). He then discusses other early creators such as 'Charles' [Carl] E. Schulz and Winsor McCay, and 'classic' strips from the pre-First World War period (such as Bud Fisher's *Mutt and Jeff* and F. Opper's *Happy Hooligan*) alongside contemporary strips such as *Gasoline Alley* and *Blondie*. He concludes by discussing the comic book format, tracing its evolution and ending with several predictions of where we are headed 'comically speaking'. These have not all proved correct (e.g. the return of the gag strip), but they stress the importance of audiences to comics and the impact these have on the medium's content.

In *Love and Death: A Study in Censorship* (1949), Gershon Legman argues the other side of the case and vehemently attacks comics. He claims that 'the perversion of children has become an industry' (33), citing antecedents and contemporaries such as Disney, cartoons, comics, and Punch and Judy as examples of the 'violent popular arts' given to children of all ages, where menaces are created solely in order to justify ever-increasing violence. He also draws on the historical development of comics to justify his argument: focusing on the removal of state laws against the production and distribution of 'any book, pamphlet, magazine, newspaper or other printed paper [...] made up of criminal news, police reports, or accounts of criminal deeds, or pictures, or stories of deeds of bloodshed, lust or crime' in 1948. He claims that the number of crime comics in circulation rose from twenty to over one hundred during the following year.

Legman argues that violence is camouflaged in many other genres of comics, such as the talking animal comics aimed at younger readers; or adaptations of classic literature for older readers that are cut and abridged to emphasize action sequences. He similarly claims that Superman is the opposite of what he appears – rather than teaching bravery and respect for the law, he represents vigilante justice and thus lives 'in a continuous guilty terror, projecting outwards in every direction his readers' paranoid hostility [against corrupt Government, other countries]' (n.p.). Similarly, in *Parade of Pleasure* (1954) Wagner criticizes the violent content of cinema and comics. He focuses on the ratio of violence in various comics titles (e.g. noting twenty-six acts of violence in twenty-one pages of one title). Although Wagner's introduction says the book is intended as a defence of American popular entertainment, his argument primarily focuses on its unsuitability for children.

The predominance of violence in crime and horror comics is also the focus of Dr Fredric Wertham, a psychiatrist who was a major voice for the anti-comics lobby from 1948 onwards. In 1948 *Colliers* magazine published an article titled 'Horror in the Nursery' by Judith Crist (available online), which drew attention to Dr Wertham's clinical studies on comics and juvenile delinquency and quoted from him extensively. Five years later, Wertham published *Seduction of the Innocent* (1953), which claimed that 'Comic books are death on reading' (121), and coincided with the Senate investigations at which he was a key speaker.

Wertham's book is now more often used as a primary text in itself, rather than a piece of comics criticism, since it represents a pivotal moment in American comics history. He aims his attack primarily at the crime comics and the violent plots and images they present to children, although he finds superhero comics, romance and other genres almost as offensive in promoting undesirable values and acts. He argues passionately that comics contribute heavily to child illiteracy and delinquency, and he puts forward numerous examples of unsuitable themes. Wertham also criticizes the comics advertisements for promoting neuroses about body image or selling items utterly unsuitable for children. For both Legman and Wertham, the young age of readers and the comics' promotion of unhealthy fantasies are crucial factors.

Sexuality is another point of concern, and Legman notes homosexual themes at both an overt level (declarations of love, kissing, boy sidekicks, tight outfits, phallic symbols and giant biceps) and also, he claims, at a deeper thematic level, as 'the weak and fearful righteousness' of heroes who 'accept their power passively' (43). Wertham also draws attention to the sexual violence that appears in crime comics and the eroticism that he claims underpins superhero titles such as *Wonder Woman* and *Batman*. Wagner also points to Wonder Woman's display of 'a curt and colourful masculinity', and describes Robin as an 'adoring' foil to Batman's character. By contrast, Waugh's early examination of the superhero genre, and early 'He-Men' such as Popeye and L'il Abner, does not find these sorts of themes or concerns present.

Legman, Wertham and Wagner also foreground other social issues such as racism, drug use and fascism. It is important to note that their concerns are not limited to the controversial crime and horror comics but extend to other genres such as the superhero. Wagner describes Superman as a 'fascist', and for Legman, superheroes as role models are insidiously damaging and offer a literature of violence and sexual frustration.

Although these critics focus their arguments around similar areas, their style and methodology differ widely. Waugh's tone is easy and conversational and as a whole *The Comics* gives an anecdotal (although sometimes fictionalized) history, supported by sample pages from most of the strips he discusses and by reader statistics. In *Parade of Pleasure*, Wagner claims simply to have examined the influences he sees in American movies, comic books and pin-up magazines, with no political angle or axe to grind. He draws on many other studies and takes pains to include the issue number and title of every example he cites. By contrast, although *Seduction* gives statistics on juvenile delinquency and draws on seven years of research working with children at the Lafargue clinic (a free psychiatric clinic in Harlem, New York), most of Wertham's evidence is in the form of brief quotations from conversations with individual patients, presented anecdotally with no referencing. The textual analysis it contains is also very superficial, and Wertham misunderstands the plots of some comics stories. His approach and language are revealing: sixteen pages of images from comics are also included at the centre, without context, along with sardonic captions. His language throughout tends towards the impassioned and emotional: he describes the comics as 'worse-than-rubbish' (276) and 'offal' (282) and makes heavy use of metaphor (such as biblical quotation, gardening analogies and even a simile that compares comics to rape [272]). The extreme nature of this moment of controversy is evident in the debates these texts offer. They all stress the importance of taking comics seriously: Wagner argues that the tendencies he identifies are apparent worldwide, but most visible in America due to its freedom of speech. However, by focusing their arguments around media effects and child protection, these critics had a key role in defining comics of all genres as childish entertainment.

While such impassioned arguments characterized the early 1950s, a few shorter articles would follow that took a more moderate and nuanced approach. In 'The Middle Against Both Ends' (*Encounter* [1955]; reprinted in *Arguing Comics*), literary critic and Fulbright lecturer Leslie Fielder surveys criticisms of the comics medium. He asks why no strategic methodology or serious consideration of comics, in order to understand the medium or create taxonomies of different subgenres, has ever been attempted. He justifies the comics' content by comparing it to many other media artefacts, and claims that their stories are no more sensational than almost all the other art produced in America: 'There is no count of sadism or brutality which could not be equally proved against Hemingway or Faulkner or Paul Bowles – or, for that matter, Edgar Allan Poe' (20). Fielder situates the criticisms of comics in the social class struggle that surrounds them: arguing that the 'problem' posed by popular culture (and the cause of attacks upon it) is a consequence of class distinction in a democratic society. He stresses that popular entertainment should not be considered as a conspiracy by profiteers aimed at a deprived but innocent people; pointing out that these artefacts often simply reflect what people want. He describes the situation as 'bewildering' and 'complex', because 'the people have not rejected completely the notion of cultural equality; rather, they desire its symbol but not its fact' (23). A hierarchy of taste and values thus becomes unacceptable to readers at every level, and provokes equal outrage from highbrow, middlebrow and lowbrow consumers. In 1960 Fielder would continue this argument in

Love and Death in the American Novel, deconstructing assumptions about this concept and analysing the American literary tradition (and, later, genre fiction).

Robert Warshow also writes about the horror comics in a personal and anecdotal article bemoaning his son Paul's love of them ('The Study of Man: Paul, the Horror Comics, and Dr Wertham', 1954, available online) while acknowledging that the EC titles in particular have 'imaginative flair' (596). He critiques Wertham for his moral confusion and for not recognizing the complexities of regulation and/or suppression. Overall he takes a moderate stance and tone, reflecting on effects arguments, gatekeeping and responsibility. He concludes that the comics are not affecting his son (who is doing well and defends them with gusto and intelligence) but that he would nonetheless 'be happy if Senator Kefauver and Dr Wertham could find some way to make it impossible for Paul to get *any* comic books. But I'd rather Paul didn't get the idea that I had anything to do with it' (604).

Retrospective evaluations and revisionist readings

For those interested in finding out more, the history of comics censorship in both the UK and the United States has been extensively revisited by scholars in the intervening decades. In particular David Hajdu, Amy Kiste Nyberg and Martin Barker have produced landmark texts that contextualize and reflect upon the chain of events and stakeholders in the controversy around American comics. Hajdu's *The Ten Cent Plague* (2008) covers the build-up to the Senate investigation in America, focusing primarily on the people and companies within the industry, rather than the proceedings themselves. He begins by summarizing the birth of American comics at the start of the twentieth century: defining the earliest newspaper comic strips (*Yellow Kid, Happy Hooligan* and *The Katzenjammer Kids*) as earthy, anti-authoritarian and unsophisticated. He notes the development of new and experimental formats from pioneering creators over the next two decades, detailing the rise of original comics and the growth of a flamboyant and highly commercial industry from this. He then surveys the rapidly expanding audience for comics in the 1930s and 1940s, which was accompanied by criticism in the national press from journalists such as Sterling North. Hajdu offers a detailed account of the way the industry moved towards publishing controversial content, and the key players from several companies who were involved in this. While he looks closely at the role of Bill Gaines and his company EC Comics, Hajdu puts this within the bigger picture of the many other comics publishers also active at the time. When he comes to discuss the rise of crime comics and the Code, his focus is on how Wertham's argument was staged and manipulated by the press. There is a close focus on grassroots initiatives such as the book burnings that took place, with first-hand evidence from readers, students and other participants.

The book traces the evolution of controversial comics through the crime, romance and horror genres, to satirical and humorous publications such as *Mad* and *Panic*. Hajdu points towards the large number of high-profile artists that worked on these titles and draws on the words of professionals to demonstrate the realities of the industry at the time (such as pay, ownership, conditions). He argues that the context of McCarthyism was crucial to the panic about comic books. He gives detailed descriptions of the initial arrests (including EC's receptionist) and of the Senate investigation itself, accompanied by a selection of photographs from the hearings. He then describes the subsequent formation of the Comics Magazine Association of America (CMAA), the body responsible for enforcing the Comics Code, and gives examples of the types of changes that were made to panels and content under these guidelines.

Hajdu's concluding chapters then discuss the impact of the Code – the emergence of EC's New Direction line, and their ongoing difficulties with aggressive censorship that led to Bill Gaines resigning from the industry, only continuing to publish *Mad* magazine. Hajdu also notes the complete collapse of many other publishers in 1955 and 1956, such as Starr, Sterling, Toby Press, United Features' comic book section, Eastern Color, Ace, Avon, Premier and Superior. Finally, he references the way the industry recovered by retrenching and shifting its focus to superheroes in the 1960s, and ends with an anecdotal epilogue in which R. Crumb speaks about the influence that *Mad* Magazine and EC Comics had on him. The book's appendices include an extensive list of the artists, writers and others who never again worked in comics after the purge of the 1950s and notes on the documentaries, interviews, first-hand conversations and other resources that were used in Hajdu's research. Accessibly written in a journalistic and anecdotal style, *The Ten Cent Plague* is well substantiated and referenced and provides a lively account of the circumstances and individuals that led to the censorship of the industry.

Amy Kiste Nyberg's *Seal of Approval* (1998) is a similarly detailed investigation into the creation of the Comics Code from an industry perspective. Nyberg examines the events leading up to the Code's creation;

the ways it was devised and implemented; and the impact on comics publishers. She challenges the widespread belief of fan-historians that the Comics Code caused the decline of the industry, arguing that the rise of television; the negative publicity attached to comics; and an unrelated antitrust suit that forced America's leading comics distributor to pull out of national distribution in 1955 (*United States* v. *American News*) were more direct causes of the loss of sales that forced many publishers out of business.

Nyberg draws on previous scholarship and readership studies to show that the primary audience for comics in the 1940s and 1950s were children, and that comics were easily available at drugstores and grocery stores. She situates concerns about comics within a longer timeline that includes dime novels, newspaper strips, and movies, and traces the emergence of attacks on comics in the popular press and from gatekeepers such as librarians and educators, noting that public attention and outrage was limited until the postwar period, when comics became linked to rising concerns about delinquency (James Gilbert's *Cycle of Outrage* (1986) offers a wider picture of this aspect of this cultural moment). Organizations such as the National Office of Decent Literature (from the Catholic Church) incorporated comics into their list of objectionable materials, drawing on elitist literary arguments of the type discussed at the beginning of this chapter, as well as the new fears about media effects. Nyberg looks closely at some of these organizations, noting the ways in which their initially modest goals changed as the issue gathered momentum, going from simply removing images of sex and violence to monitoring the content as a whole for unsuitable themes. She offers a detailed narrative of the investigation conducted by the Senate Subcommittee for Juvenile Delinquency, which took place over three days in New York in Spring 1954, and which forced the industry to agree to self-regulation by forming the CMAA and producing the initial six-point Comics Code.

Like Hajdu, Nyberg draws attention to the context of the investigation. She argues that the Senate Committee was less concerned with fact finding than with being seen to respond to public outcry, but that their activities, and pressure from distributors, wholesalers and retailers, forced the industry to commit to the above Code, changing the landscape of comics publishing as crime and horror comics virtually disappeared from newsstands. She surveys Wertham's body of work as a whole, noting that *Seduction* is just one manifestation of his lifelong concerns about children, media and violence and his wholehearted belief in the value of social psychiatry, which appear throughout his work (*The Circle of Guilt*, 1956; *A Sign for Cain*, 1966). She draws particular attention to his later work *The World of Fanzines* (1973), in which he finds genuine value in these publications and suggests they can offer an escape from the commodification of mass culture (see further below). Nyberg then goes on to trace the incorporation and development of the CMAA and the fortunes of the various publishing companies involved. She notes that the revisions of the Code in 1971 and 1989 have loosened restrictions each time in a manner that reflects the changing nature of society, the industry and the audience. While the process of Code review has remained the same, and the 'seal of approval' indicates that a comic's contents are suitable for all ages, the number of titles submitted for Code approval has also diminished over the years, acknowledging anew that comics are suitable for all ages. Nyberg's conclusion suggests that if this had been considered when the Code was hastily devised (rather than the blanket assumption that all comics were for children and therefore required approval), the consequences for the industry would have been very different. Overall she adopts a moderate position on its impact on the industry as a whole and draws attention to numerous other forces and factors that have affected comics and mass entertainment: including internal and external competition for audience, a changing distribution system and the direct market, and new creative practices and notions of intellectual property and ownership.

Martin Barker's *A Haunt of Fears* (1984) traces a similar path through the anti-comics panics in Britain between 1949 and 1955, which culminated in the Children and Young Persons (Harmful Publications) Act. Barker argues that the campaign that made it happen was in fact not about comics but about 'broader post-war societal concerns and anxieties and conceptions of society, children and Britain' (6). In the case of the comics this was founded on misconceptions that relied on very selective and superficial readings of the material. The accepted view of the British campaign is that it was a large grassroots organization led by ordinary folk who wanted to see the offensive material in these comics banned, but Barker offers an alternative point of view. His opening chapters detail the accepted history of events, which were led by the Comics Campaign Council (CCC) that emerged in 1952 out of an organization called the National Council for Defence of Children (NCDC) and would liaise with large organizations such as the National Union of Teachers (NUT) to achieve the campaign goals. Barker is concerned, however, with exposing the invisible influences and institutions that shaped the campaign, in particular the largely unreported role of the British Communist party, which was heavily involved in the background of the campaign as they sought to remove American influences from

British entertainment. He also revisits the key voices in the debate, drawing attention to the ideological, methodological and conceptual problems in Wertham's approach and argument, and comparing his claims with the work of Wagner, Legman, and, in Britain, George Pumphrey. Barker demonstrates that Legman is the most radical, critiquing society and the child's lack of power; Wagner is elitist, troubled by the rise of mass culture; and Wertham and Pumphrey are concerned liberals, wishing to protect children.

The impact of censorship on British and American comics has been vast, and many similar revisionist accounts of this period in American history have appeared, such as Bart Beaty's *Fredric Wertham and the Critique of Mass Culture* (2005), and Mark Evanier's titular essay in the collection *Wertham Was Right!* (2003). Both seek to reassess Wertham's position and ideals, reinterpreting these in accordance with context and additional evidence. Beaty considers Wertham's published work alongside private papers, correspondence, and notes, and reclaims his legacy as a progressive and nuanced thinker, focusing particularly on his positive reaction to the fanzines he encountered in the 1970s (see Chapter 10). Evanier compares Wertham to the supervillain of the comics industry and offers a fuller picture of his life. He argues that the appeal of *Seduction* to parents was that it absolved them of responsibility, and draws attention to the way in which its critics have focused on a few paragraphs rather than addressing the book in its entirety. But it is Evanier's description of his year-long correspondence with Wertham (who contacted him when researching *The World of Fanzines*) and Wertham's subsequent publication of this book that sets it apart. He highlights the ways in which *The World of Fanzines* is a rebuttal of *Seduction* and Wertham's own seeming unawareness of this. He concludes with an emotional imagined conversation between himself and Wertham, in which the doctor acknowledges the negative impact he has had on the industry and expresses regret: 'I will never be remembered for reforming prison conditions or fighting racial discrimination [...] I will always be that nutty doctor who wanted to ban *Tales from the Crypt*' (194).

Finally, John Lent's edited collection *Pulp Demons* (1999) assembles essays examining the global impact of the post-war anti-comics campaigns, following Barker in pointing out that these took place in at least twenty countries across four continents during the 1940s and 1950s. Lent's introduction contextualizes the controversy, pointing out that it far predates Wertham and that it led to some unusual alliances in different countries. Government investigations and hearings took place in America, Canada, Germany and the UK, producing legislation based around a commitment to self-censorship. Australia, Korea, Taiwan and the Philippines also introduced self-censorship to stave off government intervention; in counterpoint to Japan, where public outcries had little effect on government or industry. Lent rightly points out that, like much comics scholarship, research into this period of censorship has focused primarily on a few countries. His essay collection contains contributions from Nyberg and Barker that summarize their monographs, alongside chapters from Osborne, Barker and Reibman that focus on Fredric Wertham and draw attention to the doctor's humanist and liberal beliefs.

The remaining chapters explore other countries and cultures. In 'The Comics Debate in Germany', Jovanovic and Koch draw on analysis of press reports to demonstrate that between 1954 and 1956 (although beginning much earlier, as in the Bundestag's 1949 request for a Federal Act Against Dirt and Rubbish), the arguments over comics reflected the country's social, cultural and political landscape. In particular they note the casting of comics as an American invention (despite the existence of German comic strips prior to the Second World War) and the paradoxical definition of the United States as both modern/progressive and also symptomatic of moral decay. The debates about the comics' effects were dominated by teachers and educators and focused on comics' supposed negative impact on children and teenagers: by normalizing violence and hampering mental development. The authors argue that any new cultural novelty would have met with similar rejection and hostility, given the country's fragile national self-image after the Second World War. In the following chapter, Mona Gleason similarly explores the motivations behind anti-comics rhetoric in post-war Canada, identifying undertones of class prejudice and misogyny (as particular types of family were praised or attacked), and arguing that the debate can be read as an attempt to shore up the hegemony of middle-class Anglo-Celtic society in the country. Graeme Osborne examines the Australian debates, arguing that these were symptomatic of several larger concerns, including censorship, perceptions of the influence of mass communication, conflicting religious and secular interests, tensions over cultural identity, struggles between protectionists and free traders, and conflicts over values and standards which were part of an underlying struggle for authority and power between different generations and sociocultural groups. John Lent's subsequent chapter explores the 'Comics Controversies and Codes: Reverberations in Asia', arguing that these were felt most in areas with a strong American presence (the Philippines, Taiwan, South Korea and Japan), where the comics were criticized for their portrayals of crime, violence and sex, and their harmful effects on children. The result was that in the Philippines the industry created a self-censorship Code, while Taiwan and South Korea established government guidelines, although Lent argues that these were as much about stopping the prevalence of Japanese comics (which deprived local cartoonists of work) as they were about curbing depictions of sex and violence. These chapters all agree that anti-comics sentiment in these countries far predated Wertham's concerns about crime comics and give fascinating details of the different contexts and stakeholders that informed the debates, alongside extracts from the various codes, investigations and legislations. They demonstrate that the negative reaction to comics was a global event, which was primarily social and political in nature and arguably had little to do with the publications themselves.

The particular controversies of Scandinavia and Finland are explored in more depth in Helle Strandgaard Jensen's (2010) article 'Why Batman was Bad' and Ralf Kauranen's chapter 'Transnationalism in the Finnish 1950s debate on Comics' (*Cortsen, La Cour and Magnussen*, 2015). Jensen analyses the public discourse and debates around comics in Denmark, Norway and Sweden, situating these within the 'consumption politics' of the 1950s. Rather than reading these events as a 'moral panic' (a term Jensen critiques as it predisposes us to doubt the authenticity and validity of the claimed concerns), she argues that we need to assess the way in which communities in these countries connected particular moralities to these comics (and who was responsible for doing so), what role children's products were supposed to play in their lives (and who was responsible for policing this), and what notions were attached to childhood (and by whom). Jensen argues that children's consumption of inappropriate reading material (from Blyton to comics) was seen as a threat to the norms and aspirations of post-war Scandinavia, and that superhero comics in particular were criticized for giving a distorted and violent picture of a world where physical force and weapons dominate. As the main debaters were teachers, politicians, librarians and psychologists, the distribution of the comics (through a marketplace rather than libraries or schools) also came under attack, and fears were shared through the membership of global bodies such as the International Board on Books for Young People (IBBY).

The Scandinavian and American debates share many themes: Jensen cites the work of Lorentz Larson (*Barn och Serier* [Children and Comics], 1954), Evald Fransson ('The Comics – a Reading Problem', 1953) and Nils Bejerot's *Barn-serier-samhalle* ([*Children Comics Society*], 1954). Like Wertham, Larson interviewed hundreds of children, painting these participants as innocent and vulnerable and thus finding their identification with comics characters obsessive and alarming. Fransson, a teacher, claims the medium causes illiteracy, and Bejerot's work focuses on the perceived negative influence of popular culture more generally, arguing that children tend to imitate. Jensen points out that the debaters consistently refused to recognize children's competence to choose what was best for themselves, and concludes that the apparent unsuitability of superhero comics arose from their inability 'to teach children about the cultural and social values of the Scandinavian societies, and thus could not fulfil the educational function children's cultural products were supposed to fulfil in children's lives' (65).

Kauranen also draws attention to the integration of nationalist sentiments in the debate, by considering the way in which Finnish society viewed comics as a foreign cultural element. He explains that the first reports of global debates on comics appeared in Finland around 1952, conceptualized as problems that would soon make their way to this country, and details the way the debate gathered momentum as a transnational event. It took place in an international context and drew on national identities and traditions to frame and make meaning of events as the types of comics available in Finland were repeatedly contrasted with those elsewhere. In many ways, Kauranen's article echoes Barker's thoughts about the role of British national identity in the UK campaign, and matches the scope of Lent's collection by drawing attention to the way in which various instances of the global comics controversy shared the same concerns (a 'new', often foreign form of media that was a threat), the same odd combination of players (educators and psychologists as prominent critics, aligned with conservatives and socialist in opposition to the comics), and similar legislative solutions and reactions.

Bande dessinée publication in France was restricted by the law of 16 July 1949, which applied to all youth and children's publications.[4] This, however, did not hinder, and probably even fuelled a relatively early debate around comics legitimation propelled by fans' memories of their childhood comics reading. In addition to tracing the contributions of comics fandom (*bédéphilie*) to comics criticism, this chapter will now turn to the rise of bande dessinée criticism and the consequent move towards comics legitimation. Introducing key texts on the legitimation of French-language comics,[5] it also discusses secondary literature on the interaction between English- and French-language comics and on changes and grey areas in the notion of comics legitimation.

Legitimizing the 'Ninth Art'[6]

In contrast to the intellectuals and authors who produced some of the earliest writings on American comics, fandom or bédéphilie played a crucial role in generating the first instances of comics criticism in France. The initial consolidation of Francophone comics fandom occurred with the *Club des bandes dessinées* (*CBD*). Launched in 1962, it boasted well-known personalities such as philosopher Edgar Morin, filmmaker Alain Resnais and journalist Francis Lacassin (Groensteen, 2006: 110–111; Miller, 2007: 23–24). The club was inspired by an article on the pre-Second World War comics in the science-fiction monthly *Fiction* (July 1961) by Swiss speleologist and fan collector Pierre Strinati (Gabilliet, 2016: 140). This article resonated deeply with readers and the magazine received an unprecedented number of letters from readers longing to re-acquire and re-read those forgotten (and often discarded) comics magazines. When the conversation in the magazine turned to offers to buy or borrow comics, the editors of *Fiction* suggested that another forum should be created to facilitate such exchanges. As a result, Lacassin, who had helped with answering readers' letters about comics, set up the *CBD*. Within months the club began publishing its newsletter-turned-magazine *Giff-Wiff*. The publication's initial purpose was to facilitate the Club's two main aims: republishing inaccessible pre-war comics and establishing a network of comics collectors. It also encouraged the birth of early, often fannish, comics criticism, which initially focused on comics from 1930s to the 1940s (Groensteen, 2006: 112–116).

By 1964 the *CBD* had become the *CELEG* (*Centre d'études des littératures d'expression graphique* [Study Centre for Graphic Literatures]), a name that emphasized the key role that comics criticism had started to play for the club members. Some of its members branched off to form *SOCERLID* (*Société civil de l'étude et la recherche en bande dessinée* [Research Society for Comics]) because they wanted to include contemporary comics instead of focusing exclusively on comics from the 'golden age'. Like the other two clubs, *SOCERLID* consisted of members from diverse walks of life and included Pierre Couperie, Claude Moliterni and Maurice Horn, all of whom went on to publish extensively on comics, ranging from exhibition catalogues to histories of comics, usually with a strong focus on American comics. As of October 1966, *SOCERLID* published *Phénix,* an 'international magazine on comics', edited by Moliterni, which continued to be published until *SOCERLID*'s dissolution in 1977. Moliterni eventually became responsible for one of the earliest university courses on comics in 1969 at the University of Vinciennes. Lacassin would start giving his course on comics history and aesthetics at the Sorbonne in 1971 (cf. Demange 2017). Jean-Philippe Martin's 2012 article '*La théorie du 0%. Petite étude critique de la critique en bande dessinée*' ['The Theory of 0%. Small Critical Study of Comics Criticism'] provides a brief overview of the transformation of comics criticism from its early days in fanzines and amateur publications to its formalization with critics such as Bruno Lecigne and Thierry Groensteen, who also edited the *Cahiers de la bande dessinée* from 1984 until the last issue in 1988. In the 1970s, the *Cahiers de la bande dessinée* merged with the *Schtroumpf fanzine*, a fanzine started in the 1969 by an adolescent Jacques Glénat, who later founded one of the biggest bande dessinée publishers, Glénat. With the help of crowdfunding, the *Cahiers* were relaunched by the journalist Vincent Bernière in 2017.

Bande dessinée was hailed as the ninth art in the French-speaking world as early as 1964 in a column in the comics magazine *Spirou*. The column was written by cartoonist Morris (Maurice de Bevere), creator of *Lucky Luke*, and the collector Pierre Vankeer. Running until 1967, the column *9e art: Musée de la bande dessinée* [*9th Art: Comics Museum*] offered a fairly international history of comics: it went as far back as the late eighteenth-century *images d'épinal* (named after a press in Épinal known for publishing popular, colourful prints) and included well-known cartoonists from all over the world, ranging from Wilhelm Busch (*Max und Moritz*) to Oscar Jacobsson (*Anderson*) and Alex Raymond (*Flash Gordon*).

The epithet of the ninth art was most famously attached to comics in 1971 with Lacassin's book, *Pour un neuvième art, la bande dessinée* [*Comics, A Ninth Art*], which was the culmination of his legitimation efforts including founding comics clubs, festival work and university courses on comics. This legitimation was not as straightforward or glorious as the notion of the 'ninth art' might suggest. There is a tendency to forget that the arts that precede and follow this rank, all belong to the popular sphere: cinema is the seventh art, the 'media arts' [*arts médiatiques*] such as radio, television and even photography are part of the eighth art, and video games are the tenth art. As such, the legitimation of bande dessinée remains somewhat dubious, as Éric Maigret suggested in his 1994 article.

Legitimation issues

Scholarship on bande dessinée legitimation often takes as a central reference point sociologist Luc Boltanski's seminal essay 'La constitution du champ de la bande dessinée' ['On the Constitution of the Comics Field']. Originally published in Actes de la Recherche en Science Sociales (1975), the essay was translated into English in Beaty and Miller's The French Comics Theory Reader (2014). Boltanski, a student of Pierre Bourdieu, was heavily influenced by Bourdieu's notion of fields (champs) of cultural production and related theories including the dynamics of the hierarchies in the arts and the acquisition and augmentation of cultural capital (see for instance Bourdieu's La distinction: critique sociale du jugement [Distinction: A Social Critique of the Judgement of Taste] [1979; trans. 1984]). Seen through this Bourdieusian lens, bande dessinée legitimation has often been regarded as a struggle for recognition that unfolds through the channels used by the higher arts (fine arts, literature). These channels include the establishment of exhibitions, festivals (see Benoît Mouchart's 2017 article on the role of the Angoulême festival in comics legitimation in the special issue of Le Débat edited by Natalie Heinich), prizes, inclusion in university syllabi, academic publications and the rise of dedicated journals.

Soon after Boltanski's article, the sociology journal Communications published a special issue on comics in 1976 titled La bande dessinée et son discours [Comics and Its Discourse]. Edited by Michel Covin, Pierre Fresnault-Deruelle and Bernard Toussaint, this issue assembles articles by researchers from diverse domains (semiotics, literary theory, psychoanalysis) and includes seminal essays, such as Pierre Fresnault-Deruelle's 'Du linéaire au tabulaire' ['On Linearity and Tabularity'] on page layouts in comics, which has been translated in The French Comics Theory Reader and Umberto Eco's 'Le myth de Superman' ['The Myth of Superman', published in the critical theory journal Diacritics in 1972]. This special issue captures the interdisciplinarity of comics research and the important place occupied by semiotics in early studies, many of which are concerned with reading and narrative possibilities, genres and of course word-image hybridity. All these elements, as already discussed in this Guide's opening chapter on formalist approaches, continue to play a central role in comics theory.

More recent comics scholarship continues to question and problematize the notion of comics legitimation through Bourdieusian channels. Most notably, Thierry Groensteen considers comics 'an unidentified cultural object' and challenges the submission of comics to principles associated with the fine arts (museum exhibitions, catering to an adult audience) and its disassociation from its mass cultural essence. In his 2006 book, *Un objet culturel non identifié: la bande dessinée* [*An Unidentified Cultural Object: Comics*], Groensteen writes that the recognition of comics is hindered by the following biases:

1. Comics is a mixed medium, combining, almost heretically, both image and text

2. While it may cater to adults, it does not go beyond resurrecting their childhood memories since its message is inherently infantile

3. It is linked to caricature which does not enjoy a respectable standing amongst the visual arts

4. Comics did not follow the artistic movements of the twentieth century

5. Images in comics are devalued because of their small size and their multiplicity (2006: 23).[7]

In his article 'La reconnaissance en demi-teinte de la bande dessinée' ['The Mitigated Recognition of Comics'] (1994), Maigret suggests that the Bourdieusian notions of the cultural field and legitimation processes gloss over key constituents of comics such as its essence as a mass medium and reproduce the elitist criteria used in the canonization of the high arts. This results in a denial of the diversity and the specificity of comics. It also results in a certain banalization of comics: Maigret draws a parallel between comics and rock music since both have become assimilated into the higher echelons of culture and hence made acceptable (117–118). Nathalie Heinich has similarly proposed considering the 'artification' of comics, the processes that aim to transform comics into an art (Heinich, 2017: 5–9). For Heinich, the artification of comics, which mirrors its legitimation, is also incomplete (9).

In a more recent edited volume that proposes comics as a 'mediaculture', Maigret offers the notion of postlegitimacy to reconsider the contemporary status of comics in a cultural hierarchy that is more accepting of outsider elements (Maigret, 2012: 130–148). For Maigret, comics remains an invisible art. However, while McCloud uses this term to explain how comics stories are connected in reader's minds (see Chapter 2 on formalist approaches for more details), Maigret uses the post-colonial notion of invisibility to refer to oppressed cultures. For Maigret comics have been invisible because the medium's diversity has not been fully embraced (138) even though it inhabits a more tolerant climate (140).

In his 2009 article on the institutionalization of comics, '*L'illégitimité de la bande dessinée et son institutionnalisation: le rôle de la loi du 16 juillet 1949*' ['Comics Illegitimacy and Its Institutionalisation: The Role of the Law of 16 July 1949'], Jean-Matthieu Méon suggests that comics legitimation is caught between the more recent impulse of canonization and the older impulse to restrict and even demonize comics. He reminds us that the law of 16 July 1949 which applies to publications aimed at children and adolescents and is enforced by the *Commission de surveillance et de contrôle* [Commission of Surveillance and Control] is still in force and has played an important role in the semi- or incomplete legitimization of comics.

Maigret continues the contextualization of comics legitimation in light of consumption and production practices and their regulation, by discussing the impact of the conflation between comics and the entertainment sector in his chapter for *La bande dessinée, quelle lecture, quelle culture?* [*Comics, Which Reading, Which Culture?*] (2015). Edited by Benoît Berthou and Jean-Philippe Martin, this anthology gives a detailed overview of comics readerships across age groups and gender, social class, comics readers' interests in other cultural activities, and informal and formal distribution networks and modes of publicity. Based on a 2011 survey supported by the French Ministry of Culture, the volume takes an important step in delineating the broader context of comics readership in France and its relationship to legitimation impulses (for a detailed discussion of scholarship on fandom in other countries and regions, see Chapter 7).

In a two-part article 'Genre et légitimité dans l'édition de bande dessinée' ['Genre and Legitimation in Comics Publishing'] (2018), Sylvain Aquatias considers the role of genre in the legitimation process. The first part considers legitimation in comics magazines and series. The second turns to the rise of the graphic novel and the consequent undoing of traditional genres as independent, non-mainstream publishers launched series that were not related to specific genres. While Aquatias notes the success of the graphic novel in the French-speaking sphere, which is underscored by the increasing number of major, literary publishers such as Flammarion and Seuil publishing graphic novels, Jean-Paul Gabilliet suggests that the graphic novel phenomenon and its success in the English-speaking world – which then had international reverberations – can be seen as the result of a Europeanization of the American comic book (2005). This Europeanization is manifested through the gradual changes in American comics publishing and distribution practices as well as its reception.

Transatlantic interactions between comics and bande dessinée

It is noteworthy that one of the first instances of transatlantic convergence occurs in one of the earliest, landmark comics exhibitions in a museum: *Bande dessinée et figuration narrative* [Comics and Narrative Figuration], organized at the Musée des arts et métiers in Paris by *SOCERLID*. In focusing on American cartoonists such as Milton Caniff (*Terry and the Pirates*) and Burne Hogarth (*Tarzan*), the exhibition valorized American rather than European comics. It was accompanied by a catalogue also written by *SOCERLID*, subtitled: *Histoire/Esthetique/Production et Sociologie de la Bande Dessinée Mondiale Procedes Narratifs et Structure de l'Image dans la Peinture Contemporaine* [History/Aesthetics/Production and Sociology of World Comics, Narrative Processes and Image Structure in Contemporary Painting]. Painting and comics are juxtaposed, as are the numerous elements that evoke academic subjects (history, aesthetics, sociology, narrative). As the long-winded subtitle of the catalogue and its 250-page length suggest, *SOCERLID* attempted to go far beyond merely cataloguing an exhibition via the publication: they sought to establish and share their interest in comics and their conceptualization of comics history and to validate comics criticism.

Another moment of transatlantic convergence occurs in Strinati's above-mentioned fandom-inspiring article in the science fiction magazine *Fiction* no. 62 (1961); its subtitle transposes the 'golden age' used to refer to early American comics from the 1930s and the 1940s to France. Comics artist and connoisseur Jean Claude Forest (best-known for his adult comic *Barbarella*) responded to Strinati in *Fiction* no. 63, where he affirmed the shorter period Strinati had attributed to the golden age of French comics by declaring that nothing worthwhile was published in France after 1940 (Gabilliet, 2016: 141). Several magazines inspired by American comics appeared in the 1940s in France but their popularity and stark contrast with the existing children's press resulted in the prohibitive law of 1949, which hindered the 'Americanisation' of French comics.

Gabilliet points out that comics fandom in America was also sparked by a nostalgic interest in the pulps (especially science fiction publications) of the 1930s and the 1940s which sparked the first use of the 'golden age of comics' a mere few months before Strinati used the term. It appeared in an article by Dick Lupoff in *Comic Art* and was, like Strinati's article, a means of nostalgically reviving childhood reading. It took another decade for fandom in France to turn to Francophone comics, often published in the *Spirou* and

Tintin magazines. The 'golden age' of comics eventually acquired far more flexible dimensions in the Franco-Belgian sphere, often covering comics until the 1970s (148).

Marc Atallah and Alain Boillat's critical anthology, *BD-US: Les comics vus par l'Europe* [*The Comics Seen from Europe*] (2016), elaborates on the various kinds of interactions between American and European (especially Francophone and Italian) comics cultures, beginning with Francophone fandom's fascination for golden age comics and covering influences of the American underground on the rise of adult comics in France (see also Chapter 6 on creators and titles), the Italian *Donald Duck* and the lasting influence of *Flash Gordon* on Franco-Belgian comics.

A brief summary and comparison of recent trends in comics legitimization in Francophone and Anglophone spheres is provided in Maaheen Ahmed and Jean-Louis Tilleuil's introduction to the bilingual anthology, *The Cultural Standing of Comics: Ambiguities and Evolutions* (2016). Their main conclusion is that although the paths of comics legitimation have unfolded very differently in the English- and French-speaking worlds, a certain degree of convergence is noticeable in recent years with the rise of the graphic novel. The editors discern two kinds of interactions with the canonical hierarchies: one, the juxtaposition of intermedial references from diverse echelons of the arts, which opens up a space of dialogue between the different forms of expression and consequently places them on a comparable – albeit not equal – footing; two, embracing and entering the hierarchy through reprinting and thus revalorizing old, often forgotten, and previously inaccessible comics. The latter results in a rewriting and repositioning of comics history and, ultimately, the establishment of a distinctive comics heritage. It encompasses practices such as Chris Ware's editing of Frank King's *Gasoline Alley* volumes and Art Spiegelman's inclusion of late nineteenth-century and early twentieth-century newspaper comics in *In the Shadow of No Towers* (29–30).

The volume also considers the figuration of the comics artist and its relationship to legitimation (Lund; Odaert). Odaert discusses the different author personas cultivated in the French artist's collective L'Association, ranging from the mass culture craftsman to the legitimized author or artist. Jean-Matthieu Méon examines the role of French comics exhibitions in legitimizing comics and its makers through the notion of the 'polyvalent' artist. Sabrina Messing examines the prominence of comics in the popularizing magazine on the fine arts, *Beaux-Arts* from 1983 to 2013. Like several scholars mentioned above, Benoît Berthou problematizes comics legitimization but does so through focusing on analysing the habits and predilections of French comics readers. He argues for rethinking the concept of legitimation for comics. In the volume's final chapter, Florie Steyaert and Jean-Louis Tilleuil consider the official discourse surrounding the use of comics in Francophone Belgian schools. On both sides of the Atlantic, comics legitimation remains a tricky affair since it raises the issue of applying existing modes of artistic and literary canonization to the popular medium of comics.

Comics exhibitions

The pertinence of the above debates on bande dessinée criticism and legitimation issues is mirrored by a recent exhibition running from June 2019 to February 2020 at Bordeaux's Museum of Contemporary Art which highlights the extent to which legitimation biases continue to affect the curation and perception of comics. Titled 'Histoire de l'art cherche des personnages: de la figuration narrative à la bande dessinée contemporaine' ['Art History Searching Characters: From Narrative Figuration to Contemporary Comics'], the exhibition brings together renowned Anglophone and Francophone comics artists including Art Spiegelman, Chris Ware, Charles Burns, David B., Lewis Trondheim, Chantal Montellier, Jochen Gerner and also André Franquin. Known for his work in the *Spirou* magazine and strips, Franquin was also an eager fanzine collaborator (see Chapter 10). The exhibition places the works of these comics artists in dialogue with contemporary artists from diverse strands of post-Second World War art (conceptual art, object art, *art informel*) and includes On Kawara, Keith Haring, Richard Serra and Pierre Soulages. Although the exhibition offers a panoply of diverse comics artists and incorporates one popular comics artist (Franquin), it remains haunted by the issues concerning legitimation, especially the imposition of standards of the fine arts on comics. To counter this, the exhibition introduces the notion of character, a central concern for literature and much of popular culture, but dispensable for the fine arts. Such juxtapositions exemplify how comics exhibitions can be useful sources for understanding legitimation practices and transcultural and transmedial interactions.

Many other high-profile exhibitions have contributed to the legitimization of comics, including 'Manga!' (Louisiana Museum, Copenhagen, 2009),

'Comics Unmasked' (British Library, London, 2014), 'The Story of British Comics So Far' (The Lightbox, London, 2016) and 'Comic Invention' (Hunterian Museum, Glasgow, 2016). However, reflecting the movement towards comics legitimization and its contradictions, comics exhibitions remain novel phenomena in the cultural contexts discussed in this chapter. Hence, even though the process of legitimizing comics began decades ago, much work still needs to be done for comics to be recognized in their own right. Such work entails better understanding comics history, including the rise of comics criticism, the diversity of comics art and its interactions with, and differences from, the other arts. Chapter 3 on ideological and material approaches to comics has also offered insight into the comics legitimation debate in the English-speaking world through focusing on the rise of the graphic novel.

Conclusion

The early writings on comics demonstrate that from its very inception the medium has attracted criticism for its alleged negative impact and its low-cultural status. The earliest scholarship, especially in America and in Britain, speculated about the potential impact of comics and the way the medium's stories were developing, while defences of comics most often drew upon the historicity of folklore or myth to legitimize these stories. Moral panic peaked in the mid-twentieth century and many countries implemented some sort of censorship to manage this growing industry. Stakeholders such as educators and psychologists were passionate about their causes although in retrospect it seems they were responding primarily to changes in society rather than the comics themselves. Most recently, the critical work around this period has been revisionist and challenges simplistic cause-and-effect assumptions. As the scholarship on bande dessinée suggests, many early valorization efforts stemmed from comics fans, comics makers and other cultural actors. The channels of comics legitimation have been the topics of increasingly nuanced discussions in both Anglophone and Francophone scholarship. Comparing both highlights the cultural specificities that have determined the forms of comics legitimation and exposes sometimes forgotten sites of interaction. The role of cultural specificity is now explored further in our next chapter, which discusses publications that have applied a historical and regional focus to the study of comics.

Notes

1. Criticisms of comics can be read as part of wider fears of popular culture that are evidenced by Michael Vassallo's online historical blog Timely Atlas Comics, which cites a 1739 report of a parliamentary bill to ban plays that might corrupt the morals of youth (*The Edinburgh Courant* on Thursday, 5 April 1739).

2. This is, of course, comparable to the Frankfurt School's critique of mass culture (see for instance *Arguing Comics*, p. 38).

3. They develop this idea further in their subsequent book *The Myth of the American Superhero* (2002).

4. Loi du 16 juillet 1949 sur les publications destinées à la jeunesse.

5. For general introductions to bande dessinée, see *Comics in French: The European Bande Dessinée in Context* (2010), where Laurence Grove provides an overview of the history and legitimation of bande dessinée (229–245), Ann Miller's *Reading Bande Dessinée*, Charles Forsdick, Laurence Grove and Libbie McQuillan's anthology, *The Francophone Bande Dessinée* (2005) and Matthew Screech's *Masters of the Ninth Art: Bandes Dessinées and Franco-Belgian Identity* (2004).

6. For more information on bande dessinée and comics, the French-language website of neuvièmeart2.0, the journal of the Cité international de la bande dessinée et de l'image at Angoulême, edited by Thierry Groensteen is worth a visit. In addition to the journal, the website also hosts a dictionary of key comics terms, thematic articles, information and interviews on diverse authors as well as several research aids. It also includes links to documents digitized by the museum's library, including many early, out of print and hard to find comics magazines and prints.

7. Here Groensteen revises and increases the reasons proposed in his essay, 'Why Are Comics Still in Search of Cultural Legitimation?' in Magnussen, Anne and Christansen, Hans-Christian (eds) (2000) *Comics Culture: Analytical and Theoretical Approaches to Comics*. Museum Tusculanum Press, 29–41.

Works cited

Ahmed, Maaheen and Tilleuil, Jean-Louis. 'Introduction'. In Maaheen Ahmed, S. Delneste and Jean-Louis Tilleuil (eds), *The Cultural Standing of Comics: Ambiguities and Evolutions/La statut culturel de la bande dessinée: ambiguïtés et évolutions*. Louvain-la-Neuve: L'Harmattan, 2016, pp. 23–36.

Aquatias, Sylvain. 'Genre et légitimité dans l'édition de bande dessinée – partie 1: Le poids de la légitimité, des revues aux collections'. *Comicalités*, 2018. http://journals.openedition.org/comicalites/2639

Aquatias, Sylvain. 'Genre et légitimité dans l'édition de bande dessinée – partie 2: Le roman graphique ou la négation du genre'. *Comicalités*, 2018. http://journals.openedition.org/comicalites/2677

Atallah, Marc and Boillat, Alain (eds). *BD-US: Les comics vu par l'Europe*. Gollion: Infolio, 2016.

Barker, Martin. *A Haunt of Fears*. London: Pluto Press, 1984.

Beaty, Bart. *Fredric Wertham and the Critique of Mass Culture*. Jackson, MS: University Press of Mississippi, 2005.

Beaty, Bart and Miller, Ann (eds). *The French Comics Theory Reader*. Leuven: Leuven University Press, 2014.

Berthou, Benoît (ed.) *La bande dessinée. Quelle lecture, quelle culture ?* Paris: Éditions de la bibliothèque publique information/Bibliothèque Centre Georges Pompidou, 2015. https://books.openedition.org/bibpompidou/1671

Boltanski, Luc. 'The Constitution of the Comics Field'. In Ann Miller and Bart Beaty (eds), *The French Comics Theory Reader*. Leuven, Belgium: Leuven University Press, 1975, pp. 281–301.

Boltanski, Luc. 'La constitution du champ de la bande dessinée'. *Actes de la recherche en sciences sociales* 1, 1975: 37–59.

Campbell, Joseph. *The Hero with a Thousand Faces*. New York: Pantheon, 1949.

Couperie Pierre et al. *Bande dessinée et figuration: Histoire, esthétique, production et sociologie de la bande dessinée mondiale, procédés narratifs et structure de l'image dans la peinture contemporaine*. Paris: Musée des arts décoratifs, 1967.

Covin, Michel, Fresnault-Deruelle, Pierre and Toussaint, Bernard (eds). *La bande dessinée et son discours*. Communications 24. Paris: Seuil, 1976.

Crist, Judith. 'Horror in the Nursery: A Crisis of Innocence'. *Colliers*, 27 March 1948: n.p.

cummings, e.e. 'A Foreword to Krazy'. *Sewanee Review* 54:2, 1946: 216–221.

cummings, e.e. 'A Foreword to Krazy'. In Jeet Heer and Kent Worcester (eds), *Arguing Comics: Literary Masters on a Popular Medium*. Jackson, MS: University Press of Mississippi, 2004, pp. 30–34.

Demange, Julie. 'Bédéphilie'. In *Dictionnaire esthétique et thématique de la bande dessinée*, 2017. http://neuviemeart.citebd.org/spip.pp?article1169

Dupuy, Philippe and Sellier, Rémy. *Histoire de l'art cherche des personnages....* Bordeaux. CAPC/CIBDI/Fondation Grandur pour l'Art, 2019.

Eco, Umberto. 'The Myth of Superman. Review of *The Amazing Adventures of Superman*'. Transl. Natalie Chilton. *Diacritics* 2:1, 1972: 14–22.

Evanier, Mark. *Wertham Was Right!* Raleigh, NC: TwoMorrows Publishing, 2003.

Fielder, Leslie. 'The Middle against Both Ends'. *Encounter*, August 1955: 16–23.

Fielder, Leslie. *Love and Death in the American Novel*. Chicago, IL: Dalkey Archive Press, 1960.

Forsdick, Charles., Grove, Laurence and McQuillan, Libbie (eds). *The Francophone Bande Dessinée*. Amsterdam and New York: Rodopi, 2005.

Gabilliet, Jean-Paul. 'Du comic book au roman graphique: l'européanisation de la bande dessinée américaine'. *Image [&] Narrative* 12, August 2005. http://www.imageandnarrative.be/inarchive/tulseluper/gabilliet.htm

Gabilliet, Jean-Paul. "'Âge d'or de la BD' et 'golden age of comics'": comparaison des notions fondatrices de la bédéphilie dans l'aire franco-belge et aux États-Unis (1961–2015)". *Les Temps de médias* 2:27, 2016: 139–151.

Gibson, Mel. *Remembered Reading: Memory, Comics and Post-War Constructions of British Girlhood*. Leuven, Belgium: Leuven University Press, 2015.

Gilbert, James. *Cycle of Outrage: America's Reaction to the Juvenile Delinquent in the 1950s*. Oxford: Oxford University Press, 1986.

Groensteen, Thierry. *La bande dessinée: objet culturel non-identifié*. Angoulême: Éditions de l'An, 2006.

Grove, Laurence. *Comics in French: The European Bande Dessinée in Context*. New York: Berghahn, 2010.

Hajdu, David. *The Ten Cent Plague: The Great Comic Book Scare and How It Changed America*. New York: Picador, 2008.

Heer, Jeet and Worcester, Kent (eds). *Arguing Comics: Literary Masters on a Popular Medium*. Jackson, MS: University Press of Mississippi, 2004.

Heinich, Nathalie et al. (eds). *Le sacre de la bande dessinée*. *Revue Le Débat* 195. Paris: Gallimard, May–August 2017.

Howe, Irving. 'Notes on Mass Culture'. *Politics*, Spring 1948: 120–122.

Inge, M. Thomas (ed.) 'In Depth Section: The Comics as Culture'. *Journal of Popular Culture* 12:4, 1979: 630–754.

Jensen, Hilde Strandgaard. 'Why Batman Was Bad: A Scandinavian Debate about Children's Consumption of Comics and Literature in the 1950s'. *Barn* 21:3, 2010: 47–70. Available at https://cadmus.eui.eu/bitstream/handle/1814/14922/ Why%20Batman%20was%20Bad%20Helle%20Strandgaard%20Jensen. pdf?sequence=1&isAllowed=y. Accessed 31 October 2019.

Jewett, Robert and Lawrence, John Shelton. *The American Monomyth*. New York: Doubleday, 1977.

Jewett, Robert and Lawrence, John Shelton. *The Myth of the American Superhero*. Grand Rapids, MI: Eerdmans, 2002.

Lacassin, Francis. *Pour un neuvième art: la bande dessinée*. Geneva: Slatkine, 1982.

Legman, Gershon. *Love and Death: A Study in Censorship*. New York: Hacker Art Books, 1949.

Lent, John (ed.) *Pulp Demons: International Dimensions of the Postwar Anti-Comics Campaign*. London: Associated University Presses, 1999.

Maigret, Éric. 'La reconnaissance en demi-teinte de la bande dessinée'. *Réseaux* 67, 1994: 113–140.

Maigret, Éric and Stefanelli, Matteo (eds). *La bande dessinée: une médiaculture*. Paris: Armand Colin, 2012.

Martin, Jean-Philippe. 'La théorie du 0 %. Petite étude critique de la critique en bande dessinée'. *Comicalités*, 2012. http://journals.openedition.org/ comicalites/827

McLuhan, Marshall. *The Mechanical Bride: Folklore of Industrial Man*. New York: Vanguard Press, 1961.

McLuhan, Marshall. *Understanding Media: The Extensions of Man*. London: Routledge Classics, 2001.

Méon, Jean-Mathieu. 'L'illégitimité de la bande dessinée et son institutionnalisation: le rôle de la loi du 16 juillet 1949'. *Hermès, La Revue* 54:2, 2009: 45–50.

Miller, Ann. *Reading Bande Dessinée: Critical Approaches to French-language Comic Strip*. Bristol: Intellect, 2007.

Morris and Vankeer, Pierre. *Neuvième Art, musée de la bande dessinée. Spirou* 1392, 1964: 85–86.

Nyberg, Amy Kiste. *Seal of Approval: The History of the Comics Code*. Jackson, MS: University Press of Mississippi, 1998.

O'Day, Stephen. 'Seduction of the Innocent.Org', 2012. http://www.lostsoti.org/SOTIRelated.htm. Accessed 11 January 2015.

Pumphrey, George H. *Children's Comics: A Guide for Parents and Teachers*. London: Epworth Press, 1955.

Screech, Matthew. *Masters of the Ninth Art: Bandes Dessinées and Franco-Belgian Identity*. Liverpool: Liverpool University Press, 2004.

Seldes, Gilbert. *The Seven Lively Arts*. Mineola, NY: Dover Publications, 1924. Available at http://xroads.virginia.edu/~HYPER/SELDES/ch15.html. Accessed 21 August 2019.

Seldes, Gilbert. *The Great Audience*. New York: Viking Press, 1950.

Vassallo, Michael. J. 'Part 1: Fredric Wertham, Censorship & the Timely Anti-Wertham Editorials'. *Timely Atlas Comics*, 2011. http://timely-atlas-comics.blogspot.com/2011/02/frederic-wertham-censorship-anti.html. Accessed 12 August 2019.

Wagner, Geoffrey. *Parade of Pleasure*. [1954]. Atlanta, GA: Pure Imagination, 2010.

Warshow, Robert. 'Woofed with Dreams'. *Partisan Review* 13, 1946: 587–590.

Warshow, Robert. 'The Study of Man: Paul, the Horror Comics, and Dr. Wertham'. *Commentary*, 1 June 1954: 596–604. https://www.commentarymagazine.com/articles/the-study-of-man-paul-the-horror-comics-and-dr-wertham/. Accessed 14 July 2019.

Waugh, Coulton. *The Comics*. New York: Macmillan, 1947.

Wertham, Fredric. *Seduction of the Innocent*. New York: Rinehart, 1954.

Wertham, Fredric. *The Circle of Guilt*. [1958] Jackson, MS: University Press of Mississippi, 2007.

Wertham, Fredric. *A Sign for Cain*. Basingstoke: Macmillan, 1966.

Wertham, Fredric. *The World of Fanzines: A Special Form of Communication*. Carbondale, IL: Southern Illinois University Press, 1973.

CHAPTER 5
HISTORICAL APPROACHES

This chapter summarizes various historical accounts of comics. It begins with a selection of publications that offer a global history of comics. It then examines scholarship that has documented the development of comics in particular regions (Europe, America, Asia and Africa). The concluding section on transnationalism considers publications that have explicitly focused on the links that have developed between regions.

Global

Roger Sabin's *Comics, Comix and Graphic Novels* (1996) sets out a coherent and extensive historical view of comics, describing the 'rise, fall and resurrection of the medium' (1) across generations, primarily focused on Britain and America. While Sabin notes the presence of sequential art and comics antecedents in the Middle Ages, his analysis really begins with the invention of the printing press. He analyses early predecessors such as 'penny dreadfuls' (cheap popular serialized pamphlets that told lurid tales) and magazines such as *Punch* and *Ally Sloper* (and their American equivalents *Puck, Life* and *Judge*). He considers early woodcut illustrations, noting the use of modern comics conventions such as word balloons, speed lines (streaks that give a sense of speed) and juxtaposed words and images. Sabin storifies comics' pre- and early history as a process of reorientation that, from around 1930, reframed low-quality satire as brightly coloured slapstick, transforming comics' audiences from adults to children. Sabin's subsequent chapters explore the emergence of new titles and genres, including adventure stories, television/film adaptations, the superhero comics that took America by storm after *Action Comics* #1 launched 'Superman in 1938 and the 1940s controversy over American crime and horror comics. Other chapters also consider the history of British girls' comics, which Sabin combines with a discussion of Wonder Woman.

Sabin draws attention to the backlash against early comics (as vulgar, coarse and gauche) and their transition into newspaper strips, and the subsequent attacks on the comedy publications as violent and illiterate. He flags up that the discourse around comics has frequently been contradictory, as comics are often both sentimentalized and criticized: tolerated as humorous or childish entertainment but deemed not respectable. He claims children's comics have never escaped this set of contradictions until the present moment, the pathway to which is traced through the book's latter chapters, beginning with the emergence of underground comix in the 1960s and then the attempts of the comics industry to revitalize itself and the ways this has shaped the fan market that exists today. From *2000AD* and *Heavy Metal* to *Watchmen* and *The Dark Knight Returns*, and the emergence of companies such as Image Comics and titles such as *Raw, Maus* and *Love and Rockets*, Sabin traces how the industry has tried to bounce back and fight against the restrictions and assumptions that have historically been directed at it. Although not truly global in its scope, Sabin's history puts British and American comics in dialogue with each other within a coherent timeline and draws conclusions based on detailed historical knowledge and analysis of the styles and subjects that comics were offering at various points.

Other works, such as Paul Sassienie's *The Comic Book* (1994) or Ron Goulart's *Comic Book Culture: An Illustrated History* (2000), offer similar histories but have slightly different emphases. Both seem aimed at comics collectors or enthusiasts. Goulart's book focuses on the American industry, starting with 'Famous Funnies', and with its main emphasis on the golden age and the superhero genre. There are chapters devoted to key creators, the impact of the war, artistic style and a section on collecting that closes the book. Sassienie's book has four sections, which cover comics history, comics culture, comics collecting and grading and assessing the value of comics. The historical section focuses almost entirely on America (plus a small section on Britain's golden age) and takes us through the dates when key titles and characters first appeared. It contains many cover illustrations but no reprints of interior pages. Sassienie's history is informative but largely descriptive: summarizing content or tone but without analysis or reflection. His practical advice on collecting is now somewhat outdated, but his comments on unscrupulous dealers give an interesting picture of the exploitation that was common in the 1990s comics market, which (due to the well-publicized sales of a few *Action Comics* #1) preyed on gullible collectors and amateurs unable to distinguish between a good and bad investment. The second half of his book is devoted to an index of creators, listing their date of birth and their best-known work, a glossary of terms, and an extended index of comics titles and their publishers, which contains a large number of imprints or subsidiaries although its time period is not well delineated.

More recently, Tim Pilcher and Brad Brooks' *The Essential Guide to World Comics* (2005) and Paul Gravett's *Graphic Novels: Stories to Change your Life* (2005) offer more truly global histories of comics. Pilcher and Brooks' *World Comics* is aimed at the casual reader or fan and aims to extend their knowledge beyond the basics (which they define as American superheroes, British humour titles, a smattering of continental books such as *Tintin* or *Asterix*, and the use of manga as a catch-all term). Although it suffers from space limitations, this book considers many countries: Thailand, Indonesia, Malaysia, China, Hong Kong, the Philippines, Korea (and the work of cartoonists who have fled from areas such as Vietnam and Cambodia); the Netherlands, Italy, Switzerland, Germany, Spain and Portugal; the smaller comics cultures of Eastern Europe (Serbia, Croatia, Slovenia, Central Europe and Poland); South American countries such as Argentina, Brazil, Mexico and Cuba; Scandinavia; Australasia and the development of homegrown comics in India (which it claims began in 1969), and Africa (where the industry has struggled due to a lack of finance, poor distribution and negative perceptions). While many of its sections are very brief, *World Comics* does well to address so many underwritten regions. It does not provide much analysis of individual titles, but instead summarizes the historical development of the comics industry in each country, noting major publishing houses and the names and works of the most famous creators.

Paul Gravett's lavishly illustrated *Graphic Novels: Stories to Change Your Life* (2005) explores the historical development of the comics medium from the perspective of the recent graphic novel movement. Gravett explains the development of the term, analysing its connotations and responding to common 'things to hate about comics'. He goes on to discuss different aspects of the medium, with each chapter focusing on pages and extracts from key texts. His book covers a great deal of ground, from superheroes to underground to autobiography to crime and many more genres and key texts. While the main case study of each chapter is a well-known text, Gravett also offers multiple 'following on' suggestions of lesser-known works: bringing in comics from all over the world and in many different styles and formats. These extracts are all annotated: explaining plot events but also drawing the reader's attention to moments where the medium is used effectively, or giving additional information about the style, language or artwork. As such, the book provides analysis as well as acting as a reference book or cultural history.

Most recently, Gravett's *Comics Art* (2014) explores and explains the diversity of styles, media and approaches now possible in comics. It flags up the intersections of comics and fine art through key figures such as Picasso and Dali and then investigates the particular properties of comics (speech balloons, panelling, etc.), noting that the medium's flexibility makes it difficult to arrive at a clear definition, which has consistently led to debates about 'the first comic'. These stylistic features structure the rest of the book, as subsequent chapters examine silent comics (which have a much larger presence in countries such as Germany and with independent publishers); the use of page layout, panel composition and reading order (to affect pace, mood and meaning); the tensions and controversies that have arisen around the medium (such as accusations of classist, racist and sexist stereotyping); and the strengths of comics' treatments of genres such as autobiography. The final two chapters analyse the breadth of possible artistic styles and techniques, and the impact of the digital revolution on comics. The book is an engaging combination as each chapter explores comics history alongside a different aspect of the medium's formal properties, using anecdotal background combined with close analyses of individual titles that demonstrate the points being made.

Gravett's *1001 Comics You Must Read Before You Die* (2011) also deserves a brief mention. It is obviously and deliberately global in its scope, compiled by sixty-seven experts in twenty-seven countries. While it does not offer any critical commentary or analysis, it is a fantastic list of titles that new (and old) comics readers should make themselves aware of. These include brief summaries and accompanying illustrations of selected titles which are arranged historically (in chapters such as 'Pre-1930', '1930–49' and so forth, up until '2000–present'), and so this book can also be read as providing a historicist summary of the development of the comics medium, although there is no linking narrative.

In addition to the above critical resources, Dan Nadel's richly illustrated volumes *Art Out of Time: Unknown Comics Visionaries, 1900–1969* (2006) and *Art in Time: Unknown Comic Book Adventures, 1940–1980* (2010) reprint often forgotten comic strips and stories. These volumes are a precious source of material that often remains overlooked by comics histories. Additional reference books include Dan Mazur and Alexander

Danner's *Comics: A Global History, 1968 to the Present* (2014). Finally, the Bibliographies and Indexes in Popular Culture series published by Praeger includes a number of 'international bibliographies' of comics compiled by John Lent, beginning with *Comic Art of Europe: An International, Comprehensive Bibliography* (1994); *Animation, Caricature, and Gag and Political Cartoons in the United States and Canada: An International Bibliography* (1994); and *Comic Books and Comic Strips in the United States: An International Bibliography* (1994). These were followed by *Comic Art in Africa, Asia, Australia, and Latin America: A Comprehensive, International Bibliography* (1996), followed by a subsequent set of six volumes covering the period up until 2000 in Europe (two volumes), the United States/ Canada (three volumes), Africa, Asia, Australia/Oceana and Latin America/ Caribbean (one volume). These books are hard to get hold of and are not discussion-based, but instead are lists of critical citations relating to comics published in these countries (and taking in animation, caricature, strips, gags, political cartoons, magazine appearances and so forth). They include citation details for scholarly pieces as well as news articles, reviews, magazine features, fanzines and so forth. Although no detail, summary or analysis is given of any of these pieces, the lists may provide a useful (albeit dated) starting point for those needing to research a topic to its fullest.

Europe

David Kunzle's *History of the Comic Strip* (two volumes, 1973 and 1990) is a landmark text in the historical analysis of comics, although sadly out of print and hard to obtain. In Volume 1 (*The Early Comic Strip*) Kunzle examines comic strips taken from European broadsheets between 1450 and 1825. He defines 'comic strip' as a sequence of four or more images with accompanying text conveying 'moral' or 'topical propaganda'. These subjects include religious propaganda, crime and punishment, public vices and follies, and additional chapters focus more closely on various countries such as France, the Netherlands and England, and on artists such as Hogarth and Goya.

Volume 2 (*The Nineteenth Century*) then considers the period 1827–1896; an endpoint that emphasizes Kunzle's key argument, which is that European comics far predate the 'first' American strip of 1896. While the book has a strong focus on Western Europe, it also incorporates some insights on developments in other countries such as Russia, Spain, Italy and Austria. Kunzle examines the work of Swiss artist Rodolphe Töpffer, the French artists Honoré Daumier, Cham (Charles Amédée de Noé), Gustave Doré and Léonce Petit, and the German artist Wilhelm Busch. He takes the contexts of industrial and social revolutions into account and argues that the work of many of these artists makes social comments, for example by mocking social norms (Töpffer), addressing propaganda (Doré), articulating a clash between the bourgeoisie and the peasants (Petit) or satirizing religion (Busch).

Kunzle's history contends that processes of cultural exclusion led to the development of the political cartoon, morality tales and the association of caricature with humour and lower prestige. He stresses, however, that the comic strip audience intersected generations and social classes. He also uses his analysis to deconstruct the development of visual language in comic strips, identifying the appearance of elements such as the depiction of motion (e.g. the presence of speed lines in the earliest works from Töpffer), oscillation and rotation, and the employment of different angles of perspective or framing choices. He also discusses the changing relationship between image and caption (initially duplicative, but in more satirical works sometimes contradictory for humorous effect). Overall, his survey demonstrates the emergence of new formats and the crossing of different styles between countries. Both books are oversized hardbacks, packed full of detail of different artists and titles, including numerous extracts and illustrations.

Kunzle's emphasis on the development of comics vocabularies in the light of the burgeoning nineteenth-century visual culture makes his book particularly exciting. It can be complemented by art historian Patricia Mainardi's work on the rise of the illustrated press in France and Britain in *Another World: Nineteenth-Century Illustrated Print Culture* (2017). Mainardi's art-historical perspective, however, often overlooks important details regarding the transformation of comics culture. In contrast, Thierry Smolderen's *Naissances de la bande dessinée* (2009), translated by Bart Beaty and Nick Nguyen as *The Origins of Comics: From William Hogarth to Winsor McCay* (2014), covers a temporally and geographically broader slice of visual culture with a strong focus on comics. This includes the relationships between comics and early instances of caricature and other undisciplined drawing: Smolderen draws connections with the graffiti that appear in some of Hogarth's masterfully drawn prints and with the rise of caricature. He also uncovers the implications of drawing styles and their relationship to their cultural and media contexts. While comparable in its contextually detailed and embedded nature to studies such as Ian Gordon's *Comic Strips and Consumer Culture* (see below), *Origins of Comics* stands out in its focus on the visual nature of comics drawing. Smolderen also introduces the concept of 'polygraphy', a graphic pendant to Mikhail Bakhtin's 'polyphony', the coexistence of multiple voices in the novel. For Smolderen, polygraphy is an indispensable part of comics vocabulary and highlights the complexity of the medium, particularly the historical and cultural depth of drawing and style as it references and reworks the connotations of other visual practices. The key message from these works is that comics develop and thrive in a rich constellation of cultural and media influences.

The French Comics Theory Reader (2014), edited by Ann Miller and Bart Beaty, reprints selected key articles and extracts, including some historicist accounts of French comics history. Gérard Blanchard's 'The Origins of Stories in Images' (a short extract from his 1969 book) seeks to unmoor bande dessinée from a narrow Americocentric definition. He traces the pre-history of comics art back to its earliest days of prehistoric 'picture stories', noting the use of both 'art' (which portrays events and actions and things) and 'the sign' (which indicates words, thoughts, feelings) in these images and stating that these two main means of communication, the concrete and the abstract, promote a double reading and recur constantly through the history of stories in pictures. He extends this to pictographs and alphabetic writing, also taking in religious iconography and the Bayeux Tapestry (whose allegorical borders of scenes from Aesop's fables enhance the emotional meaning of its scenes). Medieval iconography, books of religious teachings and phylactera (speech scrolls used in art that contained scriptures, which Blanchard likens to speech balloons) are all discussed as forerunners of the comic book. With the invention of the printing press and the emergence of woodcut religious tracts, these 'pamphlets' or 'episodes' become even more reminiscent of comics as Blanchard stresses that both needed an interpreter who 'knew' how to read them and could explain the story or fill in the rest from the fragment of scripture given. He argues that the subsequent emergence of printed books is significant in establishing certain patterns of reading, but also stresses the relevance of the stream of pamphlets, seditious songs, lampoons and political and religious activism that developed alongside it. From medieval folklore to today's popular traditions, he argues, people's need for the supernatural has been ever-present and satisfied in one form or another.

In 'Graphic Hybridization' (2014), Thierry Smolderen looks back to the mid-nineteenth century to trace the evolution of modern comics. He calls the comic strip

> an obvious example of graphic hybridization [...] the intersection of two artistic practices that had developed in unrelated environments: thus the ancient phylactera grafted onto sequences of images inspired by the new technique of chronophotography, engendered, after a period of experimentation, an *audiovisual stage on paper*.
>
> (47, italics in original)

Situating this new format within the visual culture of the period allows Smolderen to consider the ways in which early cartoonists incorporated 'new ways of seeing (the Daguerre plate, the view through a microscope, instant photography, the kinetoscope, X-rays, the artistic avant-garde, Japanism, etc.)' into the language of their cartoons (48). In 1857, *The Illustrated London News* printed a woodcut of the view through a microscope and in 1870, its competitor, *The Graphic*, published a parody piece, 'Pantomime Microscope', offering similar examples based on the telegraph, the X-Ray and electricity (where the electric wire becomes the panel border). Smolderen explains 'how the image of the cartoon worked, how the familiar and the new mutually illuminated each other, producing meaning by means of an image that is all the more memorable for being unexpected – because it is created by *hybridization*' (51). He stresses that the result is not merely an observation of contemporary society and its new technologies, but rather an application of its techniques to visual style, enlivening the medium and empowering the public to play with these ideas.

Other articles in *The French Comics Theory Reader* also consider the more recent history of comics publishing and its evolution in the twentieth century. Barthélémy Schwartz writes 'On Indigence' (1986) and notes the lack of author function in comics prior to the 1960s, when anonymous stories were published by stables such as *Spirou, Tintin* and *Mickey*. Continuing his racing metaphor, he then cites the numerous 'horses' that overtook the stables (such as Pratt, Tardi, Caza and Moebius) and the 1970s boom in '*little* magazines' such as *Charlie Mensuel, L'Écho des Savanes and Métal Hurlant* which was then followed by market expansion. He thus denies the distinction between 'auteurist' and 'commercial' comics, claiming they are both cultural commodities and noting the rise of a market around this in the 1980s. He critiques artists who do not expect to be treated like workers and argues that the market is run by salesmen and thus accords with this ideology. His ideas echo Boltanski's (1975) sociological analysis of the expansion of the industry (see Chapter 4) in drawing attention to the troublesome position of comics as situated between artistic aura and commercial object.

Other scholars offer historical analyses that look at particular periods of significance in French comics history; for example Pascal Ory's book *Le Petit Nazi Illustré* [*The Nazi Boy's Own*] (2002) first considers the impact of American comics on the French market during the 1930s when they were imported and distributed by Paul Winkler's agency Opera Mundi and their popularity heavily reduced the sales of French titles. The war itself then damaged sales of all comics and by 1942 the handful of surviving publishers had amalgamated their publications into just fifteen or so magazines, with a notable drop in print quality and regularity. The content of the comics was also affected by wartime and nationalist ideologies, as American strips were banned, and in the early 1940s all the popular heroes (Tarzan, Mandrake) disappeared mid-action and without explanation, to be replaced by homegrown imitations. Ory looks closely at the historical figure Marshal Pétain (who stands for both the Empire and rural France) and the magazine *Benjamin* (launched July 1940), self-described as a 'Completely French Magazine'. He demonstrates how these nationalist characters and publications led to comics such as *Le Téméraire* [*The Bold One*] (41 issues, 1943–44) which was the sole children's magazine published in Paris at this time. Ory gives data on the fascist ideologies found in the various pages of the magazine and exposes the private funding through which the German occupying power controlled the media and notes the employment of local artists and writers.

Along similar lines, Erwin Dejasse and Philippe Capart explore the Belgium comics market via what they term the 'loss of serialisation' from publishers Dupuis and Lombard. Noting the pre-1960s incarnations of strips such as *Spirou* or *Tintin* in two-page instalments within a bigger comic, they argue that this created 'a mode of reading that was essentially fragmentary' (313). The gap in time and space between each issue contributed to comics as 'an art of discontinuity' (314) that stimulates the reader's imagination between panels and between issues and offers a 'live' experience of reading the strip. *Tintin*'s move to 'maxi chapters' of around ten pages each in 1969 had consequences for the creators (who could not produce material at this rate) and the publication (which could not print its 'star' strips in the same issue any more due to limited pagination). While there were positive benefits (space to develop sequences that would have been compressed in the old format), this change 'broke up an almost biological rhythm' (317) and destroyed the ritualistic element of its audience's habitual reading. Subsequent collection and republication, and the dominance of the 48- or 64-page album placed artificial breaks into the narrative, leading Dejasse and Capart to conclude that the album itself is now a fragment and that the readership has been conditioned to accept the restrictions of format offered, no matter how unsuitable they might be.

In terms of Nordic comics, Fredrik Strömberg's *Swedish Comics History* (2010) surveys this industry's development from around the end of the eighteenth century (although also touching on much earlier examples such as Viking stone etchings), with numerous translated examples and lavish illustrations. Numerous books exist focusing on other European countries, ranging in style and approach. For example David Roach's *Masters of Spanish Comic Book Art* (2017) briefly summarizes the history of Spanish comics and the main agencies and publishers, but then takes a primarily biographical approach, showcasing the work of the many significant artists who contributed extensively to British and American comics.

One notable text here is Santiago García's *La novela gráfica* (2010), translated by Bruce Campbell as *On the Graphic Novel* (2015), which is one of the few histories to put European and American history in dialogue. Discussed in Chapter 3, it draws parallels between the changing cultural positions of comics in Spain and America in particular. Moving on to consider the Russian context, two key works are José Alaniz's *Komiks: Comics Art in Russia* (2009) and John Etty's *Graphic Satire in the Soviet Union: Krokodil's Political Cartoons* (2019). While Alaniz provides a history of Soviet and post-Soviet comics that explores their varying fortunes during the turbulent collapse of the USSR, Etty nuances the propagandist image of the long-running illustrated satire magazine *Krokodil*.

Finally, the Internet also contains some historical summaries of individual countries' comics industries. Marcos Farrajota (2015) summarizes the development of Portuguese comics, arguing that the industry has not developed in a smooth and linear manner, but through a series of starts and interruptions, beginning with Rafael Bordalo Pinheiro's satires, albums and autobiographical cartoons (1881) and the work of his contemporaries such as Carlos Botelho. Magazines such as *Visão* (1975–76) and *Lx Comics* (1990–91) picked up the baton after the April 25 Revolution, but for Farrajota the Portuguese industry today is characterized by individuals working in isolation and a lack of interest from the public at large.

Turning to the UK, scholarship on early comics is limited. Books such as Denis Gifford's *Happy Days: A Century of British Comics* (1975) are predominantly collections of illustrations (in this instance taken from comics between 1870–1970). Gifford's short introduction names *Funny Folks* (1874) as the first British comic, although this accolade remains in dispute.[1] Joyce Goggin's chapter 'Of Gutters and Guttersnipes: Hogarth's Legacy' (2010) in *The Rise and Reason of Comics and Graphic Literature* looks closely at the commercial underpinnings of Hogarth's work, arguing that it stands as both high and low culture, thus resolving issues of commerciality that have been problematic for comics theorists.

James Chapman's *British Comics* (2011) traces the development of the British comics industry from the late nineteenth century to the present day. He is particularly concerned to situate the country's most famous titles in their cultural context and covers a diverse range of publications and genres in individual chapters: Ally Sloper, *Eagle*, anthology cartoon comics (*Beano, Dandy*), girls' comics (*Girl, Bunty, Misty*), boys' adventure and war stories (*Battle, Action*), science fiction (*2000AD*) superheroics (*Marvelman/ Miracleman, Zenith*), and the adult and alternative (*Escape, Viz, Warrior*). Chapman argues that British comics and characters strongly reflect their culture and eras, although he only describes the British cultural moment in the broadest of strokes and his theoretical backing is mostly implied; instead, he supports his claims with numerous comparisons to film, television and literature.

Chapman opens by considering comics' redefinition from adult to child literature in the context of the world wars, using the primary case study of 'Jane' in the *Daily Mirror*. Subsequent chapters also provide a contextual focus as he examines the ways in which the British censorship campaign set the stage for more moral titles such as the *Eagle*, and the rise of domestic television in the 1960s as evidence of an overarching visuality in entertainment media at this time. His focus in early chapters is on the adventure comics of this time and the ways in which they redefine masculinity: as sports comics exploit the rhetoric of Empire-building and British dominance and war comics demonstrate the 'pleasure culture of war' (cited from Paris 2000). This is contrasted with the marketing of girls' comics through processes of differentiation rather than with ideological motivations. Chapman puts the comics within this genre in dialogue with each other, for example citing *Bunty*'s lower-class protagonists and social plotlines as a response to titles such as *Girl* and *School Friend*. He also considers the controversy over the content of titles such as *Action* and offers a detailed account of the British anti-comics campaigns. The rise of behemoths such as *2000AD* is contextualized against the backdrop of dystopian cinema, and he also considers the British superhero and alternative comics. An overarching argument that the failure of the British adult comix market led directly to American imprints such as DC Vertigo links the last few chapters.

While other books such as Graham Kibble-White's *The Ultimate Book of British Comics* (2005) are more encyclopaedia-type reference books that list titles along with summaries of their creators and content, Chapman's book is the first analytical history to focus exclusively on British comics. It does an admirable job of covering much ground while still giving detail through case studies and reprints of primary material. Chapman draws on theses from UK academics and offers clear cause-and-effect arguments that are retrospectively apparent for many of the changes and notable trends, although some of his claims, for example about adult/child readerships, are disputed. Although *British Comics* does not move far beyond the areas already covered by Sabin (see above in this chapter) and Barker (see Chapter 3), it does offer both range and depth.

Other books that focus on particular aspects of British cartooning history include Nicola Streeten and Cath Tate's *The Inking Woman* (2018). This illustrated hardback shines a light on female creators working in particular subgenres and at particular times, with chapters dedicated to artists such as Mary Darly and Marie Duval, and others on more general topics like 'Women's Suffrage in Cartoons', Zines/DIY, postcards and groups such as Laydeez do Comics. Each chapter is made up of short biographies and summaries of the work of relevant female creators, accompanied by full-colour illustrations of their art (women comic artists are discussed further in Chapter 6).

North America, Canada and South America

Historical surveys of American comics generally keep a tight focus on a particular time-period or aspect of the industry. Les Daniels' *Comix: A History of Comic Books in America* (1973) is an illustrated summary of the development of the industry in North America, beginning with Outcault's *Yellow Kid* in 1896. Subsequent chapters discuss the creation and emergence of comic books, dating back to *Funnies on Parade* (1933), and then examine in turn the 'funny animal' comics and strips; EC Comics and the pre-Code horror comics; the Comics Code controversy; the subsequent 'New Direction' comics; Marvel Comics; and the underground (see also Chapter 10). Daniels combines wider anecdotal summaries of the industry with close textual analysis and reprints of full stories. He concludes that comics' mixed media and fantastic subject matter have led to them being marginalized and treated condescendingly, but that their freedom of form and content makes them key to the American character.

Other writers have examined overlooked aspects of the North American industry's development, such as Trina Robbins' *From Girls to Grrrlz: A History of Women's Comics from Teens to Zines* (1999). Robbins summarizes the (often forgotten) range of titles aimed at women, such as the teen titles that grew from the success of *Archie* in the early 1940s and the subsequent boom in romance comics. All these female titles, however, fell victim to the slump of the late 1950s, and although the 1960s saw the romance comics try to cash in on rock and roll and the hippie movement, they struggled to engage with women's liberation and by 1964 superhero titles dominated.

Robbins then considers the following two decades, explaining how an explosion of feminist underground newspapers all over America in the 1960s led to her own involvement in creating *It Ain't Me, Babe* (1970). This was the first all-women comic to take on the mostly male world of underground comics and was followed by many more, dealing with themes such as liberation; masturbation; menstruation; abortion; and, a few years later, lesbianism. Robbins notes that attempts to put out anthologies dealing with women's sexuality were always problematic and attracted censorship and outrage, even against the taboo-exploding backdrop of the male underground. Her final chapter, on the 1990s, summarizes the mainstream's continued divergence from political and underground work. She bemoans the lack of comics for children or women and discusses some self-published zines and a few outstanding examples of romance comics, alongside the formation of initiatives such as the Friends of Lulu. Throughout, Robbins' book combines brief plot summaries and direct quotes, and is liberally scattered with colour illustrations of pages and covers, giving a strong sense of what these comics were about.

Jumping forward, several more recent books have surveyed the development of the North American industry from various angles. Jean-Paul Gabilliet's *Des Comics et des hommes: histoire culturelle des comic books aux États-Unis* (2005), translated by Bart Beaty and Nick Nguyen as *Of Comics and Men: A Cultural History of American Comic Books* (2009), focuses on the social and economic relationships that have structured the development of the American comics industry. Gabilliet considers both internal and external types of consecration and explores their contribution to the visibility, recognition and cultural legitimacy of comics. In summarizing, he points out that, while the graphic novel format has shifted comics towards the field of adult culture, the inertia of the monthly market has simultaneously trapped the medium in adolescent culture.

Gabilliet book remains one of the most thorough historical accounts of American comics from the mid-nineteenth century until today. The first and longest part of the book covers the rise of comics and comic books from the mid-nineteenth century until the early twenty-first century. The second section discusses comics creation and publishing as well as comics readers. The book's final section considers the issue of comics legitimation. *Of Comics and Men* also provides a bibliographic essay that covers archives and databases as well as thematic and historical studies. While Gabilliet moves through the nineteenth century and early twentieth century fairly quickly, Ian Gordon's *Comic Strips and Consumer Culture, 1890–1945* (discussed further in Chapter 7) focuses on a shorter period to draw out the extent to which early comics were embedded in an expanding commodity culture and contributed to it. Often resorting to popular, well-known comics such as *Buster Brown* and *Gasoline Alley*, Gordon also explores the European influences on American comics, the interrogation of the supposed Americanness of comics and their racist imagery.

The Rise of the American Comics Artist (2010), edited by Paul Williams and James Lyons, assembles essays that explore the development of the industry through various lenses, including the figure of the creator and the changing contexts of creativity, publication and reception. It is split into five sections. The first considers how publishing and branding developments such as the creation of the 'graphic novel' format and an influx of international creators have been used to enhance the cultural capital of the industry. Stephen Weiner explores the history of the 'graphic novel' concept, which was famously claimed as inaugurated by Will Eisner, although clearly apparent in the works of predecessors such as Rodolphe Töpffer. Julia Round examines the material and connotative value of this term and the way it has been used to reshape the American industry, and Chris Murray argues that the 'British invasion' of US comics in the 1980s was also, in many ways, a 'lit invasion'. (This concept of a 'literary invasion' foregrounds the emphasis that was placed on British writers, although later work from scholars like Murray, Isabelle Licari-Guillaume and Christophe Dony conceptualizes this period more as a moment of transnational exchange.) The collection's second section explores the dialogue between American comics and international events, with chapters on civil liberties (Murphy) and political journalism in the work of Joe Sacco (Rosenblatt and Lunsford). Section three sets up and explores the dichotomy between employee and artist and associated cultural capital, while section four considers the politicization of identity in comics, examining depictions of national and gendered identities and sexuality in key underground texts. Finally, section five analyses the continuing legacy of landmark works such as *Maus* and the continued novelistic ambitions of comics as displayed in titles such as Chris Ware's *Jimmy Corrigan: The Smartest Kid on Earth*. While this collection does not offer a historical timeline, it does engage with many issues that are key to understanding the development of American comics and their relevance to the contemporary cultural moment.

In *Demanding Respect: The Evolution of the American Comic Book* (2014), Paul Lopes directs his gaze firmly at cultural significance: presenting an evolutionary narrative of American comics, which have developed from an industrial age into a 'heroic age' (Bourdieu), whereby comics generate their own autonomous principles. His book takes us chronologically from comics' early years up until the late 1980s. Lopes emphasizes that comics exist in the real world of cultural production, distribution and consumption and explores how comics creators and publishers have adapted the industrial logic of the culture industry to fit specific circumstances. For example, he looks at comics' pulp roots, arguing that early comics followed the same publishing model of assembly-line production, and contextualizing this against emergent moral panic and the Comics Code. The subsequent remodelling of the superhero genre is thus defined as part of comics' 'Late Industrial Age' in which the figure was made socially relevant, alongside the adoption of comics by the underground and by a left-wing college readership.

Lopes then focuses on the role of fandom in leading comics towards their 'heroic age' and shaping their creation, production, distribution and reception: for example by seeking out and extolling the auteur creator, resulting in better deals for writers and artists, creating the direct market, and privileging collection over consumption. In particular, he details the creative and critical work from artists such as Will Eisner, Scott McCloud and Art Spiegelman, alongside scholars such as Kent Worcester, Ray Mescallado and Charles Hatfield, and the role of publications such as *The Comics Journal* in arguing for a new definition of comics as Literature and Art. Lopes notes, however, that symbolic value was largely reserved for the graphic novel, and that alternative comics in general remained marginalized and excluded both from the mainstream comics readership and from high art more generally. Lopes concludes by considering the impact of manga on American comics publishing, the boost that cinematic adaptations gave to the industry, changing attitudes of librarians and teachers, and the potential impact of the World Wide Web.

Overall, Lopes argues that comics' path towards the critical and commercial position that the medium holds today has been based on its development of principles of autonomy, and its interpretative communities. His cultural history points primarily towards the ways in which comics fandom and the underground and alternative movements have repeatedly fought to bestow credibility on the medium. The changing priorities of creators and readers have established autonomous principles of comics storytelling, and led to changes in the creation, production, distribution and consumption of the medium. While dividing American comics history into just two phases might seem reductive, this dichotomy lets Lopes consider the changes that have occurred as reactions to the previous status quo, rather than identifying a continuum of textual features that are superhero-centric (as in the more established terminology of golden age, silver age, etc.). He argues that the tension that continues in today's comics between dominant fan pulp art appreciation and a more literary or marginalized appreciation is a state that also applies to fiction more generally, but is rendered more visible in this field due to its size and status.

John Bell has written several of books on the history of Canadian comics, including *Canuck Comics* (1986), *Guardians of the North* (1992) and *Invaders from the North* (2006). While *Canuck Comics* is a retrospective guide and price list (edited by Bell) and *Guardians* focuses entirely on the Canadian superhero genre, in *Invaders* Bell traces a fuller development of the English Canadian comics industry, from its claimed first comic *Punch in Canada* (1849). It opens with brief biographies of early practitioners, before moving to consider the 'golden age' of Canadian industry (1941–46), which is situated as a response to the import restrictions on American comics that were introduced in 1940. An examination of the superhero makes up the first few chapters of *Invaders,* beginning with characters such as The Iron Man and Freelance and noting their lack of any Canadian characteristics. He contrasts this with subsequent characters such as Nelvana, Johnny Canuck and Canada Jack, who respectively personified Inuit traditions (albeit whitewashed) and national identity, although their popularity faded as the war ended. Bell then considers the next crop of emergent Canadian superheroes as responses to an increased sense of Americanization that he finds in American silver age comics. He notes the comedic aspects of these first 'silver age' heroes (Captain Canada et al.), followed by the emergence of more serious figures (such as Northern Light, Captain Canuck and the Alpha Flight team). Overall, Bell concludes that while the superhero dominated Canadian comics publishing for a time, creators have struggled with uncritical depictions of heroism, power and patriotism, which has prevented a truly convincing character from ever emerging.

Invaders from the North also explores other genres of Canadian comics, putting together a narrative of the decades in which comics 'grew up'. This includes reprints of American crime and horror comics by companies such as Bell and Superior, the educational/promotional free comics produced in the 1950s and 1960s by Ganes Productions and Comic Book World (free tracts which warned of dangers such as alcohol, cigarettes, sexually transmitted diseases, etc.), and the Canadian alternative scene that emerged in the late 1960s. While the Canadian underground paralleled the American comix, peaking around 1970 (see *The Canadian Alternative* [2017], edited by Dominick Grace and Eric Hoffman, for more on this), Bell looks more closely at 1975–88, which he argues could be characterized as Canada's own silver age in terms of the quality and quantity of titles, including cult series such as Dave Sim's *Cerebus the Aardvark*, and a revised *Captain Canuck*. Bell identifies this period as one in which English Canadian comics became a (contested) adult form amid great changes to their production, distribution and content. The remainder of the book turns a spotlight on what Bell defines as the industry's three main areas: mainstream, alternative and small press, and the key creators working in each field. There is lengthy analysis of the career of Chester Brown, and of Chris Oliveros' founding and development of publishers Drawn & Quarterly. Bell's conclusion, echoing the narrative applied to many other countries, is that after six decades of struggle, comics in Canada have now finally come of age.

In *A Political History of Comic Books in Mexico* (1998), Anne Rubenstein examines Mexican comic books (*historietas*) in the cultural and political context of Mexico between the 1930s and the 1970s. In particular, she considers the relationships between comics' producers, audiences and critics, and the Mexican government. As in other countries, Mexican comics grew from the Sunday supplements (*dominicales*) of the 1920s; the first comic book was *Adelaido el Conquistador* (1934). Rubenstein notes the diversity of the *historietas*, which were sold on newsstands and were popular with a wide and varied audience. They told melodramatic and adventurous stories set in a familiar world, without superheroes. Rubenstein argues that reading these comics felt like a patriotic act and uses close analysis of the content of key titles such as *Pepín* (1936–55) to demonstrate the variety of narratives, showing how these titles tried to connect to their readers by using 'generic stories, local settings, real people and events, and reader contributions' (27) – inviting audiences to imagine themselves as creators or protagonists.

Rubenstein situates the emergent comics industry in a cultural context of increased education and literacy, which connected modernity and reading (including comics) in the public mind. She points out, however, that cultural critics and ethnographers were still keen to frame comics reading as corrupting. Effectively, comics became the centrepoint of a bigger argument about modernity versus tradition that would end in stalemate for both sides – while paradoxically reinforcing the positive aspects of both viewpoints. Rubenstein argues that the political discourses of modernity and tradition were enacted primarily through the *historietas'* representation of women. Comics first became central in shaping a narrative of revolutionary modernity and progress, for example by the creation of the stock figure of the *chica moderna,* or revolutionary girl. The moral panic of the 1940s, however, and the language the protestors used drew on the rhetoric of nationalist tradition and conservatism, in counterpoint to the modernizing discourse that they claimed the comics represented, and mobilized the stereotype of the patient, long-suffering Mexican wife/mother. Rubenstein uses close analysis of story content to demonstrate similarities across titles and notes that both figures began as political tools, although today they have developed into stereotypes.

Drawing on censors' records and government documents, Rubenstein then explores the workings of the Comisón Calificadora de Publicaciones y Revistas Ilustradas, which has monitored Mexican periodicals and illustrated magazines for slang, crime and sexual content since 1944, and analyses the comics publishers' range of responses to their actions. She argues that the commission unintentionally both enabled the incorporation of conservatives into the Mexican state and protected comics from foreign competition. She also looks closely at the wording publishers used to advertise their products and employs case studies to explore the ways they were enabled to flout the law (focusing on the Lombardini brothers) and the limitations placed on political expression (focusing on the work of Rius). Overall, Rubenstein's analysis gives a history of how the comics industry developed in Mexico, with a strong focus on the Government's involvement.

Her argument is a broad cultural and ideological one that demonstrates how the Mexican comics industry became a central point of debate within the cultural struggle of modernity versus tradition.

Asia

The rise of manga over the past century has been both a Japanese and a global phenomenon. Frederik L. Schodt's *Manga! Manga! The World of Japanese Comics* (1983) was a landmark text in summarizing the history and breadth of Japanese comics. Schodt notes the origins of the term ('man' meaning 'involuntary', and 'ga' meaning 'picture') and flags up manga's tendency towards the melodramatic, exaggerated and emotional in its drawn line; echoed in its experimental use of layouts and sound effects. He explores the development of Japanese pictorial storytelling over the past thousand years: from illustrated scrolls and religious texts, through simple four-panel newspaper strips, to longer serialized works. He stresses the impact of artists such as Osamu Tezuka (who provides a foreword to the book), who began publishing in the 1940s and whose popularity changed the face of the manga industry, which by the 1960s had assumed its present dominant position in Japanese entertainment culture. Schodt's discussion is contextualized with political analysis, which also informs his exploration of the popularity of themes and archetypes such as samurai, sports and romance. He provides a clear introduction to the idiosyncrasies of the genres, formats and conventions of manga (such as enlarged eyes, inconsistent colouring, stereotypes such as the 'salaryman', and the extensive range of emanata – lines and squiggles emerging from a character or object – to indicate emotional states). Other chapters also discuss the mechanics of the industry, such as editorial processes, the emergence and contributions of female artists, the social standing of artists and their work, formats and additions, and the difficulties of translating and exporting manga. The book is illustrated throughout and concludes with some longer extracts from significant works, reverse-printed and translated for the western reader.

Schodt continues his analysis in *Dreamland Japan* (1996), a more text-heavy book that focuses on the development of manga since the 1980s. As well as recapping the growth of the industry in the twentieth century, Schodt expands his focus to consider conventions (particularly those selling *dōjinshi*, or fanzines, which have an overwhelmingly female audience). He engages more closely with the sociocultural backdrop to manga's success, alongside discussions of its fandom, the legislation and treatment of erotica, and controversy and stereotyping. Subsequent chapters look more closely at publications for younger male and female readers, with a particular focus on their use of franchising and multimedia. There are brief summaries of lists of titles, grouped by publisher, and fuller descriptions of major ongoing manga magazines, characters and their creators. Schodt concludes with a discussion of manga's place in the English-speaking world, identifying the popularity of anime [animation], positioning of key publishers, and developing formats such as video cassettes as precursors to its initial success and successful emulation by Western artists (a subject that Casey Brienza picks up in subsequent work – see below).

In *Adult Manga: Culture & Power in Contemporary Japanese Society* (2000), Sharon Kinsella touches on many of the same topics as Schodt in a historical discussion of the development of manga in Japan from the 1960s to the millennium. Her methodology entails field work with official and more unofficial and less structured interviews with actors in the Japanese manga publishing business including publishers, editors and creators and she candidly introduces this research as a very immersive experience where she has spent large amounts of time in editing offices. Kinsella also notes, however, a possible bias because big manga publisher Kodansha funded some of the research and allowed her into their publishing meetings and discussions. Kinsella provides insight into the history of manga in the time period and into some of the censorship discussions such as the *otaku* [nerd] panic and she comments on the *dōjinshi* [fanzine] culture mentioned above. The post-Second World War cultural landscape of Japan, Kinsella contends, saw a development of manga from an artistically and politically progressive medium to a more commercial and conservative business that linked Japanese 'good' manga with the utmost in Japanese culture. This development was helped along by censorship and very active editors taking over much of the creative content and stylistic choices. *Adult Manga* provides a look into the business of manga publishing in an important period for the medium and offers some explanations for the way the Japanese manga scene looked in the early 2000s.

Paul Gravett's *Manga: Sixty Years of Japanese Comics* (2004) addresses various aspects of this medium's development in Japan. Each chapter opens with a short essay setting out its main point and arguments, followed by extracts from significant works, captioned with short creator biographies or descriptions of their relevance. Chapter 1 describes manga's historical evolution into the formats available today and contextualizes these against

Japan's culture and history. The second chapter explores the way in which the medium has developed Japan's long tradition of narrative art, dating back to the twelfth century. 'Father Storyteller' Osamu Tezuka (1928–89) is the subject of Chapter 3, which looks closely at his most famous works and their cultural and media influences. The next chapter explores the darker period of post-war recovery in the 1940s and the highly political publications of the 1950s, followed by two chapters that examine manga genres for boys and girls, respectively. Chapter 7 then explores manga created for an adult audience, considering tropes of sex and horror (and the strategies used to depict these), but stressing that such titles are not limited to these genres. Chapter 8 ('The All-Encompassing') extends the discussion into manga aimed at large demographics, such as older women, and Chapter 9 complements this with a discussion of niche publishers, fanzines and cult titles (while acknowledging that the borders between mainstream and underground are not terribly clear). The final chapter explores the country's attempts to export manga and attract international creators, which have resulted in a vibrant, transnational and post-imperialist publishing culture.

Moving beyond Japan, Paul Gravett's *Mangasia* (2016) is a more recent project with an impressive breadth that aims at surveying the history of Asian comics from 'no further west than Pakistan and no further north than Mongolia and the very top of Japan'. Gravett traces the development of manga from its roots in late nineteenth-century Japan through a wide range of different formats (comics, cartoons, animation). His history spans over a century but instead of a country-by-country geographical approach, it is organized thematically: 'Mapping Mangasia', 'Fable and Folklore', 'Recreating and Revising the Past', 'Stories and Storytellers', 'Censorship and Sensibility' and 'Multimedia Mangasia'. This allows for comparative comments and the inclusion of national examples that are not as abundant as the dominant comics countries in the region. Although the cover boasts 'The Definitive Guide to Asian Comics' the breadth of the survey necessitates a surface level dip into this part of comics culture, but its coffee table format and great emphasis on reproduction of a diverse set of samplings from so many countries not usually highlighted when Asian comics are discussed, function to give a visual impression of the many instances of comics from Asia that goes well beyond the Japanese manga, Chinese manhua, and Korean manwha often showcased.

Similarly, John A. Lent's *Asian Comics* (2015) covers material from regions other than Japan to highlight the diversity of publications beyond Japanese manga. It is divided into three sections considering East Asia,

Southeast Asia and South Asia, with each chapter focusing on a specific country or region. The introduction gives an overview and pre-history, and the following chapters trace the historical development of comics work in each locality, drawing on creator and publisher interviews, analysis of strips, and extensive scholarly research. Lent has also edited a collection, *Southeast Asian Cartoon Art* (2014), which contains chapters on Indonesia, the Philippines, Thailand, Cambodia, Vietnam, Singapore, Burma and Malaysia. These cover multiple different themes and formats, including humour magazines, political cartoons, newspaper comic strips, comic books of many genres and book-length comics or graphic novels. While individual chapters focus on different aspects, the collection as a whole traces a history from the late nineteenth century that engages with political struggle and censorship from authoritarian governments; economic problems; material issues such as newspaper publication; and themes of transnationality, national identity and chauvinism.

Turning to China, John Lent and Xu Ying's *Comics Art in China* (2017) draws on extensive interviews and existing scholarship to offer a historical overview of Chinese comics art and contextualize this with respect to politics, culture, society and economics. Lent and Ying take a broad approach to comics art, which includes *liánhuánhuà, xinmanhua,* manhua, comic books, newspaper strips, political cartoons, humour magazines, pictorial periodicals and animation. They pose four main questions: (1) Are there common threads throughout the history of Chinese art? (2) What outside factors played roles in development of Chinese comics art? (3) How is Chinese comics art linked historically to the country's wider structure of artistic and literary professions? (4) What is the relationship of Chinese comics art to society? They create a linear pathway through Chinese comics history that focuses primarily on the People's Republic of China. Early chapters explore the historical development of Chinese comics art, tracing the prehistory of caricature as far back as 5000BC and drawing attention to the debates and disputes in existing scholarship (Bader, 1941; Parton, 1877; Murck, 2000). They also explore the history of illustrated and visual storytelling, tracing this back to 206BC, and note the Western influences that produced cartoon periodicals in the late nineteenth century, leading to the emergence of *liánhuánhuà* (palm-sized paperbacks presenting one image per page with accompanying text). The subsequent chapters explore 'Manhua's Golden Age' in the 1920s and 1930s, which saw the expansion of *liánhuánhuà* alongside the first successful newspaper comic strips, increased numbers of cartoon/humour magazines, attempts to professionalize comics art, and a movement towards a more precise definition of comics. The impact of the war, the rapid changes of the following decades and the years after the Cultural Revolution are all discussed. These chapters focus on the ways cartoons were used for propaganda and resistance, the difficult circumstances of the cartoonists, and the attempts to open up comics art to a wider audience and circle of practitioners. The development of Chinese animation is also traced, from its handmade beginnings to a leading global industry.

The book's conclusion returns to its research questions, arguing that the many crises of twentieth-century China form a common thread in the development of its comics art, and have shaped its cultural position and purpose. Lent and Ying argue that Chinese comics art has repeatedly been used for propaganda and satire, although at times creators have had to employ subtlety or restraint. They draw attention to additional outside influences, such as periodicals from other nations and other artistic media, and the manifestations of these, for example through comics' appearances in high-culture magazines or defences of the medium. The relationship of Chinese comics art to society is thus characterized as tightly entwined, with cartoons taking on various roles (critic, watchdog, promoter) and directing their messages at mass audiences, adapting their formats and methods to gain greater reach. Lent and Ying conclude that while it is not the prerogative of the Chinese cartoonists to determine these social ills (which remains the role of the state), their work nonetheless comments on these perceived issues once the state has defined them. Overall, *Comics Art in China* is densely packed with historical information and offers an impressive attempt to create a linear narrative out of thousands of years of history, with its focus mainly set on the last century. The primary research is extensive (a complete list of interviews conducted is included at the end) and the scholarly research is equally wide ranging – the bibliography alone is an invaluable resource.

Other critics have explored aspects of Chinese comics art history, including the development of particular formats, styles or eras. Hwang (1978), Chen (1996) and Andrews (1997) trace the development of *liánhuánhuà* from the 1930s onwards, noting the format's evolution, such as the addition of speech balloons to emulate sound movies (Chen, 1996: 66). Taylor (2014) considers the rise of newspaper strips, and Hung (1994) looks closely at wartime cartooning. These papers have a tighter focus on individual periods or features of Chinese comics art and demonstrate that the genre is fast gaining scholarly prominence.

Turning to India, comics began in the mid-1960s, developing from the syndicated Western strips that featured in 1950s newspapers, with indigenous titles then appearing in the 1970s. English-language scholarship is limited, with key work coming from scholars such as Emma D. Varughese, whose book *Visuality and Identity in Post-millennial Indian Graphic Narratives* (2018) focuses on contemporary graphic novels from India. Varughese explores the intersections of visuality and Indian culture, particularly relating to notions of the inauspicious. Some chapters in edited collections also explore the Indian comics industry. Suhaan Mehta's 'Wondrous Capers: The Graphic Novel in India' (*Multicultural Comics*, 2011) examines the methods used by non-mainstream creators in a selection of contemporary titles to give a voice to those marginalized by caste or sexuality.

In *India's Immortal Comic Books* (2009) Karline McLain examines the history of the long-running series *Amar Chitra Katha* (*ACK*), founded by Anant Pai in 1967 in response to reprint culture as an attempt to create a homegrown Indian comics series. McLain analyses the historical development of *ACK* to argue that Indian comics are a vital site for studying the ways in which ideological discourses of national identity are negotiated. She draws on interviews and surveys with company employees and readers to detail *ACK*'s publishing and distribution history and combines this with close analysis of the comics themselves. McLain demonstrates that Indian comics draw on long traditions of Indian visual culture, and frequently combine mythology and history, for example by recasting traditional Sanskrit narratives. She reads the comics as reflecting their surrounding context, for example initially de-emphasizing religious miracles to accord with the new, modern India of the 1950s and 1960s, but subsequently re-engaging with spirituality after Pai realized his Hindu readership saw the comics as a legitimate source of spiritual material. Other chapters focus on significant figures such as Shakuntala, the first female comic book heroine, the Warrior-King Shivaji and Mahatma Gandhi. McLain notes the ways in which the treatment of these characters enacts the difficulties of negotiating history, mythology and tradition, for example regarding female suffering and martyrdom, accusations of religious or anti-Muslim propaganda, and the colonial narrative. Overall, McLain's study uses historical analysis of *ACK* to explore the relationship between media, religion and culture in South Asia, arguing that the series has established a canon of characters that define what it means to be Hindu and Indian for a vast middle-class readership throughout the transnational Indian diaspora.

Expanding the focus to the wider region, *Arab Comic Strips* (Douglas and Malti-Douglas, 1994) also takes a political critical approach: analysing comics across multiple countries from this region as a response to imported materials from America and France. Despite its title it surveys Arab comics across all formats, noting the dominant form of the children's book. It observes that Arab comics exist in a vastly intersectional space, leading to multiple points of complexity. These include accessibility issues due to the range of spoken dialects, which means that the formal language *fushâ* is used in many – emphasizing their pedagogical potential. Douglas and Malti-Douglas analyse many examples, such as the UAE's *Mâjid* and Egypt's *Samîr*, grouping their discussion around key themes such as Disney imperialism, secular nationalism, subversion and state propaganda, censorship, Islamic movements, and the nuance needed to successfully blend religious and political elements and negotiate local and regional identities. A particular emphasis is placed on the depiction of women, which must draw from three competing visions (the leftist secular, the Islamic and the Western). The writers foreground the unique position of Arab comic strips as an imported and adapted Western cultural product, yet one whose place in the Arab cultural world is vastly different from their Western situation: Arab comics creators are integrated into a larger class of intellectuals, and many are established fiction writers, painters or editorial cartoonists. Rather than belonging to popular culture, Arab comic strips thus straddle the elite world of art and literature, and that of journalism. They contain legitimizing power by depicting state leaders and ideologies, although the strips in general cohere around consensus values (rather than propaganda) and more general ideological positions such as Arab solidarity, anti-imperialism and anti-Zionism, the glory of Arab heritage, and respect for Islamic legacy and morals. Overall, these scholars argue that the development of many contemporary Arab strips demonstrates that it is possible to sustain national identity and tradition without abandoning the modern world.

Africa

Published scholarship on African comics is more common in French than English, presumably due to this continent's many Francophone countries such as Algeria, Congo and Gabon.[2] Considering South Africa in general, a tradition of political and satirical cartooning dominates over graphic novels and more diverse genres. Andy Mason's *What's So Funny? Under the*

Skin of South African Cartooning (2010) surveys the historical development of the country's cartoon industry, with a particular emphasis on the depiction of ethnicity and associated experience. The book is oversized and lavishly illustrated with the cartoons that he discusses. Mason looks back as far as the 1800s, bookending his study with George Cruikshank's 1819 depiction of cannibalistic natives, and Zapiro's notorious 'rape of justice' cartoon attacking presidential candidate Jacob Zuma (2008). In Part 1, 'The Illustrated Other', Mason takes a historical approach. His analyses are nuanced and contextualized, as he resituates the Cruikshank cartoon as political satire aimed at the British Government, rather than the racist stereotyping it is remembered for. He surveys a wide range of misleading images from the early 1800s, indicating that their inaccuracies constitute a kind of mythologizing, as they often appeared in ethnographic books. He then discusses the emergence of new, more warlike, stereotypes after the arrival of the 1820 settlers, and the use of these by contemporary white Afrikaaner cartoonists who have revisited the country's bloody history and interrogated its telling. Mason draws attention to the predominantly white ethnicity of the South African cartoonists (with notable exceptions such as writer Alex La Guma, 1959) and the omission of Black experience from these satirical strips. This leads him to discuss Len Sak's *JoJo* (created 1958) as a counterpoint that engages with a Black everyman character, despite its use of visual stereotyping.

Mason takes care to situate the cartoons within their political and social context, offering revisionist readings of some, and acknowledging his own personal relationship with comics. The second part of the book explores the development of comics in the 1970s as a medium for protest and political propaganda. Mason's analysis characterizes the subsequent decades as ones that saw the increasing publication of Black writers and artists: to oversimplify, he argues that these Black voices were often equated with realism while white liberal writers experimented with postmodernism, resulting in many political pamphlets and the return of stereotypes such as Hoggenheimer (a rich industrialist getting fat from the profits of the country). Thus, a South African alternative publishing scene arose, based in Johannesburg, with the aim of reaching new audiences and sparking discussions about social inequities. Mason contrasts this with the role of the mainstream press in shielding its audience from the realities of apartheid, and the rise of popular resistance in the 1970s: the violence of which informed the style of satirical artists such as Dov Fedler, Andy (Dave Anderson), Derek Bauer and the early work of Zapiro. Importantly, Mason draws attention to the continued lack of Black South African cartoonists throughout the twentieth century, even in modern satirical works, and situates this against the explosion of Black voices in other media (such as the poets, authors, dramatists, journalists and musicians of the *Drum* generation). Mason concludes that the legacy of racism in comics has made it hard for this medium to gain any traction, alongside the financial difficulties of making it as a cartoonist.

Overall, Mason's analysis suggests that historically the denigration of Black characters in cartooning is not a South African trait but emblematic of colonial attitudes across Europe. His consideration of contemporary cartoons demonstrates that the country's cartooning has focused on sharp political satire, although book-length publications are on the rise. His epilogue revisits the influence of British heritage on the country, via its links with his own ancestry, summarizing the creation and development of imagery of the Other that has permeated its cartooning. Mason's revisionist approach chimes with some of the later comics scholarship surveyed in Chapter 4, of this Guide which revisits the Comics Code and draws attention to the nuance and detail of its creation. He also combines the story of his own discovery and investigations into South African cartooning with analysis of the history and cartoons themselves: a personal approach also seen in much of the research discussed in Chapter 10 of this Guide.

While Mason's book gives a comprehensive overview, isolated articles exploring individual South African strips do also appear in some collections, such as Feurle's examination of the highly successful strip 'Madam and Eve' (*Cheeky Fictions*, 2005), which explores its depiction of complex racial dynamics and the clash between old and new South Africa. Feurle points towards the ways in which the strip looks back to the country's history as well as forward, and creates humour by playing with stereotypes, flouting taboos and foregrounding the nation's contradictions. She concludes that even if there is no shared national perspective, this laughter is unifying and a step towards democracy.

There are also several very useful online resources. The 'Encyclopaedia of African Political Cartooning' (https://africacartoons.com/cartoonists/map/south-africa/) allows users to select individual countries from a map of the continent, then bringing up a list of creators from this area, with thumbnails and biographies where known. The 'Africa Comic' project (http://www.africacomics.net/project/) is a physical and online archive of the comics themselves, which began in 1999 and has since collected over 2500 drawings from all areas of the continent. Online users can search for keywords or browse the collection, revealing colour scans of the comics (mostly in French) that can be scrolled through. Each is accompanied by details of publication and creator, and a summary (in English) of its plot.

Australasia

Panel by Panel: A History of Australian Comics (John Ryan, 1979) is the main historical survey of the development of Australian comics. The book proceeds chronologically through the history of Australian comics, showing how these developed in the pages of newspaper supplements and emphasizing their popularity. Ryan pairs detailed description of the strips with biographical summaries of the main artists who created and worked on them, summarizing debates about black-and-white versus colour strips, imported versus indigenous, and the fluctuating formats of the newspaper colour supplements.

Part 1 focuses on the evolution of newspaper strips, and Ryan begins with forerunners such as *Melbourne Punch*, which printed four-panel strips as early as 1870, although he names the first recognizable Australian comic strip as Norman Lindsay's work in *The Lone Hand* magazine (1907), followed by regular (and coloured) strips in the comic magazine, *The Comic Australian* (1911–13). Notably, male and female artists feature prominently in this early history: Hugh McCrae's work appeared alongside Nelle Rodd's in *The Comic Australian*, followed by May Gibbs' cartoons in the Perth *Western Mail*. These early strips were comedic, also giving way to more political fare in *The International Socialist*, and roughly drawn (excluding Lindsay's highly professional draftsmanship). The country's comics tradition began to consolidate in the 1920s in *Smiths Weekly* (launched 1919), which originally reprinted US strips and then initiated 'You & Me', a domestic humour strip originally by Stan Cross. Its success spawned imitators, and the format got another boost when 'Sunbeams', a children's supplement, was introduced into the Sydney *Sunday Sun*, and developed to include pages of comics from artists such as David Souter. 'Sunbeams' was the birthplace of some of Australia's most famous comics characters and the 1920s provided various additional news publications to further develop the comic strip format. Ryan examines how a syndicated market developed, along with serialized continuity strips and longer supplements, aided by the import restrictions that marked the start of the Second World War and prevented imported strips from taking over the market. He also explores the use of comic strips as propaganda, and the Australian underground comix scene, which emerged in the early 1970s.

In the second half of his book, Ryan examines the emergence of comic books, noting that before the 1930s this was dominated by material from the UK and claiming the first local comic as *Vumps* (1908), although this was drawn in a British style. *Fatty Finn's Weekly* began in 1934 and lasted until 1935. It was followed by *Wags* in 1936, which reprinted American newspaper strips, and during the 1930s other contemporary American titles made their way to Australia, alongside compendiums of comic sections from American Sunday newspapers. As Ryan summarizes:

> As Australia moved towards its involvement in World War II, the choice of comics lay between imported English comics, imported US ones, imported *Wags*, imported International Comics, imported backdated comics dumped on the market, and Fidgett Brothers' reprints of US strips.
>
> (154)

As with the newspaper strips, however, enforcement of import legislation gave local publishers an opportunity to enter the market, although it was often circumnavigated, for example by bringing US comics in via the UK, or licensing properties (K.G. Murray began releasing *Superman* in 1947). Local heroes, however, were popular too (such as *The Raven*, 1946; *Jet Fury*, 1948; and *The Phantom*, 1948), and indigenous imitations of famous American titles also appeared, such as *The Phantom Ranger* (1949), based on *The Lone Ranger*, and *Yarmak – The Jungle King* (1949), based on *Tarzan*. Finally, Ryan considers the 1950s and the 1960s, in which the comic book industry followed a similar trajectory to the newspaper strips: experiencing censorship and financial problems (e.g. the rising cost of newsprint) in the 1950s, and stagnation in the 1960s.

Graeme Osborne's 'Comics Discourse in Australia' in *Pulp Demons* (1999) gives a short and digestible summary of the early history of Australian comics, which dates back to the mid-nineteenth century when strips first emerged, and he summarizes the main points Ryan raised. Osborne explains how, after Lindsay's early work, and following the First World War, the creations of artists such as Stan Cross, Charles Banks and Syd Nicholls grew wildly popular during the 1920s, faltered in the 1930s depression, but regained and increased its popularity during the Second World War, which restricted imports. During this time, Australian comics turned away from their original 'knockabout' humour and towards the American-style adventure strips. After the war, however, American strips again began to dominate, both as individual books and syndicated strips in newspapers, and this led, Osborne argues, to concerns and debates about comics' effects in the 1950s, in line with many other countries (see Chapter 4).

Amy Louise Maynard's 2017 PhD thesis, *A Scene in Sequence: Australian Comics Production as a Creative Industry 1975–2017*, is available online and contains a chapter focused on the historical development of the Australian comics industry which picks up where John Ryan's *Panel by Panel* ends. Maynard breaks this period into two distinct phases. She argues that the first period of production (1890–1960) was initially characterized by reprinted American fare or comics that were strongly modelled on these templates, which appeared in newspapers. These early comics publications first appeared in June 1915 and were self-published 'troop publications' circulated by Australian soldiers. Comics publications in wider circulation such as *The Kookaburra* then emerged from 1931 onwards. While production was focused around the cities, most stakeholders worked autonomously rather than as part of a production line as in the American industry. Maynard defines these two approaches as industrial (American) and artisanal (Australian). She notes that the Australian comics scene was largely imitative of American content and that the controversies of the 1950s were thus shared in this country, with a distinct lack of political and cultural support for comics. Maynard then defines the 1960s–1970s as a 'period interlude' where both America and Australia turned their innovations to the underground, producing lowcost, sociopolitical and explicit content for adult readers. This underground 'magazine' movement in Australia, however, did not last beyond the decade and declined alongside its countercultural movement.

Maynard then explores the second period of Australian cultural production, commencing in 1975, which is characterized by fans becoming producers. She draws attention to two distinct schools of production: the Melbourne scene which followed the 1970s underground magazines and was characterized by adult themes and sociopolitical comment; and the scene that emerged in Sydney in the 1980s which was more closely inspired by the superhero and fantasy genres. Although Australian comics production still lacked a shop system and corporate publishers, distribution and networks emerged through regular meet ups which enabled collaboration through comics jams (Melbourne) and serial titles (Sydney). The 1980s then saw an explosion of comics shops and the emergence of comic-cons (annually, beginning 1979), leading to the international distribution of homegrown titles such as *Inkspots*. In the 1990s comics scenes began to appear more widely in other cities, although national distribution remained a problem. Since the millennium, Maynard argues that there have been three key changes:

1. Graphic novels have appeared from both independent comics publishers and larger book publishers, changing the cultural value of comics and their visibility.

2. Software development and online publishing have allowed for increased production, distribution and marketing of indigenous comics, and media convergence, such as crowdfunding and social media, has given creators more agency and control.

3. Consequent diversity has moved comics out of a subcultural space and made them highly visible in literary festivals, galleries, institutions and so forth.

Maynard's conclusion is that the Australian comics scene has adopted a creative industries framework that adapts international practice and develops indigenous production and circulation methods as a consequence of the divergences and time lag between these first and second periods.

Other specific historical sources include Philip Bentley's memoir *A Life in Comics* (2013), which reflects on the 1970s comics culture from the perspective of a writer, editor and publisher. Bentley explores how Australian comics production during this decade challenged the cultural stigmas attached to comics and sought to compete with international comics. For more contemporary discussions of the Australian industry, websites such as *Comicoz* (comicoz.com) and *Comics Down Under* (comicsdownunder. blogspot.com) provide blog posts and news updates.

Transnational

While the above sections have summarized works that analyse the development of comics in a particular place, several more recent collections have taken a global perspective. The four edited collections below draw particular attention to the interplay of ideas and practices that are shared between different comics cultures, and approach comics as a global, rather than national, industry. In this, they take a transnational approach; examining the interconnectedness of comics at the borders, interstices and exchanges between different cultures (rather than an international perspective which would survey multiple distinct national entities).

Transnational Perspectives on Graphic Narratives (2013), edited by Shane Denson, Christina Meyer and Daniel Stein, collects essays that chart the ways in which comics have been shaped by aesthetic, social, political, economic and cultural intersections across the globe. The editors argue that it addresses a blind spot in comics studies, which often treats national comics industries as selfcontained entities. They define their transnational approach as complementary to national and international analyses, and aim to go beyond simplistic assumptions that comics are predisposed to transnationality due to their combination of words and pictures, which aid understanding, and that transnational approaches can erode global hierarchies. Instead, the collection is divided into three parts that discuss different angles on cultural exchange, although these are all focused around American productions and genres.

The first part, 'Politics and Poetics', examines the ways in which formal comics tropes are used to explore complex questions of identity and nation. Michael Chaney's personal and rigorous article 'Not Just a Theme: Transnationalism and Form in Visual Narratives of US Slavery' considers some of the fallacies of formalism (such as the tendency to privilege meaning in the gutter, or the imagined community of readers), using the depiction of the Middle Passage in children's books and comics. Chaney argues that it is this subject's potential as a catalyst for African American creative arts and its ontological ability to create new dialogues that is significant, rather than its transnational historical content. In the following chapter on Gene Luen Yang's *American Born Chinese* (2006), Elisabeth El Refaie also considers the unstable nature of formal analysis by exploring the use of shape shifting as a metaphor for transnational identity, arguing that this symbol aptly represents the instability of highly abstract notions such as cultural identity. El Refaie notes the dominance of the shapeshifting trope across many genres of comics and visual arts history and argues that its potential to hold multiple meanings and connotations demonstrates that transnationality is complex and always more than the sum of its parts. The following chapters in this section continue this focus on the relationship between politics and formal storytelling strategies. Georgiana Banita examines the concept of 'graphic silence' in comics journalism from Guy Delisle, Joe Sacco, Jean-Philippe Stassen and Ari Folman, creating a taxonomy of three different types of silent panel and exploring their significance for the ethics of the foreign gaze. In *Footnotes in Gaza* (2009), Aryn Bartley examines Joe Sacco's use of 'critical cosmopolitanism' (rather than empathetic transnational identification), arguing that Sacco does not abandon empathy or identification but pushes beyond these concepts to create a depiction that invites a historical, critical and agnostic dialogue about the Israeli-Palestinian conflict. Finally, Iris-Aya Laemmerhirt considers the unusual perspectives on Hawaii offered by R. Kikuo Johnson's *Night Fisher*, and Daniel Wüllner explores the presence of transnationalism in the comics of the American artist Warren Craghead III.

The second section, Transnational and Transcultural Superheroes, considers adaptations of these characters that problematize simplistic ideas of imperialism and subversion. Chapters 7–9 are analyses of Batman in a global context (Katharina Bierloch and Sharif Bitar), Indian reiterations of Spider-Man (Shilpa Davé), and manga versions of Spider-Man (Daniel Stein). In chapter 10 Jochen Ecke takes a different focus and examines the transnational author figure through a close consideration of Warren Ellis, engaging with theories of authorship and performativity. Finally, Stefan Meier analyses the Muslim superhero characters that appear in *The 99*, arguing that this narrative remains uncritical of the tropes of the superhero genre, even as it achieves a significant success in presenting young Muslim cosmopolitans.

The third section, Translations, Transformations, Migrations, maps some of the changes that have shaped comics globally. Florian Groß examines the capacity of wordless comics to convey narratives of displacement. Using the works of Franz Masereel, Shaun Tan and Joe Kavalier, Groß challenges the assumption that pictures are universally understood, and instead demonstrates that they require a form of reception that foregrounds the complex process of visual translations. Frank Mehring analyses processes of remediation and omission in Frank Miller's *Sin City*, whose silhouettes, he claims, create signs without referents, removing national associations. The two following chapters consider the qualities of cultural crossovers: Lukas Etter analyses the depiction of the city as plural and fragmented in Jason Lutes' *Berlin*; Mark Berninger explores the melting pot of national influences that inform Brian Lee O'Malley's *Scott Pilgrim*. Finally, Jean-Paul Gabilliet examines the reception of *Asterix* and *Tintin* in North America, arguing that the transnational marketability of commodities such as comics is directly related to the cultural proximity of the importing and exporting countries, and affected by dialectics such as upward and downward cultural processes. The collection concludes with an afterword in which editor Shane Denson argues for a critical framework that defines comics' formal properties (the panel/gutter tension; temporal versus spatial sequences and layouts; serial formats and so forth) as a set of oppositions that connote transnationality. He draws on the preceding essays to contend that the perceptual multistability that is created as images are framed, unframed, and reframed during the reading process is a catalyst for accommodating a wide range of transnational relations within the comics medium.

Casey Brienza has produced two books exploring the transnational nature of manga today. *Global Manga* (2015) analyses the emergence of 'Japanese-style' comics that today are produced throughout the Americas, Europe and Asia. Brienza explores the cultural conditions under which this 'global manga' has flourished, interrogating the identities of emergent gatekeepers and stakeholders, considering the implications for local creative economies and the ways the genre can mix with local cultural forms and influences, and reflects on conceptions of the 'Japanese' national identity of manga. In *Manga in America* (2016) Brienza takes a deeper dive inside the American industry, drawing on interviews with industry insiders to present a sociological examination of the processes of domestication used by American media producers of Japanese manga in English. Brienza argues that these manga publishing houses and their networks can be conceptualized as faithful yet dysfunctional family units whose success is reliant on both cooperation and conflict. Her study is situated against scholarship on the production of culture and gives a detailed history of the American manga industry's development, exploring its motivations, creative practices and use of new publishing models, and concludes by reflecting on how the American remediation of Japanese culture is manifest through unequal power relations and ultimately impacts back on the production of manga in Japan.

By contrast, the collection *Drawing New Color Lines* (2015), edited by Monica Chiu, explores the interpretative possibilities and limitations of transnational narratives. Chiu draws attention to the differences in interpretation that American and Asian readers might experience, and the collection investigates and interrogates comics' use of conventions such as stereotyping, asking what happens when national stories and conventions are rearticulated from a new standpoint. Similarly, Binita Mehta and Pia Mukherji's edited collection, *Postcolonial Comics: Texts, Events, Identities* (2015), takes the standpoint that representations are necessarily always political, interweaving the production of Self and Other via discourse. This collection focuses on voices that have been neglected in discussions of the medium. They point out that there is comparatively very little criticism devoted to comics from places like Africa, India and the Middle East, and that, even in transnationally themed collections such as those above,[3] most of the texts analysed come from American or European comics traditions. Instead, the essays in this collection are split into four sections: the first focuses on comics from Gibraltar, Malta and Japan, the second on Francophone Africa (Algeria, Congo, Gabon), the third on India, and the fourth on the Middle East. As such it is a particularly useful resource for those wanting to find out more on these underwritten areas.

The collection *Cultures of Comics Work* (2016), edited by Casey Brienza and Paddy Johnston, turns its gaze to the people, rather than places, that have been overlooked in comics study. The editors argue for the importance of recognizing the numerous invisible people who participate in comics production, and the breadth of essays they present offers a strongly transnational focus. Its first chapter is an introduction from Brienza and Johnston that points towards the problems with traditional auteur-based, formalist, and definitional approaches to comics analysis, and defines their term 'comics work' in counterpoint to this, referring to the myriad of activities required to create a comic book. The following chapters are split into three sections: the first, Locating Labour, examines the local and national contexts within which context work takes place. In Chapter 2, Amy Maynard explores the Australian comic scene, arguing that its appeal is based on processes of cooperation and autonomy, rather than any financial gain. Jeremy Stoll presents a similar survey of underground comics in India. The fourth chapter examines cultures of Colombian comics, detailing events, publishers, artist collectives and historically significant events. Chapter 5 is a close reading of the comic *Nuestro Futuro* with reference to its geographic, temporal and political contexts of US/Mexican relations. Chapter 6 takes a similar perspective on Brazilian comics, and the final chapter in the section provides a case study of *Teenage Mutant Ninja Turtles* comics, a franchise that developed in opposition to mainstream American comics publishers' practices. The section offers an alternative to the auteur theories often applied to comics, by demonstrating that collaboration, community and interaction are absolutely key to the production of these works, and that multiple cultures and production systems exist around them.

The second part of the book, 'Illustrating Workers', contains case studies of individual creators and collaborative practices. Wilkins and Gray explore the various forms collaboration might take. Subsequent chapters examine particular creators such as Guy Delisle, John Porcellino, Fabien Vehlmann, and also contain reflections on practice from practitioner-scholars such as Ahmed Jameel and an analysis of the documentary *Comic Book Artists: The Next Generation* by Benjamin Woo, which draws attention to the fictionalizing processes used to visualize comics work, and the problematic exclusion of workers who fall outside a white or Asian male demographic. The book's final section brings together chapters that aim to push the current boundaries of studying comics work. Pascal Lefèvre discusses the gatekeeping practices of French publishers; José Santiago examines manga publishing in Spain, David K. Palmer analyses the distribution practices of the American industry, Alex Valente explores the translation of humour in Italian comics and Zoltan Kacsuk concludes the collection by exploring Hungarian manga production. While the focus of *Cultures of Comics Work* is primarily on developing existing methodology, its transnational content makes it useful for anybody wanting to learn more about underexplored comics cultures or practices.

Conclusion

While the existence of so many histories of the comics medium demonstrates the medium's breath and variety, such texts often follow similar debates or strategies, such as identifying the 'first' comic, and creating a subsequent timeline of development, using the contributions and biographies of key artists and publishers alongside contextual discussion of the country's industrial and political landscape. Most histories engage with publishing context to reflect on the ideological content of early comics, and the development of female characters in particular is a shared focus of writers across many different cultures (such as Mexico, Canada, India, the UK and the United States). Although comics scholarship has more recently aimed to move beyond a national and linear focus, an Anglo-American dominance remains. There seems a great need for further work in this area in the form of international and transnational collections that bring together historical analyses cohered around theme rather than geography: identifying synergies between diverse creative industries and analysing shared tropes.

Notes

1.   Gravett (2014) also notes the Lucca Comics Festival's 1989 attempt to define the first comic as 1896, using the *Yellow Kid*, and the dispute from historians such as Denis Gifford. Other contenders for the title of first comic include *The Glasgow Looking Glass* (1825), an 'illustrated newspaper' that contained a comic strip in its fourth issue.

2. See for example works by Christophe Cassiau-Haurie, Sandra Federici, Jean-Pierre Jacquemin, Sébastien Langevin, Hilaire Mbiye Lumbala, Andrea Marchesini Reggiani and Massimo Repetti, not yet translated.

3. Heimermann, Mark and Tullis, Brittany (eds) (2017) *Picturing Childhood: Youth in Transnational Comics*. Austin, TX: University of Texas Press, which is discussed in Chapter 7, is also mentioned.

Works cited

Alaniz, José. *Komiks: Comics Art in Russia*. Jackson MS: University Press of Mississippi, 2009.

Andrews, Julia F. 'Literature in Line: Picture Stories in the People's Republic of China'. *Inks*, November 1997: 17–32.

Bader, A. L. 'China's New Weapon – Caricature.' *American Scholar*, 10 April 1941: 228–240.

Bell, John (ed.) *Canuck Comics: A Guide to Comic Books Published in Canada*. Toronto: University of Toronto Press, 1986.

Bell, John (ed.) *Guardians of the North: The National Superhero in Canadian Comic-Book Art*. Ottawa: National Archives of Canada, 1992.

Bell, John. *Invaders from the North: How Canada Conquered the Comic Book Universe*. Toronto: Dundurn Press, 2006.

Bentley, Philip. *A Life in Comics: A Personal History of Comics in Australia 1960–1990*. Victoria, Australia: Second Shore, 2013.

Blanchard, Gérard. *Histoire de la bande dessinée*. Verviers: Marabout University, 1969.

Blanchard, Gérard. 'The Origins of Stories in Images'. In Ann Miller and Bart Beaty (eds), *The French Comics Theory Reader*. Belgium: Leuven University Press, 1969, pp. 25–37.

Brienza, Casey. *Global Manga: The Cultural Production of 'Japanese' Comics without Japan*. London: Routledge, 2015.

Brienza, Casey. *Manga in America: Transnational Publishing and the Domestication of Japanese Comics*. London: Bloomsbury, 2016.

Brienza, Casey and Johnston, Paddy (eds). *Cultures of Comics Work*. London: Palgrave Macmillan, 2016.

Chapman, James. *British Comics: A Cultural History*. London: Reaktion Books, 2011.

Chen, S. *Popular Art and Political Movements: An Aesthetic Enquiry into Chinese Pictorial Stories*. PhD Dissertation, New York University, New York, 1996. Available at https://www.researchgate.net/publication/34484084_Popular_art_and_political_movements_electronic_resource_an_aesthetic_inquiry_into_Chinese_pictorial_stories. Accessed 8 November 2017.

Chiu, Monica (ed.) *Drawing New Color Lines: Transnational Asian American Graphic Narratives*. Hong Kong: Hong Kong University Press, 2015.

Dejasse, Erwin and Capart, Philippe. 'À la recherche du feuilleton perdu'. *Neuvième Art: Les Cahiers de la Bande Dessinée* 15, 1999: 128–135.

Dejasse, Erwin and Capart, Philippe. 'In Search of the Lost Serial'. In Ann Miller and Bart Beaty (eds), *The French Comics Theory Reader*. Leuven, Belgium: Leuven University Press, 2009, pp. 313–320.

Denson, Shane, Meyer, Christina and Stein, Daniel (eds). *Transnational Perspectives on Graphic Narratives: Comics at the Crossroads*. London: Bloomsbury, 2013.

Douglas, Alan and Malti-Douglas, Fedwa. *Arab Comic Strips: Politics of an Emerging Mass Culture*. Bloomington, IN: Indiana University Press, 1994.

Etty, John. *Graphic Satire in the Soviet Union: Krokodil's Political Cartoons*. Jackson MS: University Press of Mississippi, 2019.

Farrajota, Marcos. 'Disquiet'. *Desassossego* #20, 2015.

Feurle, Gisela. '*Madam and Eve* – Ten Wonderful Years. A Cartoon Strip and Its Role in Post-apartheid South Africa'. In Susanne Reichl and Mark Stein (eds), *Cheeky Fictions: Laughter and the Postcolonial*. Amsterdam: Rodopi BV, 2005, pp. 271–288.

Gabilliet, Jean-Paul. *Of Comics and Men: A Cultural History of American Comic Books*. Bart Beaty and Nick Nguyen (trans.). Jackson, MS: University Press of Mississippi, [2005] 2010.

García, Santiago. *On the Graphic* Novel. Bruce Campbell (trans.). Jackson, MS: University Press of Mississippi, [2010] 2015.

Gifford, Dennis. *Happy Days: A Century of Comics*. London: Bloomsbury, [1975] 1988.

Goggin, Joyce. 'Of Gutters and Guttersnipes: Hogarth's Legacy'. In Joyce Goggin and Dan Hassler-Forest (eds), *The Rise and Reason of Comics and Graphic Literature: Essays on the Form*. Jefferson, NC: McFarland, 2010, pp. 5–24.

Gordon, Ian. *Comic Strips and Consumer Culture 1890–1945*. London: Smithsonian Institution Press, 1998.

Goulart, Ron. *Comic Book Culture: An Illustrated History*. Portland, OR: Collectors Press Inc, 2000.

Grace, Dominick and Hoffman, Eric (eds). *The Canadian Alternative: Cartoonists, Comics, and Graphic Novels*. Jackson, MS: University Press of Mississippi, 2017.

Gravett, Paul. *Manga: Sixty Years of Japanese Comics*. London: Laurence King Publishing, 2004.

Gravett, Paul. *Graphic Novels: Stories to Change Your Life*. London: Aurum Press, 2005.

Gravett, Paul. *1001 Comics You Must Read before You Die*. London: Cassell Illustrated, 2011.

Gravett, Paul. *Comics Art*. London: Tate Publishing, 2014.

Gravett, Paul. *Mangasia: The Definitive Guide to Asian Comics*. London: Thames and Hudson, 2016.

Heimermann, Mark, Tullis, Brittany and Aldama, Frederick Luis (eds). *Picturing Childhood: Youth in Transnational Comics*. Austin, TX: University of Texas Press, 2017.

Hwang, John C. 'Lien Huan Hua: Revolutionary Serial Pictures'. In Godwin C. Chu (ed.), *Popular Media in China*. Honolulu: East-West Center, 1978, pp. 51–72.

Hung, Chang-tai. *War and Popular Culture: Resistance in Modern China, 1937–1945*. Berkeley: University of California Press, 1994.

Kibble-White, Graham. *The Ultimate Book of British Comics*. London: Allison and Busby, 2005.

Kinsella, Sharon. *Adult Manga: Culture and Power in Contemporary Japanese Society*. Richmond: Curzon, 2000.

Kunzle, David. *History of the Comic Strip Volume 1, The Early Comic Strip; Narrative Strips and Picture Stories in the European Broadsheet from c.1450 to 1825*. Berkeley and Los Angeles: University of California Press, 1973.

Kunzle, David. *History of the Comic Strip Volume 2, The Nineteenth Century*. Berkeley and Los Angeles: University of California Press, 1990.

Lent, John A. (compiler). *Comic Art of Europe: An International, Comprehensive Bibliography*. Westport, CT: Praeger Publishers, 1994.

Lent, John A. *Animation, Caricature, and Gag and Political Cartoons in the United States and Canada: An International Bibliography*. Westport, CT: Praeger Publishers, 1994.

Lent, John A. *Comic Books and Comic Strips in the United States: An International Bibliography*. Westport, CT: Praeger Publishers, 1994.

Lent, John A. *Comic Art in Africa, Asia, Australia, and Latin America: A Comprehensive, International Bibliography*. Westport, CT: Praeger Publishers, 1996.

Lent, John A. *Comic Art of Europe through 2000: An International Bibliography. Volume 1*. Westport, CT: Praeger Publishers, 2003.

Lent, John A. *Comic Art of Europe through 2000: An International Bibliography. Volume 2*. Westport, CT: Praeger Publishers, 2003.

Lent, John A. (ed.) *Southeast Asian Comic Art*. Jefferson, NC: McFarland, 2014.

Lent, John A. *Asian Comics*. Jackson, MS: University Press of Mississippi, 2015.

Lopes, Paul. *Demanding Respect: The Evolution of the American Comic Book*. Philadelphia, PA: Temple University Press, 2014.

Mainardi, Patricia. *Another World: Nineteenth-Century Illustrated Print Culture*. New Haven, CT: Yale University, 2017.

Mason, Andy. *What's so Funny? Under the Skin of South African Cartooning*. Claremont: Juta and Company, 2010.

Maynard, Amy Louise. *A Scene in Sequence: Australian Comics Production as a Creative Industry 1975–2017*. PhD thesis, University of Adelaide, Adelaide, 2017. Available at https://digital.library.adelaide.edu.au/dspace/bitstream/2440/112807/2/02whole.pdf. Accessed 19 August 2019.

Mazur, Dan and Danner, Alexander. *Comics: A Global History, 1968 to the Present*. London: Thames and Hudson, 2014.

McLain, Karline. *India's Immortal Comic Books: Gods, Kings and Other Heroes*. Bloomington, IN: Indiana University Press, 2009.

Mehta, Binita and Mukherji, Pia (eds). *Postcolonial Comics: Texts, Events, Identities*. London: Routledge, 2015.

Mehta, Suhaan. 'Wondrous Capers: The Graphic Novel in India'. In Derek Parker Royal and Frederick Luis Aldama (eds), *Multicultural Comics: From Zap to Blue Beetle*. Austin, TX: University of Texas Press, 2011, pp. 173–188.

Murck, Alfreda. *Poetry and Painting in Song China: The Subtle Art of Dissent.* Cambridge: Harvard University Asia Center for the Harvard-Yenching Institute, 2000.

Nadel, Dan. *Art Out of Time: Unknown Comics Visionaries, 1900–1969.* New York: Abrams, 2006.

Nadel, Dan. *Art in Time: Unknown Comic Book Adventures, 1940–1980.* New York: Abrams, 2010.

Ory, Pascal. '*Le Désordre Noveau* [*The New Disorder*]. Chapter 2 of Le Petit Nazi Illustré [The Nazi Boy's Own]'. In Ann Miller and Bart Beaty (eds), *The French Comics Theory Reader.* Leuven, Belgium: Leuven University Press, 2002, pp. 303–312.

Ory, Pascal. *Le Petit Nazi Illustré* [The *Nazi Boy's Own*]. Paris: Nautilus, 2002.

Paris, Michael. *Warrior Nation: The Representation of War in British Popular Culture, 1850–2000.* London: Routledge, 2000.

Parton, James. *Caricature and Other Comic Art in All Times and Many Lands.* New York: Harper and Brothers, 1877.

Pilcher, Tim and Brooks, Brad. *The Essential Guide to World Comics.* London: Collins and Brown, 2005.

Roach, David. *Masters of Spanish Comic Book Art.* Mt. Laurel, NJ: Dynamite, 2017.

Robbins, Trina. *From Girls to Grrrlz: A History of Women's Comics from Teens to Zines.* San Francisco, CA: Chronicle Books, 1999.

Rubenstein, Anne. *Bad Language, Naked Ladies, and Other Threats to the Nation: A Political History of Comic Books in Mexico.* Durham and London: Duke University Press, 1998.

Ryan, John. *Panel by Panel: A History of Australian Comics.* Melbourne, Victoria: Cassell Australia Limited, 1979.

Sabin, Roger. *Comics, Comix and Graphic Novels: A History of Comic Art.* New York: Phaidon Press, 1996.

Sassienie, Paul. *The Comic Book.* London: Random House, 1994.

Schodt, Frederik L. *Manga! Manga! The World of Japanese Comics.* London: Kodansha International, [1983] 1986.

Schodt, Frederik L. *Dreamland Japan: Writings on Modern Manga.* Berkeley, CA: Stone Bridge Press, 1996.

Schwartz, Barthélémy. 'De la Misère'. *Controverse*, 1968. Reprinted in *L'Éprouvette* 2, June 2002: 327–331.

Schwartz, Barthélémy. 'On Indigence'. In Ann Miller and Bart Beaty (eds), *The French Comics Theory Reader.* Leuven, Belgium: Leuven University Press, 1986, pp. 321–325.

Smolderen, Thierry. *The Origins of Comics: From William Hogarth to Windsor McCay.* Bart Beaty and Nick Nguyen (trans.). Jackson, MS: University Press of Mississippi, 2014.

Smolderen, Thierry. 'L'Hybridation graphique, creuset de la bande dessinée'. In Laurent Gerbier (ed.), *Hybridations texte et image*. [Text-Image Hybridizations]. Tours: PUFR, 2014, pp. 147–175.

Smolderen, Thierry. 'Graphic Hybridization, the Crucible of Comics'. In Ann Miller and Bart Beaty (eds), *The French Comics Theory Reader*. Leuven, Belgium: Leuven University Press, 2014, pp. 47–62.

Streeten, Nicola and Tate, Cath. *The Inking Woman 250 Years of Women Cartoon and Comic Artists in Britain*. London: Myriad Editions, 2018.

Strömberg, Fredrik. *Swedish Comics History*. Malmö: Swedish Comics Association, 2010.

Taylor, Jeremy E. 'Cartoons and Collaboration in Wartime China: The Mobilization of Chinese Cartoonists under Japanese Occupation'. *Modern China*, 10 June 2014. http://mcx.sagepub.com/content/early/2014/07/02/0097700414538386. Accessed 8 November 2017.

Williams, Paul and Lyons, James (eds). *The Rise of the American Comics Artist*. Jackson, MS: University Press of Mississippi, 2010.

PART III
PRODUCTION AND RECEPTION

CHAPTER 6
CREATORS, IMPRINTS AND TITLES

This chapter introduces the work of scholars who have produced detailed studies of writers and artists, characters, titles or publishers. It begins with star creators from the eighteenth and nineteenth centuries, including Cham and Rodolphe Töpffer. It then discusses comics artists and their famous, serialized comics, such as Winsor McCay (*Little Nemo in Slumberland*), George Herriman (*Krazy Kat*), Charles Schulz (*Peanuts*) and Hergé (*Tintin*). The third section covers women comics artists, starting with Marie Duval, surveying early and mid-twentieth-century artists such as Nell Brinkley and Jackie Ormes and including contemporary women artists such as Lynda Barry and Julie Doucet. The chapter then turns back to male writers and artists known for their graphic novels, starting with key writers of what is frequently called the British invasion of American comics. It introduces a selection of critical material on key contemporary graphic novelists such as Art Spiegelman, Chris Ware, Seth (Gregory Gallant) and Joann Sfar. The fifth and final section of this chapter turns to studies of iconic imprints, magazines and publishers and covers, beginning with Sylvain Lesage's comprehensive history of Franco-Belgian comics publishing from 1950 to 1990. It covers popular children's and teenager comics magazines such as *Spirou*, *Pilote* and *Archie* to the adult comics magazine *Heavy Metal* (American counterpart to the French *Métal Hurlant*) and *(À Suivre)*.

Old masters

Scholarship on eighteenth- and nineteenth-century proto-comics artists remains limited and largely focused on the Swiss schoolteacher Rodolphe Töpffer, who indulged in recounting parodic stories through images and words. Originally self-published and intended for a limited audience, Töpffer's comics acquired international success, and even caught Goethe's eye. Broader contextualized readings and histories of the period can be found in Thierry Smolderen's *The Origins of Comics* and Patricia Mainardi's

Another World: Nineteenth-Century Illustrated Print Culture (2016). While *Origins of Comics* is focused on the precedents and evolution of comics, *Another World* is more concerned with the heady proliferation of the illustrated press and adopts an art historical approach that often overlooks existing research in comics studies (both works have already been discussed in Chapter 5 on historical approaches).

Töpffer, often hailed as the father of the (European) comic, has been the subject of two notable monographs: David Kunzle's *Father of the Comic Strip: Rodolphe Töpffer* (2007) and Thierry Groensteen's *M. Töpffer invente la bande dessinée* [*M. Töpffer Invents the Comic*] (2014). Both offer critical studies of Töpffer's *histoire en estampes,* which Kunzle translates as 'story in prints' or 'picture story' while also making a case for them as graphic novels due to their length, non-seriality and 'unity of theme' (Kunzle, 2007a: xi). These studies focus on the intense popularity of Töpffer's work, as suggested by its many counterfeit versions and lasting impact, reverberations of which persist in contemporary comics. Groensteen's monograph also considers Töpffer's theoretical writings on drawing and narrating through images (see Chapter 2 for more on Töpffer's *Essay on Physiognomy*). He also includes letters exchanged with the French cartoonist Cham (Charles Amédée de Noé) when the latter was adapting Töpffer's *M. Cryptogame* for the magazine *L'Illustration.* Kunzle's volume includes a facsimile English-language edition of all Töpffer's comics.

Kunzle has also edited a selection of twelve comics by the famous French illustrator Gustave Doré that were printed either as albums or serialized in the satirical weekly *Journal pour Rire* (1848–55). More recently, Kunzle published a selection of comics by Cham. In both books, Kunzle combines translated reprints of the original works with fine-tuned, contextualized analyses. Published in 2019, *Cham: The Best Comic Strips and Graphic Novelettes (1839–1862)* stands out in its monumental size that emulates the broadsheets in which Cham regularly published. Kunzle argues for the prominence of Cham, whose popularity is generally underestimated in comparison with that of Honoré Daumier. Kunzle begins by contrasting the careers of Cham and Daumier, emphasizing the importance Cham gave to word-image relationships through writing and incorporating jokes in his captions. Kunzle deftly interweaves details about Cham's life with his career in two eminent illustrated magazines, *L'Illustration* and the satirical *Charivari.* He then discusses Cham's picture stories to show how Cham was as gifted in storytelling as he was in making word-image jokes.

The late nineteenth and early twentieth century artist Winsor McCay has been the subject of relatively extensive scholarly interest, most of which centres on one of his most famous newspaper comic strips, *Little Nemo in Slumberland*. In *The Poetics of Slumberland: Animated Spirits and the Animating Spirit* (2012), Scott Bukatman takes *Little Nemo in Slumberland* as a starting point to contend for the centrality of animation and energy in America as a young country establishing its bearings in a rapidly changing world. Bukatman also elaborates on the close dialogue between the newly emerging comics and the even newer art of animation.

Katherine Roeder's *Wide Awake in Slumberland: Fantasy, Mass Culture, and Modernism in the Art of Winsor McCay* (2014) begins with an account of McCay's early life and multiple jobs especially in dime museums, to show how the emerging visual and entertainment culture had as much of an influence on McCay's work as the contemporaneous modernist, and often self-conscious, aesthetics. In examining *Little Nemo* alongside McCay's other successful strips such as the *Dream of the Rarebit Fiend, Little Sammy Sneeze* and *Hungry Henrietta,* Roeder shows how a growing consumer culture was both remediated and critiqued in McCay's work and how modernist fantasies coexisted with modern anxieties.[1]

Serialized comics

Michael Tisserand offers a detailed biography of Herriman, explaining the mystery of his 'coloured' status and his passing as white for most of his life. True to the book's title, *Krazy: George Herriman, A Life in Black and White* (2016), Tisserand interweaves Herriman's biography with the contemporary comics context, especially after Herriman's move to New York in 1900. The book also includes an appendix with, among other texts, an essay by Chris Ware on *Krazy Kat* and Herriman. More documentary information and reproduced strips can be found in Patrick McDonnell and Karen O'Connell's *Krazy Kat: The Art of George Herriman* (1999).

Scholarship on Hergé (Georges Rémi) and his most internationally successful comic, *The Adventures of Tintin,* is vast and predominantly Francophone with a few notable exceptions. In addition to Matthew Screech's chapter on Hergé in *Masters of the Ninth Art* (2005: 17–51), the critical anthology *The Comics of Hergé: When the Lines Are Not so Clear* (2016), edited by Joe Sutliff Sanders, explores many aspects of Hergé and his work, especially *Tintin*. These include the aesthetics of the clear line, the impact of the constraints the Nazi occupation imposed on the press, and how *Tintin* can be situated between the binaries of high and low art. The anthology also includes chapters on the continuation of Hergé's work and aesthetics into contemporary comics. Furthermore, Michael Farr's *Tintin: The Complete Companion* (2002) provides an accessible, extensively illustrated introduction to each *Tintin* adventure.

Pierre Assouline's *Hergé* (1998) offers one of the most thorough and critical biographies of Tintin's creator. Assouline recounts Hergé's life over twelve chapters (and seven hundred pages), which include in-depth coverage of Hergé's collaboration with the Nazis and his post-WWII re-assimilation into the publishing world. Another detailed biography is Benoît Peeters' *Hergé, fils de Tintin* [*Hergé, Son of Tintin*] (2002). Following a somewhat unconventional perspective, Peeters draws parallels between Hergé's life and the *Tintin* comics. Hergé was notoriously private and laconic about his childhood and personal life, but both books flesh out little-known details and the turmoil of the great comics artist.

Providing a highly original reading of *Tintin*, Jean-Marie Apostolidés' *Tintin et le Mythe du surenfant* [*Tintin and the Myth of the Superchild*] (2016) examines the ambiguity of Tintin's age and childlikeness. In 'Hergé and the Myth of the Super Child' (2007), Apostolidès suggests that Tintin is a myth because he remains open to interpretation by every reader. Moreover, Tintin is a modern myth: born in the interwar period, Tintin incarnates the increasing scepticism of authority figures accelerated by the First World War; at the same time, he retains a pre-war Christian morality.

Pierre Fresnault-Deruelle's *Hergéologie: Cohérence et cohésion du récit en images dans les aventures de Tintin* [*Hergeology: Coherence and Cohesion of Narration in Images in the Adventures of Tintin*] (2011) begins with a meticulous examination of Hergé's style. A selection of close readings of selected panels follows. Offering an alternative to the focus on images, Jan Baetens' *Hergé, écrivain* [*Hergé, Writer*] (1989) shows how the clear line associated with Hergé's art is also anchored in his writing, including the narration, the story and the dialogue. For Baetens, Hergé maintains a perfect balance between image and text in his *Tintin* comics. Baetens begins by exploring the connections between word and image and the particularities of the French used in *Tintin*. The remaining chapters focus on a specific character – Captain Hadock, Tournesol, the Duponts, Castafiore – before considering Hergé's work through the lens of constraints that channelled the transposition of the comics from magazine instalments to album. The final chapter highlights the complex positioning of Hergé as a Belgian writer of comics in French (and, for distinct purposes, in the Flemish-influenced dialect of Brussels).

Charles Schulz's *Peanuts* has recently been the subject of two critical anthologies. Gardner and Gordon's *The Comics of Charles Schulz: The Good Grief of Modern Life* (2019) highlights the many possibilities of reading *Peanuts*. Beginning with a queer reading emphasizing the recurrent motif of failure in the comic strip (Saunders) and the sublime aesthetic conveyed through a football gag (McCarthy), the chapters broach philosophical notions such as sincerity (Brialey) and sociopolitical aspects such as the engagement with post-war consumer culture (Saguisag) and the appearance of the strip's only black character, Franklin (Lehman). Finally, the anthology examines the afterlives of the comic strip (in films and in *Peanuts* cafés) and in comics homages, and its status as a work of comic art that remains, like many comics, influenced by personal value (Clarke). In Peanuts *and American Culture: Essays on Charles M. Schulz's Iconic Comic Strip* (2019), Peter W.Y. Lee collects essays that focus on *Peanuts'* roots in the cold war and post-war era. In addition to covering outcomes of the Cold War such as the space race, the chapters also examine child-adult relationships, race and, most prominently, gender. Also building on the contrast between child and adult comics worlds, Jamey Heit's *Imagination and Meaning in Calvin and Hobbes* (2012) studies Bill Watterson's long-running strip through focusing on the role of the imagination of Calvin, the child protagonist. Developing Richard Kearney's claim regarding the importance of the imagination in making connections between reader, text and possibilities of meaning, Heit offers a philosophical and somewhat unconventional exploration of the comic strip that focuses on the potential life lessons it shares. Michelle Ann Abate's 2017 essay "'A Gorgeous Waste': Solitude in *Calvin and Hobbes'* provides a more solid analysis of the strip's philosophical signification through focusing on the underlying omnipresence of solitude.

Women comics artists

This section covers scholarship on women artists from the nineteenth and early twentieth century and on contemporary graphic novelists, starting with a rare and largely forgotten women artist in a heavily male-dominated field, Marie Duval, whose phenomenally successful character, Ally Sloper, acquired his own magazine, *Ally Sloper's Half-Holiday*, in 1884. Addressing this anonymity, Simon Grennan, Roger Sabin and Julian Waite's *Marie Duval* (2018) is among the few exceptional monographs on women cartoonists from the earlier decades of comics history. This visually rich book offers insight into Duval's little-known life. In addition to being a theatre performer, Duval was a prolific contributor to *Judy, or the London Serio-comic Journal*, edited by her partner, Charles Ross. Her distinctively lively, frank style complemented her preferred themes of urban life and entertainment and matched her experience as a Londoner. She had no formal artistic training, but famous cartoonists such as Wilhelm Busch and George Cruikshank clearly influenced her work.

In *Drawn to Purpose: American Women Illustrators and Cartoonists* (2018), Martha H. Kennedy offers an overview, from the late nineteenth century onwards, of women artists in diverse domains from illustration to political cartoons, comics and graphic novels. Pointing out issues related to the term 'woman artist', *Drawn to Purpose* is among the few works to provide a historical account of women's contributions to the illustrated arts in North America. Kennedy introduces artists such as the 'Red Rose Girls', a group of women illustrators who lived and worked together in the early 1900s and included artists such as Jessie Willcox Smith and Elizabeth Shippen Green, who published in America's most successful magazines like *Harper's*. Recent comics artists discussed include Lynn Johnston (author of the long-running family strip, *For Better or Worse*); Lynda Barry; Roz Chast (author of *Can't We Talk About Something More Pleasant?*, which deals with the death of her parents); and Jillian Tamaki (author of *Boundless* among other graphic novels).

The early twentieth-century woman artist and writer Nell Brinkley is the subject of Trina Robbins' *Nell Brinkley and the New Woman in the Early 20th Century* (2001). Brinkley wrote and drew for American newspapers between 1917 and the early 1940s; she died in 1944 after a long illness. She is best known for creating the 'Brinkley girls', who rivalled the 'Gibson girl' as a reflection of the New Woman and her freshly won freedoms. In 1937 Brinkley created *Heroines of Today*, which glamorized the courage and accomplishments of real women.[2]

Nancy Goldstein's *Jackie Ormes: The First African American Woman Cartoonist* (2008) is a rare account of the mixed-heritage African American cartoonist's life and work. The book also reprints many of her famous but now forgotten comic strips. Known above all for her *Patty Jo 'n' Ginger* comics strips and the equally popular and unconventional Patty-Jo dolls, Ormes started her career with drawing a strip for the *Pittsburgh Courrier* in

1937 titled *Torchy Brown in Dixie to Harlem* and featuring a night club star. Then came *Candy*, a single panel cartoon about a pretty domestic worker that first appeared in the *Chicago Defender* in 1945. Within a month, while reporting on racist violence, Ormes began another cartoon, *Patty-Jo 'n' Ginger* (33), about a five-year-old girl and her sister. Despite the gaiety of the comics, both *Torchy Brown* and *Patty-Jo* referenced the harsh realities of racial discrimination and its protagonists supported justice for African Americans.

While women comics artists remain mostly overlooked, some contemporary graphic novelists have attracted unprecedented scholarly interest. Susan Kirtley's *Lynda Barry: Girlhood through the Looking Glass* (2012) assembles interpretations of Barry's comics (including her often overlooked early work) and of her novels and plays. Kirtley combines historical contextualization of Barry's oeuvre – her early struggles as a comics artist and later recognition – with analyses of her key and lesser-known works through the lens of negotiating identity and translating it into words and images. Also focusing on alternative women comics artists, Tahneer Oksman and Seamus O'Malley's *The Comics of Julie Doucet and Gabrielle Bell* (2020) compiles contributions on Doucet and Bell to highlight the role of autobiography and feminist engagement. It also includes several interviews with the artists.

In addition to Chute's interviews with key artists in *Graphic Women* (discussed in Chapter 10), Tahneer Oksman's *'How Come Boys Get to Keep Their Noses?' Women and Jewish American Identity in Contemporary Graphic Novels* (2016) broaches the negotiations of Jewish-American identity by contemporary female comics creators. Studying works by successful comics artists such as Aline Kominsky-Crumb, Sarah Glidden, Miriam Libicki, Vanessa Davis and Liana Finck, Oksman examines the complex intersection of autobiography, comics and the dialectics of belonging and exclusion, all of which unfold on an intersectional scale due to the artists' gender and origins. Also adopting an intersectional perspective, Deborah E. Whaley starts with the appearance in 1971 of the first Black female superhero, the Butterfly, to examine the representation of African American women in comics. Whaley's *Black Women in Sequence* (2015) encompasses the broader comics culture of manga, films and video games. She covers the creation, production and reception of Black female characters.

One rare publication in English on women's manga and women artists, Fusami Ogi and Rebecca Suter's critical anthology *Women's Manga in Asia and Beyond: Uniting Different Cultures and Identities* (2012) collects contributions by manga scholars and manga artists or *mangaka*. Pointing out that the manga industry is the world's largest cultural industry for female readers, the volume's editors situate the contributions in light of the recent manga boom and the internationalization of the creation and consumption of manga, all of which have been accompanied by a rise of women artists who question and reposition notions of gender identity. The volume begins with some of the most successfully exported manga genres targeting female readers, *shōjo*, 'boys' love' and women's manga, and explores gender and sexuality beyond conventional, heterosexual and binary constraints. The anthology also examines issues of transnationalization and glocalization of women's manga and sheds light on Asian manga artists' careers.

The diverse approaches to women comics artists range from biographical and cataloguing tendencies, especially in the case of earlier artists, to more thematic studies often shaped through the lens of female experience in the case of contemporary alternative comics artists. In contrast, the study of contemporary male graphic novelists, often writers who team up with several artists, is marked by a strong auteurist approach, usually influenced by literary studies.

Graphic novelists

The concept of 'graphic novels' is partly tied to several experimental and celebrated comics writers and artists, including the contemporary women artists discussed in the previous section and in Chapter 10. This section will briefly highlight key mentions of the comics writers of the 'British Invasion' before discussing a selection of secondary sources on renowned graphic novelists such as Art Spiegelman, Chris Ware and Seth. The 'British Invasion' refers to the group of British comics writers who revamped (American) superhero comics during the late 1980s. Jean-Paul Gabilliet transposed the term from the 1960s music scene in America to 'the tidal wave of British writers' who followed Alan Moore (2009: 104). Many of these comics were published by DC Comics' Vertigo imprint, founded and edited by Karen Berger, who was responsible for hiring writers such as Moore, Neil Gaiman and Grant Morrison. As the term 'graphic novelists' hints, the works of these writers and artists are usually discussed from an auteurist perspective that often treats each comic or graphic novel as the creation of one person, even when it is the result of a collaboration.

Alan Moore's work has attracted much scholarly attention, especially *Watchmen* (drawn by Dave Gibbons), which heavily reconfigured the superhero genre. In *Watchmen* the superheroes are flawed vigilantes wavering between good, evil and indifference in a postapocalyptic world irreversibly damaged by Thatcherism and Reaganomics. Andrew Hoberek's *Considering Watchmen: Poetics, Property, Politics* (2014) sheds light on the iconicity of *Watchmen* and its critique of both superheroes and neoliberalism. Hoberek connects this to Moore and Gibbon's deprivation of authorial rights and also explores the literary resonances of *Watchmen*. Annalisa Di Liddo's *Alan Moore: Comics as Performance, Fiction as Scalpel* (2009) examines Alan Moore's comics writing through diverse lenses including the chronotope, the connections between space and memory, issues of English identity, and intertextuality. In considering Moore's writing as performance, Di Liddo emphasizes its theatricality and, by extension, its literariness. In contrast, Maggie Gray's *Alan Moore, Out from the Underground: Cartooning, Performance and Dissent* (2017) adopts a novel approach combined with an under examined corpus by turning to the comics Moore drew for the underground comix scene of the 1970s. In emphasizing Moore's simultaneous implication in not only comics but also music, theatre and poetry, Gray underscores the historical and social contexts of comics production, its materiality and the politics associated with it. In addition to applying Philippe Marion's concept of graphiation, Gray also discusses Moore's use of Bertold Brecht's concept of *verfremdung* [defamiliarization] to highlight the 'political heart of his aesthetics, self-reflexively drawing attention to the artificial construction of his work so as to encourage acts of critical inquiry and appropriation' (11).

Marc Singer's *Grant Morrison: Combining the Worlds of Contemporary Comics* (2011) introduces the comics author as someone who straddles multiple genres (superhero, fantasy and personal, partially or seemingly autobiographical stories) in a self-conscious manner that reflects on the genres' histories, conventions and underlying ideologies (4). Singer highlights the sophistication of Morrison's writing for both mainstream (*X-Men, Superman, Batman*), and alternative comics (*The Invisibles, Flex Mentallo, WE3*). The book also considers Morrison's earlier work in Britain (such as *Bible John*) and discusses his treatise on superheroes, *Supergods: Our World in the Age of the Superhero*. To account for the postmodern complexity of Morrison's oeuvre, Singer applies two concepts: hypostasis, whereby comics characters become 'physical incarnations of fears, desires, or abstract concepts' (16); and synecdoche, which in Morrison's work is often used to incorporate metatextual references to the comic or the multiverse within individual panels.

Neil Gaiman has been the subject of two anthologies, the first of which focuses on *Sandman*, his best-known comic. *The Sandman Papers: An Exploration of the Sandman Mythology* (2006), edited by Joseph L. Sanders, tries to cater to casual readers and fans as well as scholars. Its first section covers some of the main *Sandman* books while the second considers diverse elements such as queer readings (through a linguistic analysis) of *Death: The Time of Your Life* (Joe Sutliff Sanders) and Gaiman's adaptation of Shakespeare (Levitan). By contrast, Joseph Michael Sommers and Kyle Eveleth's anthology *The Artistry of Neil Gaiman: Finding Light in the Shadows* (2019) covers Gaiman's entire oeuvre instead of limiting itself to *Sandman*. These include Gaiman's comics with Dave McKean (*Violent Cases, Mr. Punch*) and their picturebooks. The anthology also offers a set of more unabashedly academic interventions than the *Sandman Papers* including queer and gothic readings, and insights into the formal elements of Gaiman's imagetext works.

Jochen Ecke's *The British Comic Book Invasion* (2019) examines the styles and techniques of British authors, including Moore, Morrison, Warren Ellis and Garth Ennis, to highlight their distinctive, lasting contribution to American mainstream comics. Pinning down Moore's *Swamp Thing* as a game changing, influential comic, Ecke identifies narrative strategies that influenced later writers. Nuancing the idea of the British Invasion as a transformative power acting on mainstream American comics, he suggests that the innovative styles British writers developed evolved symbiotically with, and relied on, the existing techniques and stories of the mainstream (10).

Perhaps the most comprehensive reflection on an iconic graphic novelist and his oeuvre is Art Spiegelman's *MetaMaus: A Look Inside a Modern Classic* (2011), written in collaboration with Hillary Chute. It includes archival material, interviews and reflections by Spiegelman on how and why he wrote the *Maus* book and on the impact of *Maus*'s simultaneously contested and celebrated reception. Arranged according to three criticisms or questions levied against *Maus* – Why the Holocaust? Why mice? Why comics? – the volume offers unprecedented insights into the making of *Maus*.

Chris Ware, encouraged by his early submissions to Spiegelman and Mouly's *RAW* magazine, is now a renowned comics artist, whose complex works have been the subject of numerous scholarly publications. Martha

Kuhlman and David M. Ball's *The Comics of Chris Ware: Drawing Is a Way of Thinking* (2010) collects an impressive set of essays. Their topics include Ware's relationship with comics histories and the canon; his experimental language; autobiography; the combination of public and private stories; and aspects of urbanism, race and slowness. Daniel Raeburn's concise *Chris Ware* (2004) is also a useful introduction to reading Ware's complex work and the many influences and references he incorporates. Richly illustrated, Benoît Peeters and Jacques Samson's *Chris Ware: La bande dessinée réinventée* [*Comics Reinvented*] (2010) begins with a chronology of his work. In addition to Samson's analysis of *Jimmy Corrigan*, the book includes an interview and translations of Ware's texts.

The role of memory, often used to discuss Ware's work, also plays a central role in Daniel Marrone's *Forging the Past: Seth and Art of Memory* (2016). Known for situating his books in a seemingly idealized 1950s, Seth's comics exude nostalgia. Marrone interrogates the relationship between Seth's distinctive style and authenticity, the many kinds of ambivalences present in his work, and the forms of reading encouraged by the comics form. He excavates the nostalgic sheen in Seth's comics to highlight their ironic and self-conscious facets. He also considers the themes of collecting (a recurrent theme in Seth's works) and Canadian identity.

Turning to a prominent French artist who has published both graphic novels and mainstream comics, Fabrice Leroy's *Sfar So Far … : Identity, History, Fantasy and Mimesis in Joann Sfar's Graphic Novels* (2014) considers the widely acclaimed and prolific artist's works published between 2000 and 2014. As the subtitle suggests, Leroy contextualizes his readings through diverse lenses including the construction of Jewishness, anti-Semitism and France's colonial past, and the use of fantasy and magic realism in Sfar's comics. He also broaches intertextuality and meta-representation in, for instance, tracing Sfar's stylistic affinity with the painter Marc Chagall.

Many of the works discussed in this section are part of the University Press of Mississippi's 'Great Comics Artists' series, which includes several other titles on specific artists, including Charles Hatfield's seminal *Hand of Fire: The Comics Art of Jack Kirby* (2012). It combines a chronological account of the comics writer and artist's career, focusing on his superhero comics, with close readings of significant works from his vast oeuvre. In addition to paying close attention to Kirby's style and his 'narrative drawing', Hatfield examines the problematic issue of co-creation, which remains understudied, despite the traditionally collaborative essence of comics-making. However,

Hatfield is also aware that such an appraisal of a mainstream comics artist would have been impossible without the auteurist discourse built around graphic novelists.

The University Press of Mississippi also has a series devoted to interviews with comics makers titled 'Conversations with Comics Artists' and focusing on canonized creators such as Jeff Smith, Ben Katchor, Alison Bechdel, Chris Ware and many more.

Iconic magazines and publishers

While comics authors and one-shot comics or graphic novels have traditionally been the preferred topic of scholarship, comics scholars are gradually turning their attention to serialized comics and comics magazines, ranging from *Archie* and *Spirou* to comics magazines for adults, such as *Heavy Metal*. These magazines and publishers are usually analysed with reference to their historical developments and transformations, recurrent themes, relationship to comics legitimization and transnational collaborations.

Bart Beaty's *Twelve-Cent Archie* (2015) is the first book-length study of an iconic comics magazine that comics studies has by and large overlooked. Beaty offers astute readings of the *Archie* comics from December 1961 to July 1969. As the title suggests, this covers the period during which one could buy the magazine for 12 US cents. The book's innovative format of one hundred chapters of one to five pages enables a non-chronological reading, much like the *Archie* comics themselves. While the first two chapters introduce the comic and its mechanics, the rest focus on diverse aspects, from individual characters and their context to issues such as racial exclusion and juvenile delinquency. Beaty pays careful attention to the drawing styles of different *Archie* artists to highlight the significance of seemingly banal visual details and their variations.

Gert Meesters, Frédéric Paques and David Vrydagh's critical anthology *Les Métamorphoses de Spirou: le dynamisme d'une série de bande dessinée* [Spirou's *Metamorphoses: the Dynamism of a Comics Series*] (2019) takes an important step beyond the comics album to consider the serialized publications in comics magazines that traditionally preceded the album, even though the focus remains on a comics character rather than the publication format. The volume examines the iconic character, a bellhop named Spirou, first drawn in 1938 by Rob-Vel (Robert Velter) for a comics magazine named after the character. The *Spirou* magazine remains the longest running magazine to date. The volume's contributions highlight diverse aspects of the character, such as Spirou's incessant movement (Tomasovic), the lasting impact of the style and narrative technique of André Franquin, who introduced the Marsupilami among other characters during his long run on *Spirou* (Vrydaghs; Turgeon; Dejasse), and the contributions of Jijé, also known as the founder of the *École de Marcinelle* [Marcinelle School] (Paques; Glaude). Odaert's chapter draws out the influences of Martin Banner's *Winnie Winkle* as well as the influence of Rob-Vel's own slightly earlier work on *Les Aventures de Toto* (for the magazine, *Journal de Toto*). Even though several chapters discuss new versions of *Spirou*, especially the albums of Tome and Janry, the final chapters turn to recent interpretations of *Spirou* by alternative comics artists such as Rosse and Schlingo who deconstruct Spirou (Demoulin) and the archival work of albums belonging to the special series 'Le Spirou de ...' (Crucifix and Moura).

Wendy Michallat's *French Cartoon Art in the 1960s and the 1970s: Pilote hebdomadaire and the Teenager bande dessinée* (2018) provides the first comprehensive historical account of the *Pilote* comics magazine and concentrates on its publishing strategies. Launched in October 1959 *Pilote*, Michallat reminds us, was unique in its aim to cater to a broad readership including both children and school-going teenagers (9). In line with the French government's aim to exercise further control over the education of young people, *Pilote* also tried to tap into the emerging youth culture. While original, this formula was not easy to sustain and the magazine was the subject of a crisis from 1969 until 1974, which is also the period that *Pilote* has been most remembered for as it emulated the emerging alternative, adult comics. *French Cartoon Art* helps fill this gap in comics periodical history and ends with *Pilote*'s change from weekly to monthly publication. After tracing how the remnants of Vichy educational tactics seeped into comics magazines published by Catholic presses (Bayard, Lombard, Dupuis), Michallat shows how *Pilote*'s innovative formula of catering to an older readership without offending parents won over the baby-boomer generation that witnessed a changing youth culture, was more emancipated than its predecessors and constituted a significant consumer demographic. *Pilote*'s formula included educational material and exclusive 'celebrity' interviews by sportsmen and writers. It was one of the rare comics and children's magazines of its time to include news briefs, which were greatly appreciated by its readers (38). It also benefited from close collaboration with Radio Luxembourg which was popular amongst teenagers. When this formula failed to attract new readers in the 1960s, once television sets had become more affordable and widespread, the *Astérix* comics successfully won over both schoolboys and older students. Before 1968, the magazine (bought by the publishing giant Dargaud in 1960) had already succeeded in mirroring the youth's growing scepticism of education and state institutions at large. It had increased its comics content and moved towards more experimental comics catering to an older readership and introducing hitherto taboo elements such as sexuality. Paying close attention to formats, Michallat also examines the 'Astérixisation' of the market caused by the increasing number of successful comics albums and the media attention they received.

In his chapter, '*Actuel* 1970–1975: passeur transatlantique de l'underground américain de la bande dessinée pour adultes' ['*Actuel* 1970–1975: Transatlantic Trafficker of Underground American Comics for Adults'] (2016), Jean-Paul Gabilliet does not limit himself to examining the transatlantic connections between the underground comics magazine *Actuel* and American comics artists. *Actuel* published both French-language comics and translations of American underground comics. The latter were acquired through the Underground Press Syndicate, founded in 1966 and permitting its members free use of underground comics (82). Although *Actuel* only ran for five years, Gabilliet underscores its key role in introducing French adult comics readers to American artists such as R. Crumb, Gilbert Shelton and, to a lesser degree, Richard Corben (Gabilliet, 2016: 98). *Actuel,* reflecting the predilections of its editor, Jean-François Bizot, became an 'expression of a French counterculture with "an American taste"' (82). Gabilliet also points to three key reference works on *Actuel,* with Bizot being involved in the first and second: *Actuel par Actuel: Chronique d'un journal et de ses lecteurs* [*Actuel by Actuel: History of a Journal and Its Readers*] (1977); *Underground. L'Histoire* (2001); and *Les Années Actuel. Contestations rigolardes et aventures modernes* [*The Actuel Years: Amusing Disputes and Modern Adventures*] (2010) by historians Perrine Kervran and Anaïs Kien.

Nicolas Labarre's *Heavy Metal, l'autre Métal hurlant* (2017) also examines a comics magazine from a cultural history approach and incorporates a strong transnational dimension. By studying *Heavy Metal,* the American counterpart of the iconic French adult comics magazine, *Métal hurlant,* Labarre draws out the tensions and differences between two publications that shared the same name and often many of the same artists but existed in very different contexts. The original *Métal hurlant* was launched in 1975 by two comics artists known for their adult and science fiction work: Moebius (Jean Giraud) and Philippe Druillet. The American counterpart was launched just two years later by the publisher of the satiric National

Lampoon press, and outlived *Métal hurlant*. The differences not only were limited to comics traditions but also encompassed economic policies: *Heavy Metal* placed far greater importance on profit than *Métal hurlant* and prioritized attracting a large adult readership over encouraging artistic liberties. Labarre also considers the influence of Spiegelman and Mouly's *RAW*, looks briefly at the various German-language versions of *Heavy Metal*, and includes an interview with *Heavy Metal* editor Julie Simmons-Lynch. *Métal Hurlant, 1975–1987: La machine à rêver* [*The Dream Machine*] (2005), edited by Gilles Poussin and Christian Marmonnier, provides a history of the French-language *Métal hurlant* and points to the growing differences between its French and American versions. The book collects interviews, pictures, excerpts from the magazine and other documents.

In contrast to Labarre's transnational history of comics periodicals, Sylvain Lesage and Gert Meesters' *(À Suivre): Archive d'une revue culte* [*Archive of a Cult Magazine*] (2018) brings together contributions based on the Belgian publisher Casterman's archives in Tournai. It focuses on one of the most important adult comics magazines of its time *(À Suivre)* [literally '(*To Be Continued*)']. While Moine elaborates on the turbulent and morphing editorial form of Casterman, especially during the *(À Suivre)* years (1978–97), Crucifix and Lesage analyse the overseas exchanges made by Casterman's rights and permissions department. Other topics discussed are iconic authors such as Jacques Tardi and Hugo Pratt; the magazine's editorial pieces (Habrand); the short-lived Dutch-language counterpart, *Wordt Vervolgd* (Meesters and Lefèvre); the persistence of Hergé's clear line (Barros); and, of course, comics legitimation (Messing) in which the magazine played a catalysing role. The book includes a chronology of the magazine and several brief contributions ranging from notes on key comics artists and writers (Geluk, F'murr) to the magazine's irregular letters column, its continued interest in cinema, the photonovel and the novel itself, since one of the main aims of the early issues was to serialize long-form comics. Nicolas Finet, who had worked for *(À Suivre)*, recently re-edited his richly illustrated history of the magazine: *(À Suivre) 1978–1997: une aventure en bande dessinée* [*An Adventure in Comics*]. Tracing the evolution and demise of the magazine over almost three decades, Finet's book caters to a broader public, including comics fans.

Tracing the major trend-setting transformations in the French and Belgian comics publishing contexts, Sylvain Lesage's *Publier la bande dessinée: Les éditeurs franco-belge et l'album, 1950–1990* [*Publishing Comics: Franco-Belgian Publishers and the Album, 1950–1990*] (2018) covers the history of publishing since the law of 16 July 1949 regarding publications for young people (see Chapter 4). In delineating the transformation of comics publishing through diverse formats, Lesage emphasizes the importance of considering the unique format of the album and its role in preserving and connecting comics that were usually relegated to newspapers and magazines to book publishing. He argues that the establishment of the album format as a regular feature of comics publishing from 1950 until 1990 played as important a role in the current legitimation of comics as the rise of adult themes. Ending his study with the 1990s, which saw the rise of manga and independent and alternative trends in comics publishing, Lesage focuses on the changes adopted by publishers like Casterman, Dargaud, Lombard and Futuropolis that monopolized comics publishing in France and Belgium. *Publier bande dessinée* is an astutely contextualized and detailed history of the multiple publishing lives (and deaths) of comics. It highlights the importance of interrogating the key formats that comics find themselves in and considering the forms of existence acquired by comics beyond the book or album format.

Like French-language comics publications, comics magazines are gradually gaining more attention in Anglophone scholarship. A noteworthy, fresh (and at present unique) example of such research is Julia Round's *Gothic for Girls: Misty and British Comics*. Appearing weekly from 1978 to 1980 and totalling 101 issues, *Misty*, Round points out, marks a visible return to the horror genre in British comics after a gradual obsolescence of censorship policies. It was launched by comics writer and editor Pat Mills as the feminine pendant to the internationally successful *2000AD* (which was also a stepping stone to American publishing for many British comics artists and writers). Round adopts a holistic approach for analysing *Misty*: she combines interviews with *Misty*'s readers and (often anonymous) creators with a contextualization of horror and Gothic in Britain in the 1970s and close readings of the stories in *Misty* through the critical lens of the Female Gothic.

Conclusion

This chapter has interwoven diverse strands of research on comics artists from the eighteenth century until today, covering both well-known mainstream artists and writers (such as Hergé) and graphic novelists (including Alan Moore, Chris Ware and Lynda Barry). It has also covered research on the otherwise largely overlooked, but important, comics magazines in France, Belgium, the United States and Britain and points to a growing international interest in examining comics magazines and highlighting their contributions to comics history, the notion of the graphic novel and, by extension, comics legitimation.

The discussion in this chapter showed how the original focus of comics studies on certain canonical graphical novelists is changing in favour of researching different kinds of comics productions such as conventional comic strips and magazines, while also inscribing artists, both recent and old, into the expanding and diversifying 'canon' of comics. The focus on comics writers and artists is often auteurist, despite the fact that comics are often made collaboratively and rarely by a single author, although this has changed with the rise of the graphic novel. There is also a strong tendency to apply a multidisciplinary set of perspectives, especially from cultural studies and literature, to understand the writer's and artist's work, its context and impact. The literature on comics magazines seeks to inscribe the periodicals in a cultural historical account of comics offering glimpses into the often turbulent, rapidly changing publication histories of comics highlighting their economic dependence on maintaining a loyal readership. Ultimately, comics scholarship remains dominated by graphic novels and the male writer-artist even though, paradoxically enough, most of the recent women artists that have attracted academic attention are (autobiographical) graphic novelists (see Chapter 10).

While this chapter covered the production end of comics, the next chapter turns to its readers. In addition to introducing scholarship on comics readers from the perspectives of history and identity, it offers nuanced insight into the notions of fans and fan practices.

Notes

1. For more biographical insight into McCay and his comics and animation work, see Canemaker, John (2005) *Winsor McCay: His Life and Art*. New York: Abrams. Another useful source is the anthology, *Little Nemo 1905-2005: Un siècle de rêves [A Century of Dreams]* (2005). Brussels: Les Impressions Nouvelles, which combines scholarly essays on McCay's comics with homages in comics drawn by renowned artists such as Art Spiegelman and David B.

2. For more of Brinkley's comics see Trina Robbins (2009) *The Brinkley Girls: The Best of Nell Brinkley's Cartoons from 1913-1940*. Seattle, WA: Fantagraphics.

Works cited

Abate, Michelle Ann. "'A Gorgeous Waste": Solitude in *Calvin and Hobbes*'. *Journal of Graphic Novels and Comics* 10:5–6, 2017: 488–504.

Apostolidés, Jean-Marie. *Tintin et le mythe du surenfant*. Brussels: Moulinsart, 2004.

Apostolidés, Jean-Marie. 'Hergé and the Myth of the Superchild'. *Yale French Studies* 111, 2007: 45–57.

Assouline, Pierre. *Hergé*. Paris: Gallimard, 1998.

Baetens, Jan. *Hergé, écrivain*. Paris: Flammarion, 1989.

Ball, David M. and Kuhlman, Martha B. (eds). *The Comics of Chris Ware: Drawing Is a Way of Thinking*. Jackson, MS: University Press of Mississippi, 2010.

Beaty, Bart. *Twelve-Cent Archie*. New Brunswick, NJ: Rutgers University Press, 2015.

Bukatman, Scott. *The Poetics of Slumberland: Animated Spirits and the Animating Spirits*. Berkeley, CA: University of California Press, 2012.

Canemaker, John. *Winsor McCay: His Life and Art*. New York: Abrams, 2005.

Chute, Hillary and Spiegelman, Art. *MetaMaus: A Look Inside a Modern Classic*. New York: Pantheon, 2011.

Collective. *Little Nemo 1905–2005: Un siècle de rêves*. Brussels: Les Impressions Nouvelles, 2005.

Di Liddo, Annalisa. *Alan Moore: Comics as Performance, Fiction as Scalpel*. Jackson, MS: University Press of Mississippi, 2009.

Ecke, Jochen. *The British Comic Book Invasion: Alan Moore, Warren Ellis, Grant Morrison and the Evolution of the American Style*. Jefferson, NC: McFarland, 2018.

Farr, Michael. *Tintin: The Complete Companion*. San Francisco, CA: Last Gasp, 2002.

Fresnault-Deruelle, Pierre. 'Hergéologie: Cohérence et cohésion du récit en images dans les aventures de Tintin'. Tours: Presses universitaires François Rabelais, 2011.

Finet, Nicolas. *L'Aventure (À Suivre): 1978–1997*. Montrouge: PLG, 2018.

Gabilliet, Jean-Paul. '*Actuel*, 1970–1975: passeur transatlantique de l'underground américain et de la bande dessinée pour adultes'. In Marc Atallah and Alain Boillat (eds), *BD-US: Les comics vus par l'Europe*. Gollion: Infolio, 2016, pp. 79–98.

Gardner, Jared and Gordon, Ian (eds). *The Comics of Charles Schulz: The Good Grief of Modern Life*. Jackson, MS: University Press of Mississippi, 2018.

Goldstein, Nancy. *Jackie Ormes: The First African American Woman Cartoonist*. Ann Arbor, MI: University of Michigan Press, 2008.

Gray, Maggie. *Alan Moore, out from the Underground: Cartooning, Performance, and Dissent*. New York: Palgrave, 2017.

Grennan, Simon, Roger, Sabin and Waite, Julian. *Marie Duval*. London: Myriad Editions, 2018.

Groensteen, Thierry. *M. Töpffer invente la bande dessinée*. Brussels: Les Impressions Nouvelles, 2014.

Heit, Jamey. *Imagination and Meaning in Calvin and Hobbes*. Jefferson, NC: McFarland, 2012.

Hoberek, Andrew. *Considering Watchmen: Poetics, Property, Politics.* New Brunswick, NJ: Rutgers University Press, 2014.

Kennedy, Martha H. *Drawn to Purpose: American Women Illustrators and Cartoonists.* Jackson: University Press of Mississippi, 2018.

Kirtley, Susan. *Lynda Barry: Girlhood through the Looking Glass.* Jackson, MS: University Press of Mississippi, 2012.

Kunzle, David. *Father of the Comic Strip: Rodolphe Töpffer.* Jackson, MS: University Press of Mississippi, 2007a.

Kunzle, David. *Rodolphe Töpffer: The Complete Comic Strips.* Jackson, MS: University Press of Mississippi, 2007b.

Kunzle, David. *Gustave Doré: Twelve Comic Strips.* Jackson, MS: University Press of Mississippi, 2015.

Kunzle, David. *Cham: The Best Comic Strips and Graphic Novelettes, 1839–1862.* Jackson, MS: University Press of Mississippi, 2019.

Labarre, Nicolas. *Heavy Metal, l'autre Métal hurlant.* Bordeaux: Presses universitaires de Bordeaux, 2017.

Lee, Peter W. Y. (ed.) *Peanuts and American Culture: Essays on Charles M. Schulz's Iconic Comic Strip.* Jefferson, NC: McFarland, 2019.

Leroy, Fabrice. *Sfar So Far: Identity, History, Fantasy and Mimesis in Joann Sfar's Graphic Novels.* Leuven: Leuven University Press, 2014.

Lesage, Sylvain. *Publier la bande dessinée. Les éditeurs franco-belge et l'album, 1950–1990.* Villeurbanne: Presses de l'ENSIB, 2018.

Lesage, Sylvain and Meesters, Gert (eds). *(À Suivre): Archive d'une revue culte.* Tours: Presses universitaires François-Rabelais, 2018.

Mainardi, Patricia. *Another World: Nineteenth-Century Illustrated Print Culture.* New Haven: Yale University Press, 2017.

Marrone, Daniel. *Forging the Past: Seth and the Art of Memory.* Jackson, MS: University Press of Mississippi, 2016.

McDonnell, Patrick and O'Connell, Karen. *Krazy Kat: The Comic Art of George Herriman.* New York: Abrams, 1999.

Meesters, Gert, Pâques, Frédéric and Vrydaghs, David (eds). *Les Métamorphoses de Spirou: le dynamisme d'une série de bande dessinée.* Liège: Presses universitaires de Liège, 2019.

Michallat, Wendy. *French Cartoon Art in the 1960s and the 1970s: Pilote hebdomadaire and the Teenager bande dessinée.* Leuven: Leuven University Press, 2018.

Ogi, Fusami, Suter, Rebecca, Nagaike, Kazumi and Lent John, A. (eds). *Women's Manga in Asia and beyond: Uniting Different Cultures and Identities.* New York: Palgrave, 2019.

Oksman, Tanheer. *'How Come Boys Get to Keep Their Noses?' Women and Jewish American Identity in Contemporary Graphic Novels.* New York: Columbia University Press, 2016.

Oksman, Tanheer and O'Malley, Seamus (eds). *The Comics of Julie Doucet and Gabrielle Bell.* Jackson, MS: University Press of Mississippi, 2020.

Peeters, Benoît. *Hergé, fils de Tintin.* Paris: Flammarion, 2002.

Peeters, Benoît and Samson, Jacques. *Chris Ware: La bande dessinée réinventée.* Brussels: Les Impressions Nouvelles, 2010.

Poussin, Gilles and Marmonnier, Christian. Métal Hurlant *1975–1987: La machine à rêver.* Paris: Denoël, 2005.

Raeburn, Daniel. *Chris Ware.* New Haven, CT: Yale University Press, 2004.

Robbins, Trina. *Nell Brinkley and the New Woman in the Early 20th Century.* Jefferson, NC: McFarland, 2001.

Robbins, Trina (ed.) *The Brinkley Girls: The Best of Nell Brinkley's Cartoons from 1913–1940.* Seattle, WA: Fantagraphics, 2009.

Roeder, Katherine. *Wide Awake in Slumberland: Fantasy, Mass Culture, and Modernism in the Art of Winsor McCay.* Jackson, MS: University Press of Mississippi, 2013.

Round, Julia. *Gothic for Girls: Misty and British Comics.* Jackson, MS: University Press of Mississippi, 2019.

Sanders, Joe (ed.) *The Sandman Papers: An Exploration of the Sandman Mythology.* Seattle, WA: Fantagraphics, 2006.

Sanders, Joe Sutliff (ed.) *The Comics of Hergé: When the Lines Are Not so Clear.* Jackson, MS: University Press of Mississippi, 2016.

Singer, Mark. *Grant Morrison: Combining the Worlds of Contemporary Comics.* Jackson, MS: University Press of Mississippi, 2011.

Sommers, Joseph Michael and Eveleth, Kyle (eds). *The Artistry of Neil Gaiman: Finding Light in the Shadows.* Jackson, MS: University Press of Mississippi, 2019.

Tisserand, Michael. *Krazy: George Herriman, a Life in Black and White.* New York: Harper, 2016.

Whaley, Deborah Elizabeth. *Black Women in Sequence: Re-inking Comics, Graphic Novels and Anime.* Seattle, WA: University of Washington Press, 2015.

CHAPTER 7
AUDIENCES AND FAN CULTURES

It has been claimed that audience research is comparatively neglected within the Humanities (*Participations,* 2017), and comics studies is no exception. While numerous historical, textual and cultural analyses of the medium exist, data on the critical responses of readers is harder to find. This chapter will consider audience studies, looking at the work of scholars who have analysed fans and fan practices. Its focus is primarily on Anglo-American readers and global manga audiences, due to a dearth of English-language material about other cultures.

Many scholars have tried to define comics subcultures and fandoms by using genre taste or consumption patterns (Brown, 2012; Woo, 2012b; Round, 2014), social networks (Woo, 2011a), collecting practices (Woo, 2012a), or reading habits and preferences (Pustz, 1999; Hammond, 2009; Beaty, 2012). Berenstein (2012) notes these diverse approaches but instead seeks commonalities between these groups; the structure of this chapter follows his lead. It has three sections. The first summarizes the development of critical work on audiences in comics history. The second discusses newer, revisionist analyses of comics readers, with a particular focus on identity. The third explores the specific and notorious identity of 'fan', looking at the work of scholars who have focused on the labels and behaviour associated with comics fandom as cultural practice, and considering elements such as collecting, conventions and cosplay.

Historical audience studies

Many of the historical books discussed in Chapter 4 include a mention of readers in their analyses of comics, although these are often speculative claims about media effects. For example, Irving Howe's 'Notes on Mass Culture' (1948: 46) emphasizes the 'intimate' relationship between popular media and everyday life, claiming that 'daily experience and mass culture are so interlaced that it would be futile to seek causal relationships between them'. Howe claims that mass culture elicits conservative responses from its audience and suppresses the imaginative work of the unconscious, and that such texts can only ever achieve identification from everyday viewers and readers on the basis of social anonymity. This presumed divide between an intellectual elite and an 'everyday' audience (and text) also appears in Warshow's article 'Woofed with Dreams' (1946), which also notes a divide in audience ('While the intellectuals had to "discover" *Krazy Kat*, the comic strip audience just read it').

Gilbert Seldes' defence of comics in *The Seven Lively Arts* (1924) finds an equivalent in his 1950 book *The Great Audience*. This focuses primarily on the audiences for movies, radio and TV, arguing that these media actively create their own reception, shaping the 'climate of feeling' in which we all live (4). Only one small section within 'The People and the Arts' (271–289) considers comics, using the medium as a case study that demonstrates the powerlessness of the audience to impose their will on the producers. In this, Seldes speaks too soon, as the Comics Code would be introduced in 1954.

Turning to the UK, George Pumphrey's *What Children Think of Their Comics* (1964) gives a similarly passive view of the audience. While Pumphrey draws on interview material to discuss the use child readers make of their reading, he is sceptical of young readers' abilities to negotiate potential meanings and instead concludes that messages of delinquency are easily transmitted. This ideological slant is common in these early investigations of comics, particularly those linked to gender. For example, in *Magazines Teenagers Read* (1968), Alderson claims that girls' comics are little more than commodities designed to keep uneducated readers in their place, which offer amorality, anti-intellectualism, a rejection of complexity and escapism. She also identifies a divided audience due to the education system of 1960s Britain. Her work is followed by Sue Sharpe's *Just Like a Girl* (1976), a wider study of stereotyping and role models in girls' media, which critiques comics' use of stereotypes. Mary Cadogan and Patricia Craig's *You're a Brick, Angela!* (1976) contains a chapter on British periodicals from the 1930s to the 1950s, which argues their writers were forced to manipulate character and plot to accord with gendered social expectations. Similar arguments inform the work of Valerie Walkerdine (1984), who looks at popular titles such as *Bunty* and claims that these comics contain messages to prepare readers for adolescent sexuality (and thus the next tier of magazines offered by their publishers). Angela McRobbie (1978a, 1978b, 1981) focuses on the British girls' comic *Jackie*, taking a semiological approach and identifying four codes (romance, fashion and beauty, pop, and personal and domestic life) that transmit clear messages of acceptability in these fields.[1] A later piece by

McRobbie (1997) brings in the idea of negotiated and resistive reading, but initially all of these critics view the comics as tools of oppression that convey direct ideological messages about female victimization and construct a model of girlhood that is based on femininity and passivity.

After these early speculations about media effects, thinly veiled dismissals of mass culture, and ideological arguments about femininity, studies of historical comics audiences only really gained depth and traction retrospectively. For example, Ian Gordon's *Comic Strips and Consumer Culture 1890–1945* (1998) explores the publishing history of American comic books as a commercial act. Gordon argues that comics played an essential part in creating the mass culture of consumption that underlies contemporary American identity. His first chapter argues that early humour magazines helped their readers adapt to an emergent mass culture, and examines the work of artists such as Howarth and Outcault. Chapter 2 tracks the national spread of comics strips via the major newspapers and explores their development into branded properties ripe for licensing. Gordon shows how these early strips transformed a particular type of urban imagery into a national commodity, and then homes in on the texts and figures that were excluded from this commodification, scrutinizing the limitations and stereotypes attached to African American characters in strips such as *Poor Lil' Mose, Sambo* and *Krazy Kat*. The following chapters then analyse the use of comic strips in advertisements, the depiction of consumer goods and commentaries on consumer culture that appeared in the strips and the emergence of the comic book as an independent commodity in the late 1930s. Gordon's epilogue reflects on the subsequent history of the medium, noting the rise and continued commodification of superheroes. He makes some prescient observations, such as noting that DC's dominance over Marvel at the millennium was largely due to Marvel not having realized 'the full commodity potential of their characters through other media' (156). Conversely, at the time of writing this Guide, the situation has been completely reversed – *Avengers: Endgame* has ended the series of nineteen Marvel Cinematic Universe movies, and Disney has purchased Marvel's Netflix properties.

Comics readers and identities

As noted above, many early studies of comics readers did not draw on empirical research and have since been critiqued, particularly within the field of girls' comics. More recently, the work of scholars such as Mel Gibson and Martin Barker offers alternative readings of British girls' comics that object to the idea that a singular ideology can be conveyed by such a wide range of titles. In *Comics: Ideology, Power and the Critics* (1989), Barker uses *Jackie* as a case study to argue against the readings of girls' romance comics from McRobbie et al. He claims that these readings are 'almost all hostile' (1989: 139) and 'start from unsatisfactory theories of influence and ideology' (159) – basically, the mistaken assumption that these comics carry a unified message: both within the pages of an individual publication, and across the breadth of titles and many years of publishing.

By contrast, Éric Maigret (1999) explores the consumption of superhero comics in France and the United States, drawing on interviews and letters from readers. He argues that gender identities are learnt through media such as comics, which present readers with multiple insights and allow them to learn about new or complex identities (rather than directly transmitting simple roles). McLain's work on Indian comics (discussed in Chapter 5) also draws on empirical data and correspondence with real readers, noting their self-identification with a 'new generation' and the ways the comics broadened their perceptions of diversity and international contexts.

June Madeley (2010–12) extends a gender studies focus to the audience reception of English-translated manga. Using research data taken from in-depth interviews with nineteen participants, she notes that this industry publishes for targeted gender and age groups, and that a female market has been particularly targeted for translated manga, which is often freely available online. Her analysis compares the likes and dislikes of male and female readers for particular genres and characters, and reveals that 'girly' characters (across all genres) and romance genres have the lowest appeal for both groups, while many male manga characters offered something outside of the norm in North American popular culture. Madeley concludes that factors beyond gender are relevant to reading manga and that her project will develop to consider the impact of aspects such as age, tenure as a manga reader and fan communities as influences on meaning-making. In subsequent work (2015), she has continued to explore reader activity around translated texts: examining the conflict between manga readers and publishers and licencees of translated content, using survey data and forum posts. Other articles on manga audiences also focus on the female reader, such as 'Situating the Shojo in Shojo Manga: Teenage Girls, Romance Comics, and Contemporary Japanese Culture' (Deborah Shamoon, 2008).

The learnt mechanics of reading comics and manga are explored in John E. Ingulsrud and Kate Allen's *Reading Japan Cool* (2009), which studies Japanese manga literacy by interviewing Japanese school children and young adults about their experiences with reading manga. They begin their study by discussing differences and similarities between manga and comics and note that, like comics, manga is considered improper reading material by some but is very widely read in Japan. Ingulsrud and Allen insist that comics and manga have many similarities in their image/text relations and sequential storytelling, but point out differences in their graphic styles, publication practices, relationships with other media and origins. Just as with comics, it is heavily debated which manga is the first, but Ingulsrud and Allen show how, when it comes to manga, this discussion is divided between two camps: one that emphasizes the historical-cultural aspect and one that puts emphasis on the production side (2009: 35). The first traces the origin of manga way back in Japanese history to various kinds of pictorial Japanese art such as twelfth-century humorous, pictorial scrolls and woodblock prints (2009: 36–41). The second socioeconomic approach designates the period after the Second World War as the point of origin for manga and emphasizes the onslaught of magazine production, used bookstores and lending libraries as key players in the development of manga in Japan. Ingulsrud and Allen discuss the history of literacy in Japan and explore the problems of learning how to read Japanese because of the different scripts involved. This in turn impacts how children read manga; in contrast to learning how to read scripts in school, reading manga requires special skills which school does not teach (2009: 69–87).

Manga's Cultural Crossroads (2016), edited by Berndt and Kümmerling-Meibauer, examines the intercultural exchanges that have shaped twentieth-century manga and compiles recent approaches to manga reception around the world. It includes chapters on Japanese fan comics and North American fan art (Nele Noppe); the reception of Japanese manga in Korea (Chie Yamanaka); the reception of female characters by female readers (Yukari Fukimoto); and fan fiction (Jessica Bauwens-Sugimoto and Nora Renka). 'Reading Manga Fandom', the seventh chapter of Marco Pellitteri's *The Dragon and the Dazzle* (2010), also investigates the role of international audiences and surveys audience studies in Italy and Europe. The book traces the legitimation of Japanese manga since the 1990s and cites previous studies such as Sabre (2006), which identify a 'fantasised Japanesity' constructed by manga readers from cultural artefacts rather than reliable sources of knowledge. Pellitteri draws on survey data of Italian manga readers that reveals that these fans valued reading manga as more than just reading, viewing it as a practice and process of sharing with a like-minded community. Anthony Fung, Boris Pun and Yoshikata Mon's 'Reading border-crossing Japanese comics/anime in China' (2019) presents a similar study, exploring the way in which consumption practices challenge and change cultural identity and looking at Chinese consumers of Japanese manga (probably the world's biggest comics' audience with five million readers). It draws on focus groups and interviews in Japan and China alongside textual analyses of Japanese anime and comics to explore the reading, fandom and cultural impact of comics and anime on Chinese urban youth. The essay demonstrates that Chinese readers are active audiences and that, although the national identity and political ideology of the interviewees is robust, their high regard for Japanese cultural products debases the local production of Chinese comics/anime.

Many studies of manga audiences and fans combine their focus with that of anime in a similar way. For example, Marc Steinberg has explored how platform choice relates to audience reception and engagement in Japan. While Steinberg's primary focus is on anime, he has recently started to direct his gaze at manga in *The Platform Economy: How Japan Transformed the Commercial Internet* (2019) and the coedited collection *Media Theory in Japan* (2017). Similarly, in 'Looking into the "Anime Global Popular" and the "Manga Media"', Manuel Hernández-Pérez introduces a special issue of *Arts* 8(57) (2019) that examines the cross-cultural appeal and consumption of manga and anime. While the article opens with a meta-analysis of the scholarly attention paid to manga and discussion of the diverse channels through which these texts can be distributed and accessed, Section 2.3 discusses manga audiences, arguing that, although general, mainstream audiences consume manga media, their practices have more in common with those of smaller fan communities.

A key theme in these studies is the potential impact of manga and its popularity; many use reception theory and interrogate effects arguments. Jolyon Baraka Thomas's *Drawing on Tradition: Manga, Anime and Religion in Contemporary Japan* (2012) focuses on audience reception and the media impact on audiences. Similarly, Harsh Mahaseth's 'The Cultural Impact of Manga on Society' (2017) considers the various aspects of manga that have invited attack and criticism, such as violence, sexual content and blasphemy. Mahaseth draws on effects research and cites existing censorship legalization to argue for the tastes of audiences to be considered and respected so manga can move past its notoriety and flourish throughout the world.

Martin Barker has also interrogated media effects and influence across many media. 'Kicked into the Gutters: or, "My Dad doesn't read comics, he studies them'" (2002) is a deeply personal piece that reflects on his own journey into audience research through comics, and consequent identity as a reader, scholar and researcher. This grew from his interrogation of the problematic term 'identification' and his critiques of academics that had used comics to make an ideological point based on this notion. Barker explains how this shaped his research (1989, 1991, 1993) into a quest for a better way to characterize readers' engagement with their reading material, using the concept of commitment (designed to capture the different ways and the extent to which people care about and involve themselves in such materials). 'Kicked into the Gutters' then summarizes the main aims of Barker's previous works, which include: making visible the voices of readers and fans, refining methodologies for audience and quantitative research, interrogating problematic concepts and assumptions that pervade critical analysis and exploring the way in which publishers construct images of possible audiences and how these shape their productions. His *Comics: Ideology, Power and the Critics* is discussed more fully in Chapter 3 of this book; however, its Chapter 11 ('Reading the Readers') examines reader activity in the context of previous scholarship. Barker summarizes several previous studies driven by either media effects theory or uses and gratifications approaches, which have sought to prove the negative influence of comics on young readers. He uses these to introduce and argue for the book's central thesis: that the media are only capable of holding power and influence over readers to the extent there is a contract between them, the nature and type of which is widely variable and negotiated.

Mel Gibson is another significant critic who takes a revisionist approach to audience studies. Her chapter 'On British Comics for Girls and Their Readers' (2000) offers detailed summaries of the works of Alderson, Walkerdine, McRobbie and many more, along with Barker's rebuttal of their arguments. In contrast to these critics, Gibson's interviews with readers found that they primarily remembered the comics' stories as about rebellion rather than victimization, and saw characters as active and inspiring (sporting, adventurous) rather than passive. Gibson concludes that further audience research is needed when considering these underexplored titles, since 'textual analysis cannot evaluate issues of access, peer group, family, education and class and motives in reading or rejecting such publications' (226).

Gibson's subsequent work seeks to fill this gap in direct audience research. In the article '"You can't read them, they're for boys!" British Girls, American Superhero Comics and Identity' (*International Journal of Comic*

Art 5(1), 2003) she reflects on a handful of interviews with adult women in which they reflect on their memories of reading comics as young girls. She demonstrates that reading American superhero comics was a rebellious and transgressive practice for these readers, enabling them to reject girls' comics and construct an alternative identity for themselves by rejecting concepts of femininity and perhaps even Britishness. Gibson's participants performed complex negotiated readings of these titles. They felt that reading these comics put them on the periphery of female culture, but without allowing them to truly escape their gender, which continually restricted them to the periphery of the comics world. Gibson concludes that comics are consistently problematic to female readers, and that particularly those of the 1970s and 1980s were thus perhaps fans without fandom.

Gibson's chapter 'Cultural Studies: British Girls' Comics, Readers and Memories' appears in Duncan and Smith's guidebook *Critical Approaches to Comics*, which is discussed further in Chapter 11. Here Gibson suggests places where students might find potential research projects relating to audience studies and warns against some of the assumptions that often underlie such projects. She draws on Barker's work to argue that audience-based analyses of comics require, rather than media effects or 'uses and gratifications' approaches, a cultural studies approach that views media consumption as part of everyday life and as an ongoing site of struggle over meanings and pleasures.

Conflict and internal tension are characteristic findings from audience-based approaches to comics, as explored in Gibson's book *Remembered Reading* (2015), which develops her previous work in this field. Gibson draws on 126 interviews conducted with (predominantly female) adults, asking them to reflect on their childhood reading of girls' comics, and uses these 'lost texts and neglected memories' (21) to draw conclusions about the nature of memory studies, the language used to describe comics, and the ideological messages and narrative strategies these titles used and the uses to which readers put them. Her findings show that comics (of all genres) were often used as markers of different stages of childhood and the move to adulthood. The book includes a history of British girls' comics, summaries of key titles, close readings of indicative stories and extensive evidence from her interviews. Gibson argues that girls' comics are bound up in perceptions of class, identity, girlhood and femininity and offer socially approved models of behaviour, but readers could also engage in resistive readings.

These later studies foreground the individual nature of the reading experience and the myriad of possible responses. Bill Schelly takes a similarly personal approach in his memoir *Sense of Wonder: My Life in Comic Fandom – The Whole Story* (2018). Schelly reflects on the ways in which comic books shaped his life as a fan, artist and collector. His memoir is contextualized as he notes the changing perceptions of comics between the 1940s and the 1960s (by which time the Code meant that they were viewed as appropriate only for children) and reflects on his own position within a 'minority sexuality' at a time when this was much less accepted. Schelly's excitement on discovering a world of magazines about comics and adverts that gave access to back issues led him to produce his own fanzine and contact other fans. He describes the rise of comics fandom in America as a genuine grassroots movement, enabled by the postal service, and collecting as a method of expressing one's identity and personality. It is a personal book but thoughtful and reflective and paints an engaging picture of the way in which individual comics readers became a networked audience through their fandom. Scott Saavedra's *Flee Puny Humans!* (2003) is similarly personal and anecdotal, reflecting on how his lifelong relationship with comics and their culture has shaped his identity.

In addition to the above chapters and monographs, much of the research into comics readers has come from journals. The *Journal of Graphic Novels and Comics* 2(2) (2011) is a special edition, edited by Robert G. Weiner and Mel Gibson, devoted to readership and audience. It contains a selection of pieces that explore the role of dedicated spaces of comics fandom such as shops (Woo, 2011b), the impact of school-based clubs and reading groups (Sabeti, 2011), and the abilities of comics to reach and address new audiences (Demson and Brown, 2011). These sit alongside contrasting approaches that consider the impact of genre on perceptions of comics (Thomas, 2011), and investigations into the individual nature of the reading experience (Sugawa-Shimada, 2011) and the use of comics in creating personal identity (Botzakis, 2011).

Martin Barker's pioneering journal *Participations* (launched 2003) has printed several articles addressing comics (see further below) and *Participations* 9(2) contains a special section of seven papers devoted to the medium (2012). Taken together, these articles demonstrate complementary ways of approaching audience studies. They include Barker's study of the reception of Joe Sacco's *Palestine* (1993), which draws on the traces of the comic's reception in reviews and online debates, rather than direct investigation via interviews and surveys. Barker's literature review highlights the differences between audience studies, reception studies and fan studies, building on his work on fans' responses to the *Judge Dredd* movie (1988) by approaching his material as a type of discourse: 'contextually-produced and -responsive ways of speaking which have to be analysed for their working principles, concepts and moves' (2012: 61). His conclusions show that *Palestine* has moved from a marginalized position to one of relative visibility and that, while journalists' and critics' comments are framed by a hierarchical and historical understanding of comics and their value, readers' responses take place in a less judgemental environment and they are comfortable with expressing uncertainties and unsettled opinions. The issue's other articles similarly draw on different methodologies and bridge the gap between fan and audience studies. Ian Gordon's (2012: 121) exploration of fan response to *Superman* uses material from comics letters pages to argue that these fans are engaged in 'a rudimentary form of social networking, with those writing more letters forming a discursive community of sorts'. Gordon emphasizes the collegiate nature of this audience and traces the crossover between fan and creator. Sabeti explores reader response in an educational setting through interviews and ethnographic observation, demonstrating that comics lend themselves to more social forms of reading and interpretation. Burke (2012) uses surveys to catalogue viewer response to superhero movies, with a particular focus on participants' use of intertextual knowledge. The remaining articles, discussed below, consider fan identities and speech acts.

Fan studies in comics

Comics fandom goes back at least to the early 1960s (Pustz, 1999; Schelly, 2010), making this one of the oldest groups of organized fans.[2] This section will explore scholarship that has examined this fandom and its cultural practice. It first considers the work done to delineate and define fan identities in comics, before surveying critical analyses of some of the most significant forms of fan activities, including collecting, conventions and cosplay, and their intersections with key issues such as gender and ethnicity.

Several more general studies of fan culture across media provide the basis for looking at comics and fandom. Henry Jenkins' *Textual Poachers* (1992) is a landmark in the field that examines television audiences. Like many other first-wave fan studies it challenges representations of fans as mindless consumers, claiming instead that fan activities are participatory, active and creative. Shorter articles by other significant scholars, such as John Fiske's 'The Cultural Economy of Fandom' (1992), are also of interest. Fiske explores fandom's relationship to popular and official culture, drawing on Bourdieu's famous concept of culture as an economy (1984) to argue that fandom is a drive for cultural capital based on knowledge and collecting. He argues that the objects of fandom hold contradictory functions as they serve both the economic interests of the industry, and the cultural interests of fans. Matt Hills' *Fan Cultures* (2002) explores the definitions of cult fandom, arguing that 'fan' is an identity that is performed, often to contest cultural norms. Hills examines what fandom does culturally: analysing the creative spaces of fans and considering them as individuals as well as members of an interpretative community; addressing the boundaries of academia and fandom alongside the emergence of new fan cultures.[3]

Academic studies aimed specifically at comics fans emerged as the field developed. Barker's *Comics: Ideology, Power and the Critics* (1989) has already been discussed, and his subsequent work continues to examine comics audiences. Barker's (1993) analysis of *2000AD* draws attention to the split in its readership between 'casual', 'regular' and 'committed' readers, and uses interview material to reflect on their response to the label and notion of 'fan'. For Barker, 'fan' is an industry-created category (projected through editorial material and other paraphernalia) that seeks to shape and limit how readers interact with their comics.

In 'Comic Book Fandom and Cultural Capital' (1997), Jeffrey Brown takes an opposite stance, arguing for a view of fandom as a site of struggle and cultural contestation. He draws on Bourdieu (1984) and Fiske (1992) to argue that fans produce their own cultural capital, in counterpoint to what is valued by the mainstream, to compensate for a wider cultural disempowerment (e.g. economic, racial, age-related). He continues this argument in *Black Superheroes* (2001), arguing that fandom is an active identity that grows out of comics readers' genuine interest in the medium. He considers the various motivations for fan practices, such as 'compensation', 'finance' and 'love', and evaluates their authenticity using interviews with readers and professionals.[4]

Matthew J. Pustz's *Comic Book Culture* (1999) is among the first monographs entirely about comics fandom. Pustz draws on the more general work of Jenkins (1992) and Fish (1980) to explore the spaces and rhetoric of comics culture. He first identifies the 'rhetoric of cooperation' between fans and creators (xi) and focuses on the comics shop as a hangout or clubhouse. Pustz then examines historical comic-book reading communities, such as 'EC fan addicts' and 'Marvel zombies', noting early studies that divide child comics readers into fans, moderates, and hostiles (Wolf and Fiske, 1949) and tracing the emergence of an adult readership that potentially migrated from pulp fiction. He also analyses EC's use of strategies such as the use of 'insiderism' and invitations for readers to contribute, alongside Marvel's flattery of fans as intelligent and its creation of a hierarchy of commitment levels for them to attain: selling 'a participatory world' and way of life for readers (56). This is contextualized against increased attention from the mainstream press in the mid-1960s, leading to speculative purchasers in the 1970s. Pustz also looks briefly at underground comix and concludes that legislation meant that a truly adult audience with genuine synergy between creator and reader did not emerge until these appeared. He then surveys the resulting diversity in contemporary comics readers, from collectors and speculators, to selective and committed, to casual and nostalgic. In particular he explores the motivations for collecting, notes some key texts aimed at different groups, and analyses the role of fan publications such as *The Comics Journal* in sustaining divisions. Pustz argues that proximity between producers and consumers makes comics unique in American popular culture, and that the increasingly self-referential content of comics reflects this. He demonstrates how comics exploit expertise in comics literacy through features such as innovative layouts, parody, intertextuality, postmodernism and metafiction; developing tropes such as continuity and character archetypes that then become the subject of revisionist works. Finally, the book explores other spaces of fandom, such as comic-cons (conventions), letters pages, professional fan magazines, amateur fanzines and web pages. Pustz concludes that American comics culture encourages participation and gives satisfaction on multiple levels and thus may have something to teach wider popular culture about integration and engagement.

Will Brooker's *Batman Unmasked* (2000) contains a chapter on fandom and authorship, which focuses on the interwoven nature of the concepts of fan and author, and the potential for resistive reading by audiences. Brooker uses close analysis of *Detective Comics'* letter columns during 1965 to argue that fans created a 'cult of authorship' (256) by guessing at artist and writer identities, which the editors then picked up. Brooker shows that once credits appeared regularly the discussion deepened and engaged with 'complex issues arising from the nature of comics storytelling' (259) by reflecting on the contributions and dynamics of the creative team. He then explores subsequent decades, arguing that the emergence of direct sales and royalty payments in the 1970s and 1980s helped develop comics fandom and stardom. The chapter concludes by surveying the audience anticipation of, and response to, the Tim Burton and Joel Schumacher *Batman* movies; exploring the leverage that fans and creators may have and the rhetoric of ownership and emotion that surrounds such characters.

Several scholars have examined practices associated with comics fandom, such as conventions; shops; and fan behaviours like costuming, collecting and conversing. These include: Pustz (1999), Woo (2011b), Hammond (2009), Brown (2012) and Swafford (2012). Their discussions focus mainly on the American industry and its practices, although Jacobs (2013) explores the performance of queer sexuality within Japanese cosplay. One of the earliest articles to explore the drive to collect comics is Tankel and Murphy's 'Collecting Comic Books' (1998), which draws on a small-scale survey of thirty-eight collectors. They situate their findings against data on the number of comics published, audience size and average expenditure on collection and preservation, and suggest this is an act of 'curatorial consumption,' in which the value of the items is not intrinsic but results from the owner's interactions with them. Collecting comics is thus a strategy of resistance intended to create personal meaning out of an impersonal world.

Lincoln Geraghty's book *Cult Collectors* (2014) explores the appeal of collecting items of popular media culture and the reasons for its devaluation as a practice. Part 1 examines stereotypes of collectors depicted in media texts; Part 2 contrasts these with the real people who collect; Part 3 discusses the places where collecting occurs; and the final part explores the virtual spaces visited by collectors. A case study supports each section, although these come from film, television and toy franchises, rather than comics. Part 3 has the most direct relevance to comics since it contains a close discussion of San Diego Comic-Con International. Geraghty concludes that the drive to collect is an attempt to connect with one's own history, and that the materiality of toys and other collected objects is increasingly important in a digital age. Fans make direct links between their objects and personal experiences, and so nostalgia becomes a transformative and active process rather than something conservative and inhibiting, and the collecting process directly informs fan identity.

Simon Locke's 'Fanboy as a Revolutionary Category' (*Participations* 9(2), 2012) reviews the debates around terms such as 'fanboy', arguing that neither Barker (1993) nor Brown's (2001) definitions have accurately captured the complex identities that comics fans must negotiate. He applies Sacks' (1995) theory that labels like 'fanboy' are devices to control cultural activity, arguing that their adoption by comics readers is a reaction to the consistent downgrading and denigration of comics. By naming themselves as 'fanboys' and acknowledging the childish and lowbrow connotations of the label, such readers paradoxically claim authenticity and individuality for their actions, rather than being labelled as cultural dupes. This idea is prefigured in the work of critics such as Hills (2002), who argue that fans adopt and rearticulate the values of the dominant culture. Locke, however, takes a different angle and claims that the category is used with revolutionary intent. He argues that, like the classic paradox of the Cretan who stated 'All Cretans are liars',

> In ostensibly agreeing with a category that carries the inference of not really being authentic fans, they are actually managing to accomplish a sense of their deep commitment to comics – so deep that they are prepared to allow themselves to be viewed through a derogatory category, a stance that thereby quashes its derogatory charge.
>
> (Locke, 2012: 851)

Locke traces this back to the EC 'fan addicts' of the 1950s whose ironic adoption of this label was a stance against fears of juvenile delinquency and drug addiction.

Locke's article appears in *Participations* 9(2), alongside many others that interrogate fan identities. Berenstein's (2012) investigation into comic book store interactions also explores fan practices, using ethnographic observation and interviews to examine the interpersonal communication patterns of comics fans. He identifies a recurrent sequence of events as a 'recommendation ceremony' that serves the psychological needs and social functions integral to achieving a sense of community. His analysis draws on the linguistic and anthropological research of Hymes (1974) to demonstrate that a ritual encounter frequently becomes a ceremony in which participants share knowledge and recommend reading to each other through three possible methods: the reversal act, the 'educated scholarly debate', or the 'aficionados sparring'. Berenstein argues that uncovering this speech acts sequence 'is an important stage in understanding comics as a social, rather than literary or artistic phenomenon' (92).

Finally, Woo's article in this collection approaches comics audiences as participants in a set of sociocultural practices, drawing on interviews with self-identified fans. While Woo notes that several highly varied practices characterize fandom, he argues that these share two common traits: 'First, they all involve or enable forms of criticism and connoisseurship. Second, they are charged with a sense of affection, pleasure, and even commitment or loyalty' (2012b: 182–183). He thus refers to these acts as 'consummative practices' that complete cultural commodities by putting them to use within a social practice (Baudrillard). Woo develops this further by arguing that, although scholars often use 'fan' and 'collector' interchangeably, many of his respondents indicate that 'reader' and 'collector' have become distinct categories that understand comics very differently. He divides collectors into completists, hobbyists and speculators and notes that all three types oppose the idea of reading as a use-value of comics.

Woo's previous work (2011a, 2011b, 2012a, 2012b) stresses the importance of understanding the social contexts in which comics are produced and consumed. In 'Beyond our Borders' (2011a) he argues that, rather than trying to define comics (in all their variety) as a material form, it may be more productive to explore the 'where' of comics – in what kinds of spaces (institutional, contextual) do the medium and its study appear? Woo uses fieldnotes and interviews: recording mentions of comics-based people, organizations, events and venues, and plotting these as nodes in distinct themed zones. He thus produces a 'map' of connected spaces, which include media fandom; table-top and role-playing gaming; anime and manga fandom; and comics spaces. He argues that identifying these relationships reveals the importance of context to any discussion of comics aesthetics, and the dominance of 'cultural intermediaries' in constructing the comics scene. In 'Alpha Nerds' (2012b) he further explores the nature and functions of these intermediaries, using ethnographic research into the individuals and organizations (stores, clubs) that make up the 'nerd-culture scene' in a Canadian city, and arguing that these types of subcultural scenes cross industrial sectors and cultural industries.

In 2013, the online open access journal *Transformative Works and Cultures* published a special issue on the theme 'Appropriating, Interpreting, and Transforming Comic Books', focused primarily on fan practices. This considered the ways in which twenty-first-century comic book fandom has transformed comics characters, industry and the art form itself, and demonstrated that the political aspects of fan practices are particularly apparent in comics fandom, which is often a transformative act. Guest editor Matthew J. Costello (2013) argues that acts such as indexing and collecting, and the creative and critical practices undertaken by fans, frequently appropriate and transform comics characters, alter their meaning by placing them in new situations, and push against the boundaries between comics and other media. The following articles explore various perspectives on fandom. There is a particular focus on individual characters such as Captain America and on key issues that intersect with fan practices. For example, Suzanne Scott analyses the intersection of gender and fandom, arguing that 2011 and 2012 can be read as a transformative moment in comics culture, as an exponential increase of women within the industry, fandom and scholarship counterpoints the relative invisibility of women in comics. Rebecca Lucy Busker's 'Fandom and Male Privilege' also engages with gender issues by reflecting on the discourses of inequality and anger that arise in response to female-centric fan spaces online. Both articles demonstrate that comics fandom is made up of gendered spaces, which can be used as sites of transformation and reflection to expose the political potential of the medium and its practices. Similarly, Ora C. McWilliams discusses the junctions of ethnicity and fandom and evaluates colourblind approaches to comics characters by analysing the fan actions surrounding the introduction of Latino character Miles Morales as Spider-Man in 2011. Taken as a whole, the collection demonstrates the transformative and political potential of fan activities based around specific characters, titles and concepts.

Later issues of *Participations* also explore fandom: *Participations* 10(1) (2013) presents work from the Fan Studies Network, and 15(1) (2018) contains a themed section on Toxic Fan Practices. While not explicitly focused on comics, some articles have relevance, such as Jones' (2018) consideration of the relationship between fans and organizers of the *Walking Dead* convention Walker Stalker Con.

While much of the scholarship reviewed in this chapter has focused on the American and British industries, a handful of books and articles take a wider view. Patrick (2012) explores the fan practices of Australian readers of *The Phantom*, noting the strip's ubiquitous position in Australian culture and its framing as a homegrown title. After a lengthy historical account of how this came to be, he notes the emergence of Antipodean comics fandom in response to a largely one-way system of communication, driven by fanzines such as John Ryan's *Down Under* (1964). Patrick pays particular attention to the role of clubs in sustaining interest, such as the Captain Atom Fan Club (which peaked in the 1950s with 75,000 members) and the Phantom Club (launched in 1981), a licensed fan-driven venture. His article explores how these groups must negotiate with gatekeepers, and the mobilization of national identity to support claims of ownership.

Conclusion

Audience research is a comparatively overlooked field within comics studies and much of what does exist focuses on the British and American industries. Early analyses were often largely speculative and took a media effects perspective; this has given way to more integrated cultural studies-based approaches. Today varied methodologies are used to consider the work that readers do, and there has been increased focus on activities specific to comics, such as collecting or cosplaying. In particular, the notion of fandom has been explored from many angles, such as the ideological, social, cultural and economic. The next section of this Guide now moves to discuss comics' content, focusing on work that has examined recurring themes and their representation.

Notes

1. Angela McRobbie's monograph *Feminism and Youth Culture* (1991) extends this work, exploring a range of girls' titles.
2. It is, of course, arguable that comics fandom goes back much further, for example if we take as evidence the merchandising of titles such as *Ally Sloper* (1884) or *Bécassine* (1905) (see Sabin 1996 and Grove 2010).
3. The Fan Studies Network website (www.fanstudies.org, launched 2012) lists other relevant general journals and resources.
4. Bart Beaty's *Comics as Art* (discussed in Chapter 3) also touches briefly on some of the same ideas as Brown, as it seeks to define the 'comics world' and notes its move towards activities that mirror 'official' art practices, such as the respect of auteurship.

Works cited

Alderson, Connie. *Magazines Teenagers Read*. London: Pergamon Press, 1968.

Barker, Martin. *Comics: Ideology, Power and the Critics*. Manchester: Manchester University Press, 1989.

Barker, Martin. *Action: The Story of a Violent Comic*. London: Titan Books, 1991.

Barker, Martin. 'Seeing How far You Can See: On Being a "Fan" of *2000 AD*'. In David Buckingham (ed.), *Reading Audiences: Young People and the Media*. Manchester: Manchester University Press, 1993, pp. 159–183.

Barker, Martin. 'Taking the Extreme Case: Understanding a Fascist Fan of *Judge Dredd*'. In Deborah Cartmell, Ian Q. Hunter, Heidi Kaye, and Imelda Whelehan (eds), *Trash Aesthetics: Popular Culture and Its Audiences*. London: Pluto, 1997, pp. 14–30.

Barker, Martin. 'Kicked into the Gutters: Or, "My Dad doesn't Read Comics, He Studies Them"'. *International Journal of Comic Art* 4:1, 2002: 64–77.

Barker, Martin. 'The Reception of Joe Sacco's *Palestine*. *Participations* 9:2, 2012: 58–73.

Beaty, Bart. *Comics versus Art*. Toronto, ON: University of Toronto Press, 2012.

Berenstein, Ofer. 'Comic Book Fans' Recommendations Ceremony: A Look at the Inter-personal Communication Patterns of a Unique Readers/Speakers Community'. *Participations* 9:2, 2012: 74–96.

Berndt, Jaqueline, and Kümmerling-Meibauer, Bettina (eds). *Manga's Cultural Crossroads*. London: Routledge, 2016.

Botzakis, Stergios. '"To be a part of the dialogue": American Adults Reading Comic Books'. *Journal of Graphic Novels and Comics* 2:2, 2011: 113–123.

Bourdieu, Pierre. *Distinction: A Social Critique of the Judgment of Taste*. Cambridge, MS: Harvard University Press, 1984.

Brooker, Will. *Batman Unmasked: Analyzing a Cultural Icon*. London: Continuum, 2000.

Brown, Jeffrey A. 'Comic Book Fandom and Cultural Capital'. *Journal of Popular Culture* 30:4, 1997: 13–31.

Brown, Jeffrey A. *Black Superheroes, Milestone Comics, and Their Fans*. Jackson: University of Mississippi Press, 2001.

Brown, Jeffrey A. 'Ethnography: Wearing One's Fandom'. In Matthew J. Smith and Randy Duncan (eds), *Critical Approaches to Comics: Theories and Methods*. New York: Routledge, 2012, pp. 280–290.

Burke, Liam. '"Superman in Green": An Audience Study of Comic Book Film Adaptations *Thor* and *Green Lantern*'. *Participations* 9:2, 2012: 97–119.

Cadogan, Mary and Craig, Patricia. *You're a Brick, Angela! A New Look at Girls' Fiction from 1839 to 1975*. London: Victor Gollancz, 1976.

Costello, Matthew J. 'The Super Politics of Comic Book Fandom'. In Matthew J. Costello (ed.), 'Appropriating, Interpreting, and Transforming Comic Books', special issue, *Transformative Works and Cultures* 13, 2013. https://doi.org/10.3983/twc.2013.0528.

Demson, Michael and Brown, Heather. '"Aint I de Maine guy in dis paRade?": Towards a Radical History of Comic Strips and Their Audience Since Peterloo'. *Journal of Graphic Novels and Comics* 2:2, 2011: 151–167.

Fan Studies Network, 2012. https://fanstudies.org/about-us/. Accessed 19 August 2019.

Fingeroth, Danny. *Superman on the Couch: What Superheroes Really Tell Us about Ourselves and Our Society*. New York: The Continuum International Publishing Group Inc., 2004.

Fiske, John. 'The Cultural Economy of Fandom'. In Lisa A. Lewis (ed.), *The Adoring Audience: Fan Culture and Popular Media*. London: Routledge, 1992, pp. 30–49.

Fung, Anthony, Pun, Boris and Mori, Yoshitaka. 'Reading Border-Crossing Japanese Comics/Anime in China: Cultural Consumption, Fandom, and

Imagination'. *Global Media and China*, 2019. https://doi.org/10.1177%
2F2059436419835379. Accessed 20 February 2020.

Geraghty, Lincoln. *Cult Collectors*. London: Routledge, 2014.

Gibson, Mel. 'On British Comics for Girls and Their Readers'. In Julia Hallam
and Nikkianne Moody (eds), *Consuming for Pleasure: Selected Essays on
Popular Fiction*. Liverpool: University of Liverpool John Moores Press, 2000,
pp. 210–227.

Gibson, Mel. '"You Can't Read Them, They're for Boys!" British Girls, American
Superhero Comics and Identity'. *International Journal of Comic Art* 5:1, 2003:
305–324.

Gibson, Mel. 'Cultural Studies: British Girls' Comics, Readers, and Memories'. In
Matthew J. Smith and Randy Duncan (eds), *Critical Approaches to Comics:
Theories and Methods*. New York: Routledge, 2012, pp. 267–279.

Gibson, Mel. *Remembered Reading: Memory, Comics and Post-War Constructions of
British Girlhood*. Leuven, Belgium: Leuven University Press, 2015.

Gordon, Ian. *Comic Strips and Consumer Culture 1890–1945*. Washington and
London: Smithsonian Institution Press, 1998.

Gordon, Ian. 'Writing to Superman: Towards an Understanding of the Social
Networks of Comic-Book Fans'. *Participations* 9:2, November 2012: 120–132.

Grove, Laurence. *Comics in French*. New York: Berghahn, 2010.

Hajdu, David. *The Ten-Cent Plague: The Great Comic-Book Scare and How It
Changed America*. New York: Farrar, Straus and Giroux, 2008.

Hammond, Heidi Kay. *Graphic Novels and Multimodal Literacy: A Reader Response
Study*. Köln: Lambert Academic Publishing, 2009.

Hernández-Pérez, Manuel. 'Looking into the "Anime Global Popular" and
the "Manga Media": Reflections on the Scholarship of a Transnational and
Transmedia Industry'. *Arts* 8:57, 2019.

Hills, Matt. *Fan Cultures*. London and New York: Routledge, 2002.

Howe, Irving. 'Notes on Mass Culture'. *Politics*, Spring 1948: 120–122.

Hymes, Dell. *Foundations in Sociolinguistics: An Ethnographic Approach*.
Philadelphia: University of Pennsylvania Press, 1994.

Ingulsrud, John E. and Allen, Kate. *Reading Japan Cool: Patterns of Manga Literacy
and Discourse*. Lanham, MD: Lexington Books, 2009.

Jacobs, Katrien. 'Impersonating and Performing Queer Sexuality in the Cosplay
Zone'. *Participations* 10:2, 2013: 22–45.

Jenkins, Henry. *Textual Poachers: Television Fans and Participatory Culture*.
New York: Routledge, 1992.

Jones, Bethan. '"Stop Moaning. I Gave You My Email. Give Me a Solution": Walker
Stalker Con, Fantagonism and Fanagement on Social Media'. *Participations* 15:1,
2018: 252–271.

Locke, Simon. '"Fanboy" as a Revolutionary Category'. *Participations* 9:2, November
2012: 835–854.

Locke, Simon. *Comics Superheroes and Their Fans: A Sociological Analysis*.
Farnham: Ashgate Publishing, 2013.

Madeley, June M. 'Girly Girls and Pretty Boys: Gender and Audience Reception
of English-Translated Manga'. University of Regina, 2010–12. https://ourspace.

uregina.ca/bitstream/handle/10294/3092/QueenCityComics-4-June_Madeley.
pdf?sequence=1&isAllowed=y. Accessed 12 August 2019.

Madeley, June M. 'Transnational Convergence Culture: Grassroots and Corporate
Convergence in the Conflict over Amateur English-Translated Manga'. *Journal
of Graphic Novels and Comics* 6:4, 2015: 367–381.

Mahaseth, Harsh. 'The Cultural Impact of Manga on Society'. 2017. *Asian Journal
of Language, Literature and Culture Studies*, 24 January 2018: 1–5. Available
at SSRN https://ssrn.com/abstract=2930916 or http://dx.doi.org/10.2139/
ssrn.2930916. Accessed 20 February 2020.

Maigret, Éric. 'Strange Grew up with Me: Sentimentality and Masculinity in
Readers of Superhero Comics'. *Réseaux* 7:1, 1999: 5–27. http://www.persee.
fr/web/revues/home/prescript/article/reso_0969-9864_1999_num_7_1_3347.
Accessed 5 July 2019.

McLain, Karline. *India's Immortal Comic Books: Gods, Kings and Other Heroes.*
Bloomington, IN: Indiana University Press, 2009.

McRobbie, Angela. '*Jackie*: An Ideology of Adolescent Femininity'. Occasional
paper. Centre for Cultural Studies. University of Birmingham, 1978a.

McRobbie, Angela 'Working Class Girls and the Culture of Femininity'. Centre for
Contemporary Cultural Studies. Women Take Issue. London: Hutchinson, 1978b.

McRobbie, Angela. 'Just like a *Jackie* story'. In Angela McRobbie and Trisha McCabe
(eds), *Feminism for Girls*. London: Routledge and Kegan Paul, 1981.

McRobbie, Angela. *Feminism and Youth Culture: From Jackie to Just Seventeen.*
London: Macmillan, 1991.

McRobbie, Angela. 'More! New Sexualities in Girls' and Women's Magazines'. In
Angela McRobbie (ed.), *Back to Reality? Social Experience and Cultural Studies.*
Manchester: Manchester University Press, 1997, pp. 172–194.

Participations. About Participations: History and Founding Principles.
Participations, 2017. http://www.participations.org/about.htm. Accessed
4 January 2017.

Patrick, Kevin. 'The Invisible Medium: Comics Studies in Australia'. *Refractory* 17,
2010: 1–11.

Patrick, Kevin. "Phans', not Fans": The Phantom and Australian Comic-Book
Fandom'. *Participations* 9:2, 2012: 133–158.

Pellitteri, Marco and Bouissou, Jean-Marie. *The Dragon and the Dazzle: Models,
Strategies, and Identities of Japanese Imagination: A European Perspective.*
Roberto Branca and Christie Lee Barber (trans). Latina, Italy: Tunué, 2010.

Pumphrey, George. *What Children Think of Their Comics*. London: Epworth Press,
1964.

Pustz, Matthew J. *Comic Book Culture: Fanboys and True Believers*. Jackson:
University Press of Mississippi, 1999.

Round, Julia. *Gothic in Comics and Graphic Novels: A Critical Approach*. Jefferson,
NC: McFarland, 2014.

Saavedra, Scott. *Flee, Puny Humans! The Comic Book Heaven Collection*. San José:
SLG Publishing, 2003.

Sabeti, Shari. 'The Irony of "Cool Club": The Place of Comic Book Reading in
Schools'. *Journal of Graphic Novels and Comics* 2:2, 2011: 137–149.

Sabeti, Shari '"Arts of Time and Space": The Perspectives of a Teenage Audience on Reading Novels and Graphic Novels'. *Participations* 9:2, 2012: 159–179.

Sabre, Clothilde. *Le Néo-japonisme en France. Passion des mangas et images du Japon*. Master's thesis, University Lille 1: Sciences and Technology, France, 2006.

Schelly, Bill. *The Golden Age of Comic Fandom*. Ellettsville, IN: Hamster Press, 1995.

Schelly, Bill. *Founders of Comic Fandom*. Jefferson, NC: McFarland, 2010.

Schelly, Bill. *Sense of Wonder: My Life in Comic Fandom–The Whole Story*. Berkeley, CA: North Atlantic Books, 2018.

Seldes, Gilbert. *The Great Audience*. New York: Viking Press, 1950.

Shamoon, Deborah. 'Situating the Shojo in Shojo Manga: Teenage Girls, Romance Comics, and Contemporary Japanese Culture'. In Mark Wheeler MacWilliams (ed.), *Japanese Visual Culture: Explorations of the World of Manga and Anime*. New York: M.E. Sharpe, 2008, pp. 137–154.

Sharpe, Sue. *Just Like a Girl: How Girls Learn to be Women*. Harmondsworth: Penguin, 1976.

Steinberg, Marc. *The Platform Economy: How Japan Transformed the Commercial Internet*. Minneapolis, MN: University of Minnesota Press, 2019.

Steinberg, Marc and Zahlten, A. (eds). *Media Theory in Japan*. Durham, NC: Duke University Press, 2017.

Sugawa-Shimada, Akiko. 'Rebel with Causes and Laughter for Relief: "Essay Manga" of Tenten Hosokawa and Rieko Saibara, and Japanese Female Readership'. *Journal of Graphic Novels and Comics* 2:2, 2011: 169–185.

Swafford, Brian. 'Critical Ethnography: The Comics Shop as Cultural Clubhouse'. In Matthew J. Smith and Randy Duncan (eds), *Critical Approaches to Comics – Theories and Methods*. New York: Routledge, 2012, pp. 291–302.

Tankel, Jonathan David and Murphy, Keith. 'Collecting Comic Books: A Study of the Fan and Curatorial Consumption'. In Cheryl Harris and Alison Alexander (eds), *Theorizing Fandom: Fans, Subculture and Identity*. Cresskill, NJ: Hampton Press, 1998, pp. 55–68.

Thomas, Jolyon Baraka. *Drawing on Tradition: Manga, Anime and Religion in Contemporary Japan*. Honolulu: University of Hawai'i Press, 2012.

Thomas, P. L. 'Adventures in Genre!: Rethinking Genre through Comics/Graphic Novels'. *Journal of Graphic Novels and Comics* 2:2, 2011: 187–201.

Walkerdine, Valerie. 'Some Day My Prince Will Come: Young Girls and the Preparation for Adolescent Sexuality'. In Angela McRobbie and Mica Nava (eds), *Gender and Generation*. London: Macmillan, 1984, pp. 162–184.

Warshow, Robert. 'Woofed with Dreams'. *Partisan Review* 13, 1946: 587–590.

Wolf, Katherine M. and Marjorie Fiske. 'The Children Talk about Comics'. In Paul Lazarsfeld and Frank Stanton (eds), *Communications Research 1948–49*. New York: Harper, 1949, pp. 3–50.

Woo, Benjamin. 'Beyond Our Borders: Mapping the Space of Comics'. *Comics, forum.org*, 2011a. https://comicsforum.org/?s=woo. Accessed 29 July 2012.

Woo, Benjamin. 'The Android's Dungeon: Comic-Bookstores, Cultural Spaces, and the Social Practices of Audiences'. *Journal of Graphic Novels and Comics* 2:2, 2011b: 125–136.

Woo, Benjamin. 'Understanding Understandings of Comics: Reading and Collecting as Media-oriented Practices'. *Participations* 9:2, 2012a: 180–199.

Woo, Benjamin. 'Alpha Nerds: Cultural Intermediaries in a Subcultural Scene'. *European Journal of Cultural Studies* 15:5, 2012b: 659–676.

Wright, Bradford W. *Comic Book Nation: The Transformation of Youth Culture in America*. Baltimore: Johns Hopkins University Press, 2001.

PART IV
THEMES AND GENRES

CHAPTER 8
THEMATIC APPROACHES

This chapter focuses on the most recurrent and pertinent themes in current comics criticism. It begins with the documentary inclinations of comics that provide social and historical accounts of key moments in history, including contemporary history. It also broaches the analysis of comics as historical documents. The chapter then expands on works studying the representation of trauma and different kinds of memory in comics. The second section covers research on diversity in comics in the broadest sense of the word to include Latinx comics, the rise of Muslim superheroes in mainstream American comics and explorations of racial identity in graphic novels and more mainstream publications. Recent comics criticism has also shown an increasing interest in child characters in comics, which is covered in the third section of this chapter. The fourth and final section briefly introduces transmedia storytelling and intermedial approaches that situate comics in relationship to other media, alongside in-depth studies on the connections between comics and major literary and artistic movements such as Gothic and Romanticism.

Documentary, trauma and memory

Countering the association between comics and humour, many recent comics, especially graphic novels, and historical comics and political cartoons, have represented historical and contemporary events in diverse ways (realistic, cartoonish, experimental, pedagogical, politically engaged). This section turns to sources examining documentary comics and the representation of traumatic, historical and autobiographical memories.

Documentary comics cover both graphic journalism which record actual events, such as Joe Sacco's work on Palestine (*Palestine* [1996]; *Footnotes in Gaza* [2009]) and post-war Bosnia (*Safe Area Goražde* [2000]) and comics that retell historical events, for example *Maus*, which merges the family memoir with the animal fable, or the long-running *Charley's*

War [1979–1986] scripted by Pat Mills and Scott Goodall and drawn by Joe Colquhoun, which follows the experiences of a young recruit who joins the British army at the outbreak of the First World War. While Sacco remains the most well-known comics journalist, two French magazines – *La revue dessinée* and *XXI* – also promote bande dessinée reportage. Sacco's work has recently been the subject of a critical anthology, *The Comics of Joe Sacco: Journalism in a Visual World* (2015), which combines diverse perspectives, including the politics of time in Sacco's work (Jared Gardner), its performativity (Rebecca Scherr) and historical bearing (Ben Owen) and its relevance for teaching world politics (Kevin C. Dunn).

Comics, including single panel newspaper cartoons, can also serve as historical sources, as suggested by Jane Chapman's books, *Comics and the World Wars: A Cultural Record* (2015), co-written with Anna Hoyles, Andrew Kerr and Adam Sherif and *Comics, the Holocaust and Hiroshima* (2015), co-written with Dan Ellin and Adam Sheriff. In advocating for the use of comics as historical sources or 'comics as cultural record', the authors base themselves on the tenets of New Cultural History, which seeks to capture the *mentalité* [mindset] or *zeitgeist* [spirit] of an era from a democratic, non-elitist perspective attuned to the narrative nature of sources (Chapman et al., 2015: 2, 172). Comics, the authors suggest, are excellent source material for this kind of history, especially when read from a contextualized perspective that accounts for all the factors – social, cultural, economic – that influenced their making. Here the authors build on Joseph Witek's seminal work, *Comics as History*, which focused on personal, recent graphic novels (see Chapter 10). In contrast to Witek, the authors of *Comics and the World Wars* apply the methodological suggestion of comics as cultural documentation to the often anonymously authored comics appearing in newspapers, beginning with W.K. Haselden's *Daily Mirror* strips published during the First World War, selected strips published in various trench magazines, the Socialist Party's publications in the UK and beyond, and the Second World War American propaganda. Separate chapters discuss the representation of women and workers. The shorter volume, *Comics, the Holocaust and Hiroshima*, furthers the project of considering comics as cultural records. It begins by examining the representation of Nazi violence in the Second World War comics produced by the successful American publisher, the Quality Comics Group. The second chapter looks at the bande dessinée album of *Paroles d'étoiles*, [*Words of the Stars*] a collection of memoirs and other documentary material (photographs, drawings) of Jewish children during the Vichy regime. The final chapter considers Japanese alternative manga [*gekiga*] artist Keiji Nakazawa's *Barefoot Gen*, an autobiographical memoir of the Hiroshima bombing. Building on trauma theory and discussions of PTSD, the chapter argues for the 'effectiveness' of comics to represent such psychological issues. Notably, it is the autobiographical nature of the last two works that justifies the authors' consideration of them as primary sources for their analysis (Chapman et al., 2015b: 50).

This supposed effectiveness of comics to represent trauma plays a recurrent role in scholarship on trauma and memory. A good starting point is Hillary Chute's *Disaster Drawn: Visual Witness, Comics and Documentary Form* (2016). While advocating that comics have a certain uniqueness, Chute highlights the temporal and, by extension, mnemonic layers ensconced in the drawn line (21) and how the form itself 'literalizes the work of archiving' (192). This builds on Jared Gardner's study of the practices and representations of archiving and collecting in his 'Storylines' article (2012: 149–179). *Disaster Drawn* delineates a lineage of bearing witness through images starting with the seventeenth-century prints of Jacques Callot, *Les Grandes misères et les malheurs de la guerre* [*The Miseries and Misfortunes of War* (1633)] about the Thirty Years War and Francisco Goya's *Los Desastres de la Guerra* [*The Disasters of War*] (1810–1820) on the Peninsular War. In examining Kenji Nakazawa's *I Saw It* (1972), Chute points out that comics offer more atomic bomb stories than any other medium (146). Other comics discussed include Art Spiegelman's *Maus* and Joe Sacco's works. Here Chute is particularly interested in how comics narrate and represent traumatic histories in ways that are very distinct from other media. While the chapter on *Maus* discusses the archival work of comics, the section on Sacco's *Footnotes in Gaza* emphasizes how comics can offer alternatives to official histories and hence function in a 'counterarchival' manner.

Jeff Adams' *Graphic Novels and Social Realism* (2008) and Nina Mickwitz's *Documentary Comics: Graphic Truth-telling in a Skeptical Age* (2015) both closely interrogate the documentary function of graphic novels. Covering canonical graphic novels such as *Persepolis* (Marjane Satrapi), *Maus*, *Barefoot Gen* and *Jimmy Corrigan*, Adams highlights the political interventions they make and argues for their realist import. His last chapter draws out similarities between W.G. Sebald's *Die Ausgewanderten* [*The Emigrants*] (1992) and *Maus*. These include the use of the impersonal diagram to highlight the structural violence of the Nazi regime and the (pseudo-)documentary tendencies of the anonymous photographs in *The Emigrants* and their parallels in *Maus* through, for instance, the incorporation of Vladek Spiegelman's testimony.

Working with a broader and simultaneously visually attuned scope, Mickwitz's *Documentary Comics* (2016) focuses on the transposition of documentary modes onto the form of comics. She maps the documentary inclinations of graphic novels, non-fiction comics, travelogues and documentary webcomics. She applies Jay Bolter and Richard Grusin's concept of remediation to suggest that the comics she examines 'remediate [...] a documentary mode of address usually associated with certain other media' (Mickwitz, 2016: 7). In considering diverse comics, Mickwitz emphasizes their narrative and performative workings. Analysing Harvey Pekar's *American Splendor* and Emmanuel Guibert's collaboration with photographer Didier Lefèvre for *The Photographer* books, Mickwitz questions the biases towards authenticity that favour realistic representation and that can work against comics because of their drawn, stylized essence. She then delineates the role of the counter- – or to use Chute's term 'counterarchival' – narrative in Sacco's *Footnotes in Gaza* and Guibert's *Alan's War* (2008). She also examines travelogues by Craig Thompson and Guy Delisle as well as the role of travel in Satrapi's *Persepolis*. While examining Josh Neufeld's *AD New Orleans: After the Deluge* (2009), Mickwitz highlights the ambiguity and limits of agency offered to underrepresented people. Finally, she turns to 'short-form documentary webcomics' such as those published by *Symbolia Magazine* and the *Cartoon Movement* to underscore the diversity of digital documentaries while emphasizing the remnants of the documentary aesthetics of analogue media.

Mark McKinney's anthology, *History and Politics of French-language Comics and Graphic Novels* (2008), presents a gamut of ways in which to consider the historical relevance of comics. Most of the chapters examine historical themes in recent works, often with a focus on identity creation and the aftermath of French and Belgian colonization (for more on colonialism in comics, see Chapter 3). In addition, Bart Beaty studies the notion of *patrimoine* and heritage in contemporary French-language comics, covering alternative publishers such as Cornélius, Fréon, L'Association and their relationship to the 'classic' comics of the Franco-Belgian schools and comics history in general. Clare Tufts turns to French children's newspapers from the Second World War to trace the fate of popular publications during the Occupation, the use of comics and illustration to channel Nazi propaganda, and the creation of the myth of resistance in the wake of liberation and the initiation of new children's comics magazines such as *Vaillant*. The volume concludes with an essay from French alternative comics artist, Baru, on the anti-bourgeois inclinations of some comics and the game-changing role they played in transforming the image of comics while giving a voice to protagonists from working-class backgrounds. He uses his comic *Quéquette blues* to illustrate this while also highlighting its autobiographical elements.

Although the study of comics as historical sources and documentaries is rooted in the discipline of history another, arguably more prominent line of comics research stems from literary and cultural studies and focuses on how different kinds of traumatic experiences are represented in comics. The study of trauma in comics has been the subject of several monographs in recent years. In *The Trauma Graphic Novel* (2017), Andrés Romero-Jódar examines the subgenre of 'trauma graphic novels' such as Paul Hornschemeier's *Mother Come Home* (2003) and Joe Sacco's *Palestine* and *Footnotes in Gaza*; Alan Moore and Dave Gibbons' *Watchmen,* on the representation of political trauma; as well as *Maus* and *MetaMaus*. Romero-Jódar turns to trauma studies scholars such as Roger Luckhurst – who coined the term 'traumaculture' to describe the influx of trauma narratives in the 1990s – and cultural studies scholars such as Walter Benjamin. Before turning to close readings of the graphic novels, Romero-Jódar provides a concise overview of the transformations in comics production, contextualizing them in the broader cultural discourse. He suggests that in trying to represent traumatized psyches, many graphic novels take the modernist novel as a model by incorporating, for instance, fragmentation and stream of consciousness. These graphic novels are also inscribed in the 'ethical turn' pervading both critical discourses and cultural productions; the establishment of trauma studies during the 1980s and the 1990s encouraged the production of trauma narratives. Another important contribution to the rise of the trauma graphic novel is the erosion of the self-imposed censorship of comics that had been in force since 1954 (see the section on the Comics Code in Chapter 4).

Using a more specific corpus, Harriet E.H. Earle's *Comics, Trauma and the New Art of War* (2017) examines post-1975 'conflict comics' published by North American comics artists with a migration background. In addition to looking at the usual suspects of *Maus, Palestine* and *Footnotes in Gaza,* Earle also considers comics on the Vietnam war (*The* 'Nam comics, 1986–1993 and the more recent *Vietnamerica*), 9/11 (Alissa Torres' *American Widow* [2008]), generational trauma of the Holocaust (Carol Tyler's *You'll Never Know* [2009], Joe Kubert's *Yossel* and Dave Sim's *Judenhass* [2008]). Earle combines insights from trauma studies with Freudian psychoanalysis, especially the interpretation of dreams. She transposes psychological conceptualizations of the stages of grief and PTSD to the comics. The last two chapters explore comics techniques in representing trauma. Like Romero-Jódar, Earle proposes applying Bakhtin's chronotope to better understand the inextricability of space and time in comics. In considering comics as postmodern, Earle underscores the importance of play and reader participation. Maintaining the postmodernist lens, Earle also refers to Pierre Masson's description of comics as a 'stuttering art' to capture its reliance on fragmentation and repetition of images (157).

In *Ethics in the Gutter: Empathy and Historical Fiction in Comics* (2017), Kate Polak considers trauma in graphic novels through tackling their tough 'nexus of ethics and empathy' (1). Like Earle, Polak also emphasizes the role of reader participation and extends it to include the participation of comics themselves: '[r]eaders' awareness of the graphic narrative as something *produced* is embedded in the form, which gives comics the possibility of engaging in commentary on the production of history and its violences' (11). Polak mobilizes narratological tools to consider readers' potential ethical positions and the devices used to suscitate, or limit, reader involvement, especially through focalization. Beginning with *Déogratias* (2000), Jean-Philippe Stassen's graphic novel on the Rwandan genocide, Polak provides close readings of Sally Jupiter's rape scene in *Watchmen* and of Jason Aaron and R.M. Guéra's *Scalped* (2007–12) on the repression of Native Americans on a reservation during the 1960s and 1970s. After considering intergenerational, racial trauma in Jeremy Love's two-volume *Bayou* (2009), Polak turns to a *Hellblazer* issue by Mike Carey to test the extent to which reader empathy can be repelled. In this exploration of encouraging reader involvement and provoking different kinds of feelings through graphic novels, Polak contends that the 'wandering point of view' of graphic novels offers the potential to highlight the complexity and ambiguity of historical and fictionalized representations of violence (213).

Laurike in 't Veld's monograph, *The Representation of Genocide in Graphic Novels: Considering the Role of Kitsch* (2019), selects a new lens for examining comics about traumatic events. She turns to kitsch, which '[a]s a cultural and visual concept [...] is generally associated with elements like excess, aestheticization and (emotional) manipulation' that become problematic when used for the representation of historical violence (1). Elaborating that kitsch is something that is simultaneously '*too much* and *too little*' (2, emphasis in the original), in 't Veld traces kitsch's connections to the Nazi regime which operationalized kitsch in its nationalist discourse. She (like Romero-Jódar, and to a certain extent, Earle) also emphasizes the overlap between modernist aesthetics and the representation of trauma through nonlinear subjective experiences. In focusing on contemporary graphic novels on the genocides in Nazi Germany, Bosnia and Armenia, in 't Veld combines the study of canonical works and of educational or didactic ones that usually fall below the critical radar. In 't Veld's readings unfold across the visual metaphors of animals and dolls that recur in the kitsch imaginary, the ethical issues raised by both nuanced and exaggeratedly evil representations of perpetrators, the tension between showing and concealing violence, especially rape, and graphic novels' attempts to circumvent kitsch.

Golnar Nabizadeh's *Representation and Memory in Graphic Novels* (2019) also considers graphic novels on personal and historical traumas but adopts a broader focus on the representation of different kinds of interlinked memories (personal, political, social, historical). Nabizadeh is particularly interested in the representation of marginalized and minority voices and suggests that comics, because of its own marginalized status, is particularly appropriate for this. This linking of comics and marginalized perspectives is comparable to Hillary Chute's claim in her latest book *Why Comics?* (see Chapter 11). Arguing that both comics and memory are 'polysemiotic', Nabizadeh interweaves close readings of migrant memories in Henry Yoshitaka Kiyama's *The Four Immigrants Manga* from the 1930s and Shaun Tan's *The Arrival* from the early 2000s. The book then focuses on recent works including online comics on Australian detention centres, one from a guard's perspective and the other from a refugee's perspective. In addition to looking at multimodal memories (*Waltz with Bashir* and *The Photographer*), Nabizadeh reads *Persepolis* through the lens of trauma. In considering memories of illness in *Epileptic* and David Small's *Stitches* (2009), Nabizadeh focuses on the representation of gestures and highlights the role of 'the body as a living archive, and one that bears the marks of its history in visible and invisible ways' (2019: 107). In studying instances where racism is countered in *American Born Chinese* and Jul' Maroh's *Blue Is the Warmest Color* (2010), Nabizadeh shows how 'each artist explores the animating power of racist stereotypes by drawing attention to their afterlives as a form of cultural memory' (63). She also underscores the relevance of gaps, especially gutters, in challenging xenophobic and exclusionary discourses.

For a still broader engagement with the role, and not only representation, of memory in comics, see Maaheen Ahmed and Benoît Crucifix's *Comics Memory: Archives and Styles* (2018). The volume moves away from the focus on traumatic memories to consider other kinds of memories at work in comics. It brings together contributions on autobiographical, personal and personalized memories, fan memories, comics history and virtual, artistic and institutional archival practices. Proposing the tangents of style and archive to consider comics memory, the volume concludes with a user guide for thinking about different kinds of memory in comics (as personal, collective, or at the level of the comics medium). Most of the chapters in the volume show how these different strands of memory are often inseparable. Concerned with how comics remember and the roles played by different kinds of memory in comics, including how comics figure their own histories, the volume also broaches the relevance of nostalgia in contemporary graphic novels (Busi Rizzi).

Although not directly connected to mnemonic or documentary projects, Greice Schneider's remarkable study on the notion of the everyday in contemporary comics deserves mention because it highlights the possibilities of combining and extending memory and comics historical projects through close readings of a particular motif, in this case boredom. *What Happens When Nothing Happens: Boredom and Everyday Life in Contemporary Comics* (2016) starts with the rise of underground comics in the 1960s to tease out connections between notions of boredom and modernity. The concept of boredom is operationalized through insights from diverse fields, combining literature, philosophy and cultural studies to lay the ground for establishing a poetics of boredom in comics. Schneider also incorporates narratological concepts theorizing narrative tension, especially tellability (Raphaël Baroni) and narrative interest (Meir Steinberg). Analysing the works of acclaimed comics artists such as Seth, Adrian Tomine, Chris Ware and Lewis Trondheim, she weaves connections between the comic strip and its penchant for repetition – a symptom of boredom that is prominent in the comics artist's repertoire – and contemporary graphic novelists.

Generally focusing on contemporary graphic novels instead of older, more mainstream productions, current research on documentary, memory and trauma in comics has tried to tease out the specificity of comics for capturing complex memories, personal and historical situations. This trend continues in the newly initiated research on representation and diversity.

Diversity: Ethnicity and religion

While Nabizadeh's book examines marginalized voices in traumatic situations, there is a growing body of research on the representation of minorities in comics. This is complemented by scholarship on the work of comics artists and writers from underrepresented communities. In considering diversity, multiculturalism, and in particular multicultural and

Latinx comics, as well as religion and comics are the most recurrent themes. Two critical anthologies, Frederick L. Aldama's *Multicultural Comics: From Zap to Blue Beetle* (2010) and Carolene Ayaka and Ian Hague's *Representing Multiculturalism in Comics and Graphic Novels* (2014), illustrate the scope of themes associated with multiculturalism.

One of the first volumes to broach multiculturalism and comics, most of the chapters in Aldama's critical anthology focus on issues of race, migration and multiple cultures within the American context including African Americans, Latinx (the gender-neutral version of Latina and Latino) as well as Native Americans. In his introduction, Aldama situates the volume at the intersection of different cultures, race, gender and sexuality. He maps multicultural comics across several genres and hybrid genres such as coming-of-age, autobiography, biography, memoir, historical fiction and erotica. Rifas' chapter in the collection interrogates racism and underground comics. Examining Asian American graphic novels, Gardner suggests that the move from cartoon to comic strip and eventually the graphic novel propelled 'a shift away from cartoon racism toward what we might call "graphic alterity"' (135). For Gardner, the repetition that is essential to the comic strip, and through which we encounter the same characters repeatedly enables a move away from rigid, unchanging stereotypes. The volume's final chapter by Jenny E. Robb and Rebecca Wanzo reflects on the negotiations that need to be made for conducting multicultural research. The chapter also contains a list of useful comics studies resources and archives for multicultural comics research.

Representing Multiculturalism is concerned with the structures of power at work in the representation of coexisting cultures as well as the possibilities of representing multiculturalism. It considers comics as a 'nexus of cultures' rather than simply a hybrid medium (Ayaka and Hague, 2015: 3). In contrast to *Multicultural Comics, Representing Multiculturalism* strives to move beyond the usual focus on American and British-American comics and contains chapters on Romanian comics (Precup), Japanese art and comics (Grennan; Birken; Link), South African political cartoons (Mason) and Spanish comics (Harris). Many of the chapters deal with the persistence of racial stereotyping in the representation of others (Alexandru; Grennan; Harris; Horton; Mihăilescu; Oki). In addition to examining comics through the postcolonial lens (Horton; Alexandru, amongst others), the recycling of racist imagery in underground comix is also examined (Creekmur)

One of the most international volumes in its selection of comics and perspectives is Binita Mehta and Pia Mukherji's *Postcolonial Comics: Texts,*

Events and Identities (2015). It covers comics from regions often overlooked by scholarship, including India, Asia Pacific, Africa and the Middle East. The selected comics often interrogate their colonized pasts, suppression and the atrocities of war. Comics, the editors contend, can resist imperialist hegemonies through deconstructing repressive images associated with regions and cultures relegated to the periphery. *Postcolonial Comics* stands out through its geographical scope. For scholarship on Asian and Russian comics, see Chapter 5.

In *Your Brain on Latino Comics: From Gus Arriola to Los Bros Hernandez* (2009), Aldama interviews numerous Latinx comics artists and writers. He begins with a general overview of Latinx comics characters from the mainstream and beyond. This is followed by a closer reading of specific devices used by Latinx cartoonists to flesh out their stories. He also highlights the precarity of many Latinx artists and the necessity of combining jobs and other sources of income, especially when they produce comics that deviate from the mainstream and are consequently unprofitable and overlooked. In the more recent *Latinx Superheroes in Mainstream Comics,* Aldama focuses on the commercial superhero genre to critique the representation of Latinx characters and their transformations since their first appearance in the 1940s. It also includes a transmedial analysis of Latinx superheroes in film and television to show how comics' practices of simplifying and negatively connoting Latinx superheroes are perpetuated and even exacerbated. This tendency, however, is countered in digital comics. For a broader perspective on Latinx identity both within and beyond the United States, see Juan Poblete and Héctor Fernández L'Hoeste's edited volume, *Redrawing the Nation: National Identity in Latin/o American Comics* (2009), which collects insights on comics from Peru, Brazil, Mexico, Chile and Argentina as well as the Hernandez brothers.

Comics artist Tim Jackson offers a generously illustrated history of African American cartoonists from the nineteenth century to our present day. Providing a counterpoint to racist representations of African Americans, Jackson's *Pioneering Cartoonists of Color* (2016) introduces the Black illustrated press, incorporating cartoons from the late 1800s. Jackson divides his history into eight periods to cover the decades from the 1900s to the 1970s and beyond. Pointing out that there were as many as 2700 Black-owned newspapers in the United States by the 1900s, Jackson begins his introduction with Herriman's *Krazy Kat* before moving on to the lesser known *The Jolly Bean Eaters* by Fon Holly from 1911 and highlighting the importance of the *Chicago Defender.* The next chapter includes Leslie

M. Rogers' *Bungleton Green* and Roger L. Powell's Bud Billiken among many other race cartoons. This was the term employed during the 1920s, following W.E.B. Du Bois' use of race as a replacement for the derogatory terms associated with African Americans. Identifying 1940 to 1949 as the era of 'cartoon renaissance' (Jackson, 2016: 52) to capture the rich production by Black cartoonists, Jackson devotes a separate section to wartime cartoons and comics published in the Black press. It was only during the 1960s that work by Black cartoonists successfully reached a broad audience with strips such as Morrie Turner's *Wee Pals*, Brumsic Brandon's *Luther* and Ted Shearer's *Quincy*. The book ends with an index of pioneering cartoonists with brief biographical notes. Jackson however is careful to mention the many missing details in the list due to a dearth of available information. For a discussion of scholarship on the pioneering Black artist, Jackie Ormes, see Chapter 6.

Martin Lund's Re-Constructing *the Man of Steel: Superman, 1938–1941, Jewish American History and the Invention of the Jewish-Comics Connection* (2016) turns to the early *Superman* comics to question and nuance the relevance of the Jewish origins of its creators. Emphasizing how Superman incarnates New Deal efforts even after the New Deal lost its popularity, Lund goes on to show how he also remained, like other comic book heroes, a devout, fully 'Americanized' patriot. Insights into the issues of race, sexuality and, eventually, masculinity in the *Superman* comics are complemented by intertextual readings. For more on the superhero, see Chapter 4 on ideological approaches and Chapter 9 on popular genres.

Furthering studies of superhero and identity by turning to underrepresented groups, A.D. Lewis and Martin Lund's *Muslim Superheroes: Comics, Islam and Representation* (2017) is currently the only edited volume to study the rise of Muslim superheroes in comics. The contributions are not limited to American comics and encompass Egyptian and Kuwaiti comics (Kreil's and Stromberg's respective contributions) and the presence of superheroes in Islam (Rashid) to emphasize 'Muslim traditions of heroic stories' (Lewis and Lund, 2017: 208). The editors end the volume by warning against essentializing Muslim superheroes. They argue for considering superheroes such as Kamala Khan and The 99 as forms of 'autoethnography' through which a minority culture engages with its representations in a dominant culture (239). They liken such superhero comics to contact zones where different cultures meet and negotiate their identity and power dynamics. In addition to summarizing the diverse characteristics of Muslim superheroes brought out by the chapters, the editors also offer suggestions for discussing Muslim superheroes in different kinds of courses and encouraging multicultural thinking.[1]

Scholarship on ethnic and religious diversity combines issues of representing different cultures with historical overviews and comparisons of the presence and absence of minorities in comics, encompassing comics stories, the techniques of representation and comics by minorities.

Children in comics

Comics studies has traditionally tried to distinguish itself from children's literature and picturebook studies and has focused on comics and graphic novels for adults rather than children. In recent years however children in comics and, to a lesser extent, comics for children have attracted some attention. One of the earliest works to focus on children in comics (and not only children's comics) is Ian Gordon's *Kid Comic Strips: A Genre Across Four Continents* (2016). Gordon introduces and discusses 'kid comics' as a genre in its own right. He analyses and compares a diverse set of strips including the American *Skippy* and the Australian *Ginger Meggs*, the American *Winnie Winkle* and its French version (*Bicot*) as well as the very different British and American *Dennis the Menaces*. In doing so, Gordon highlights the centrality of kid comics for the development of newspaper comics and the medium of comics itself on an international scale.

In *Reading Lessons in Seeing: Mirrors, Masks and Mazes* (2016), Michael Chaney devotes his first chapter to the child in graphic novels drawn by adults (*Persepolis, Epileptic, Palestine, Nat Turner, Jimmy Corrigan*) but also, in one case by a child themselves, Ariel Schrag's *Awkward* (1999). Chaney argues for considering children in comics, especially early comics like the *Yellow Kid* as representing the medium of comics.

In *Good Grief! Children and Comics* (which accompanied an exhibition at the Billy Ireland Cartoon Library and Museum in 2016), Michelle Ann Abate and Joe Sutliff Sanders collect a selection of brief essays on diverse children in comics ranging from Winsor McCay's *Little Nemo* to Jeff Smith's *Bone*. Sanders starts by suggesting that children's comics began distinguishing themselves from mixed-audience works during the 1930s (in the English-speaking world). While they diversified in the 1940s, Sanders points out that many comics sought to strike a balance between material that would please adult authority figures and offer children the possibility of constrained rebellion.

Lara Saguisag's award-winning *Incorrigibles and Innocents: Constructing Childhood Citizenship in Progressive Era Comics* (2018) examines turn-of-the-century Progressive era American comics in light of the ongoing discourses on childhood and citizenship. In addition to close reading successful comics such as R.F. Outcault's the *Yellow Kid* and *Buster Brown*, Saguisag explores the representation of race and the roles accorded to little girls in comics. Michelle Ann Abate's *Funny Girls: Guffaws, Guts and Gender in Classic American Comics* (2018) contributes further to the history of girl characters in comics by examining strips from the first half of the twentieth century. She covers both well-known and lesser-known comics characters including *Little Orphan Annie, Nancy, Little Lulu, Little Audrey* and *Lil' Tomboy*. Abate reads these girls, who were by and large very unconventional, against the sociopolitical concerns and transformations of their times and, the rise of child psychology in the case of *Lil' Tomboy*. As comics history has often focused on boy characters, Abate's book expands on the relevance and prominence of girl characters in the early days of comics.

Broadening the potential corpora and means of studying the connections between children and comics, Mark Heimermann and Brittany Tullis's critical anthology *Picturing Childhood: Youth in Transnational Comics* (2017) has a geographically wide range and covers comics and themes ranging from *Little Orphan Annie* as a streetwalker (Woycik), the relationship between *RAW* magazine and the *Little Lit* comics edited by Mouly and Spiegelman (Saguisag) to child-animal hybridity in the *Sweet Tooth* graphic novels (Heimermann).

The newly burgeoning scholarship on children in comics covers both historical studies and analysis of child characters in graphic novels. It is noteworthy that the study of children in comics, unlike most of the other themes, is dominated by bringing to light older, often overlooked and forgotten, comics.

Intermedial and transmedial approaches

The cultural significance of the many ways comics can interact, influence and impact other media is an area of comics studies that has recently boomed. This section focuses on intermedial interactions and adaptations and the connections between comics and movements that have traversed visual and literary arts. It also broaches transmedia storytelling.

Much has been written about comics and adaptation. It has also been the subject of three anthologies, beginning with Stephen E. Tabachnick and Esther Bendit Saltzman's *Drawn from the Classics: Essays on Graphic Adaptations of Literary Works* (2015); *Comics and Adaptation* (2018), edited by Benoît Mitaine, David Roche and Isabelle Schmitt-Pitiot (translated from French by Aarnoud Rommens); and Évelyn Deprêtre and German A. Durante's *Transmédialité, bande dessinée et adaptation* (2019). Transposing Linda Hutcheon's and Robert Stam's work on adaptation theory, Tabachnick and Saltzman's volume focuses on comics versions of a wide range of literary classics ranging from *Beowulf* and Gustave Flaubert's *Madame Bovary* to Raymond Queneau's *Exercises in Style*. The other two volumes in contrast apply a broader concept of adaptation, to cover diverse kinds of transmedial connections where comics can be both adaptations (target texts) of works in other media or source texts that are adapted. Going even further, the *Transmédialité* volume inscribes itself in the discourse initiated by Henry Jenkins' concept of 'transmedia storytelling' to describe how the same story is told through different media. It also highlights the role of fandom. The volume devotes separate sections to comics adaptations of literature and cinematic adaptations of comics.

In her 2002 article, Irina Rajewsky neatly distinguishes between transmediality, intermediality and intertextuality. While intermediality refers to the 'crossing of borders between media', transmediality covers phenomena (motifs, stories) that move and coexist across media (46). In Jenkins' understanding of transmedia storytelling, media need to expand the franchise with additional stories or new aspects of the same world, for instance prequels or sequels or games that allow the audience to interact with the universe of a story but in a way where the individual story can be experienced independently (2003). He expands this *Convergence Culture* (2006) which explores how transmedia storytelling is impacted by digital media platforms and the very active and participatory role of fans in co-creating and interacting in storyworlds comprised of many stories in different media, including comics.

Looking at the field of comics, it becomes clear that many stories are not confined to the comics medium and often find new expressions across media. Similarly, stories originating in other media are reworked through text-image transpositions in the form of comics. Rarely do comics stories stay within their medium and there are many ways in which comics can find a new form. Recent scholarship has explored how stories from other media are transposed to comics (adaptation) and how comics can be situated and studied amidst these intermedial interchanges.

Armelle Blin-Roland examines adaptations across media in an original study of adaptations of two landmark twentieth-century novels: *Adapted Voices: Transpositions of Céline's* Voyage au bout de la nuit *and Queneau's* Zazie dans le metro (2015). Blin-Roland is especially interested in how the distinctive voices of Céline and Queneau are reworked or mirrored as their novels take new forms ranging from illustrated novels and comics to films, plays and even recorded readings.

Benoît Glaude's *La bande dialoguée: Une histoire des dialogues de bande dessinée (1830–1960)* [Comics in Dialogue: A History of Dialogues in Comic Strips] (2019) also focuses on the voice but, more specifically, on the representation of voice through the iconic word balloon. Beginning with Töpffer's *L'histoire de M. Cryptogame* (1846), Glaude delineates the nature and role of dialogues in different kinds of nineteenth-century imagetexts and the possible influence of the gestural and mimetic vocabulary of theatre. In addition to looking at the representation of music in comics in an interlude, Glaude considers word balloon monologues in adventure comics from the 1940s and 1960s before turning back to the 1950s, when scriptwriting for comics was recognized as a task in its own right, to highlight the centrality of the dialogue in diverse comics genres.

These two monographs are innovative additions to the discussions of comics and intermediality, which often focus on adaptations of novels into comics or comics into novels (also known as the phenomenon of novelization) as well as adaptations of comics into film. Another important intermedial dimension is the contextualization of comics in movements that spanned the arts while having their own legitimation struggles.

Julia Round's *Gothic in Comics and Graphic Novels: A Critical Approach* (2014) suggests possibilities of considering comics as a gothic medium due to its reliance on techniques that are comparable to those of gothic literature. Focusing on the comics of the Vertigo imprint, Round begins with a contextualization of British and American comics of the past few decades, highlighting their growing self-consciousness and emancipation from censorship. For her close readings, she discerns three symbols that are particularly relevant for a gothic reading of comics: the crypt, the spectre and the archive. Expanding her analysis to a discussion of communities and cultures built around comics and the Gothic, Round ends with studying the perpetuation of the quintessentially gothic (and ungraspable) figures of the vampire and the zombie.

Maaheen Ahmed's *Monstrous Imaginaries: The Legacy of Romanticism in Comics* (2019) also builds on drawing connections between a major cultural movement and comics. Examining good monsters in English-language and French-language contemporary comics, Ahmed shows how they channel Romantic elements such as the solitary protagonist; the quest; excessive emotions; the love for spectacles; and, above all, ambiguity and rebelliousness. In addition to tracing such characteristics back to Romantic classics such as Hugo's *The Hunchback of Notre-Dame* [*Notre-Dame de Paris*] (1831), she also draws out visual connections to works by Goya and Blake. While such intermedial connections are not unknown to comics, they are rarely broached outside the framework of adaptation studies.

This section provides brief insight into the variety of intermedial and transmedial approaches that can be used to deepen our understanding of comics. Such approaches underscore the importance of contextualizing comics in a broader media ecology and remembering the close connections between comics and other media.

Conclusion

This thematic discussion of comics scholarship identifies four main trends in comics criticism that have not been covered in other sections: history and memory; ethnic and religious diversity; children in comics; and intermedial approaches. The first and longest theme of documentation and memory is fed by interests ranging from comics journalism and the ethical issues and possibilities of documentation, reading history and politics in comics to trauma and memory studies. This section also provides a glimpse into the diverse possibilities of studying comics, be it through the literary and cultural studies movement of postcolonial criticism to considering comics as historical sources in their own right. The three other approaches are more recent. Studies on ethnic and religious diversity have generally focused on African American and Latinx comics, the many comics creators of Jewish heritage and, most recently, Muslim superheroes. Studies on children in comics currently have a strong focus on American comics even though Ian Gordon's pioneering *Kid Comic Strips* offers a comparatively global perspective on comics in English. Going beyond the more common trend of looking at comics adaptations of literature or film adaptations, the works discussed in the last section offer a more holistic approach to understanding the complex interactions between comics and other media.

These themes interact with the broader discourses of memory studies, multiculturalism and diversity, childhood studies, inter- and transmediality. While the corpora are dominated by graphic novels, certain themes, particularly diversity, children in comics, and the consideration of comics as 'cultural records' have attracted more historical overviews that turn to old, mainstream comics. Many of the themes discussed are closely connected to the popular genres discussed in the next chapter on popular genres. This includes the gendering of Romance comics and the novel readings of the superhero through, for instance, the lens of disability studies which builds on the growing interest in diversity.

Note

1. For further work on diversity and comics, see: Aldama, Frederick L. (2020) *Graphic Indigeneity: Comics in the Americas and Australasia*. Jackson, MS: University Press of Mississippi; Sheyashe, Michael A. (2013) *Native Americans in Comic Books: A Critical Study*. Jefferson, NC: McFarland; Foster III, William H. (2005) *Looking for a Face Like Mine*. Waterbury, CT: Fine Tooth Press; and, of course, Strömberg, Fredrik (2003) *Black Images in the Comics: A Visual History*. Seattle, WA: Fantagraphics. An annotated bibliography of indigenous comics and graphic novels by Taylor Daigneault, Amy Mazowita, Candida Rifkind and Camille Callison is accessible on the website of *Jeunesse: Young People, Texts, Cultures*. https://jeunessejournal.ca/index.php/yptc/article/view/504/395

Works cited

Abate, Michelle Ann. *Funny Girls: Guffaws, Guts and Gender in Classic American Comics*. Jackson, MS: University Press of Mississippi, 2019.

Abate, Michelle Ann and Sanders, Joe Sutliff (eds). *Good Grief! Children and Comics*. Columbus, OH: Ohio State University Press, 2016.

Adams, Jeff. *Graphic Novels and Social Realism*. Bern: Peter Lan, 2008.

Ahmed, Maaheen. *Monstrous Imaginaries: The Legacy of Romanticism in Comics*. Jackson, MS: University Press of Mississippi, 2019.

Ahmed, Maaheen and Crucifix, Benoît (eds). *Comics Memory: Archives and Styles*. New York: Palgrave, 2015.

Aldama, Frederick Luis. *Your Brain on Latino Comics: From Gus Arriola to Los Bros Hernandez*. Austin, TX: University of Texas Press, 2009.

Aldama, Frederick Luis (ed.) *Multicultural Comics: From Zap to Blue Beetle*. Austin, TX: University of Texas Press, 2011.

Aldama, Frederick Luis. *Latinx Superheroes in Mainstream Comics*. Tucson, AZ: University of Arizona Press, 2017.

Aldama, Frederick Luis (eds). *Graphic Indigeneity: Comics in the Americas and Australasia*. Jackson, MS: University Press of Mississippi, 2020.

Ayaka, Carolene and Hague, Ian (eds). *Representing Multiculturalism in Comics and Graphic Novels*. New York: Routledge, 2018.

Blin-Rolland, Armelle. *Adapted Voices: Transpositions of Céline's* Voyage au bout de la nuit *and Queneau's* Zazie dans le métro. Oxford: Legenda, 2015.

Chaney, Michael. 'The Child in and as Comics'. In *Remembered Reading: Mirrors, Masks and Mazes in the Autobiographical Graphic Novel*. Jackson, MS: University Press of Mississippi, 2015, pp. 57–94.

Chapman, Jane L., Hoyles, Anna, Kerr, Andrew and Sherif, Adam. *Comics and the World Wars: A Cultural Record*. New York: Palgrave, 2015a.

Chapman, Jane L., Hoyles, Anna, Kerr, Andrew, Sherif, Adam, Ellin, Dan and Sherif, Adam. *Comics, the Holocaust and Hiroshima*. New York: Palgrave Macmillan, 2015b.

Chute, Hillary. *Disaster Drawn: Visual Witness, Comics and Documentary Form*. Cambridge, MT: Harvard University Press, 2016.

Daigneault, (Métis)Taylor, Mazowita, Amy, Rifkind, Candida and Callison, Camille. 'Indigenous Comics and Graphic Novels: An Annotated Bibliography'. *Jeunesse: Young People, Texts, Cultures* 11:1, 2019: i–xxxvi. https://jeunessejournal.ca/index.php/yptc/article/view/504

Deprêtre, Èvelyne and Durante, German A. (eds). *Transmédialité, bande dessinée et adaptation*. Clermont-Ferrand: Presses universitaires Blaise Pascal, 2019.

Earle, Harriet E. H. *Comics, Trauma, and the New Art of War*. Jackson, MS: University Press of Mississippi, 2016.

Glaude, Benoît. *La bande dialoguée: une histoire des dialogues de bande dessinée (1830–1960)*. Tours: Presses universitaires François-Rabelais, 2019.

Gordon, Ian. *Kid Comic Strips: A Genre across Four Countries*. New York: Palgrave Macmillan, 2016.

Foster III, William H. *Looking for a Face Like Mine*. Waterbury, CT: Fine Tooth Press, 2005.

Heimermann, Mark and Tullis, Brittany (eds). *Picturing Childhood: Youth in Transnational Comics*. Austin, TX: University of Texas Press, 2017.

In 't Veld, Laurike. *The Representation of Genocide in Graphic Novels: Considering the Role of Kitsch*. New York: Palgrave Macmillan, 2019.

Jackson, Tim. *Pioneering Cartoonists of Color*. Jackson, MS: University Press of Mississippi, 2016.

Jenkins, Henry. 'Transmedia Storytelling'. *MIT Technology Review*, 2003. https://www.technologyreview.com/s/401760/transmedia-storytelling/ Accessed 20 February 2020.

Jenkins, Henry. *Convergence Culture*. New York: New York University Press, 2006.

Lewis, A. David and Lund, Martin (eds). *Muslim Superheroes: Comics, Islam and Representation*. Boston, MA: Ilex Foundation, 2017.

McKinney, Mark. *History and Politics in French-language Comics and Graphic Novels*. Jackson, MS: University Press of Mississippi, 2008.

Mehta, Binita and Mukherji, Pia (eds). *Postcolonial Comics: Texts, Identities*. New York: Routledge, 2015.

Mickwitz, Nina. *Documentary Comics: Graphic Truth-Telling in a Skeptical Age*. New York: Palgrave Macmillan, 2016.

Mitaine, Benoît, David, Roche and Schmitt-Pitiot, Isabelle (eds). *Comics and Adaptation*. Aarnoud Rommens (trans.). Jackson, MS: University Press of Mississippi, 2018.

Nabizadeh, Golnar. *Representation and Memory in Graphic Novels*. New York: Routledge, 2019.

Poblete, Juan and L'Hoeste, Héctor Fernández (eds). *Redrawing the Nation: National Identity in Latin/o American Comics*. New York: Palgrave, 2009.

Polak, Kate. *Ethics in the Gutter: Empathy and Historical Fiction in Comics*. Columbus, OH: Ohio State University Press, 2017.

Rajewsky, Irina O. 'Intermediality, Intertextuality, and Remediation: A Literary Perspective on Intermediality'. *Intermédialités* 6, Autumn 2005: 43–64. https://doi.org/10.7202/1005505ar

Round, Julia. *Gothic in Comics and Graphic Novels: A Critical Approach*. Jefferson, NC: McFarland, 2014.

Saguisag, Lara. *Incorrigibles and Innocents: Constructing Childhood and Citizenship in Progressive Era Comics*. New Brunswick, NJ: Rutgers University Press, 2018.

Schneider, Greice. *What Happens When Nothing Happens: Boredom and Everyday Life in Contemporary Comics*. Leuven: Leuven University Press, 2016.

Sheyashe, Michael A. *Native Americans in Comic Books: A Critical Study*. Jefferson, NC: McFarland, 2013.

Strömberg, Fredrik. *Black Images in the Comics: A Visual History*. Seattle, WA: Fantagraphics, 2003.

Tabachnick, Stephen E. and Bendit Saltzman, Esther (eds). *Drawn from the Classics: Essays on Graphic Adaptations of Literary Works*. Jefferson, NC: McFarland, 2015.

Worden, D. (ed.) *The Comics of Joe Sacco: Journalism in a Visual World*. Jackson, MS: University Press of Mississippi, 2015.

CHAPTER 9
POPULAR GENRES

This chapter summarizes the work of key critics who have focused on staple genres of comics. It opens with a thorough discussion of the American superhero, drawing on critical work that has approached and attempted to define this figure from a variety of angles. It also includes discussion of critical work that has focused on international superheroes. The focus is then turned to the horror genre, specifically in America and Britain. Its third section discusses scholarship on romance comics, including critical work on several American silver age titles, as well as scholarly analysis of various genres of British girls' comics.

Genre

The concept of genre is yet another contested term that has been interwoven in comics studies with the 'definition' debate and discussions about what makes a medium. Genre is a way of categorizing types of cultural expressions such as literature, film, music or comics and it can be culturally specific and mutable with time. Just as with the 'definition' discussion, genre is often used to exclude or include certain types of stories in a category, which helps manage the reader's expectations. By labelling a comic with a genre, the reader can expect certain conventions to be present just as publishers often use genre to give audiences a sense of what kind of story is being told. Catherine Abell's article 'Comics and Genre' (2012) emphasizes this understanding of genre as sets of conventions used for evaluation or interpretation of a work, but also stresses that these sets of conventions have developed within a community and that genre is both supported and challenged by this community. Sometimes, comics are themselves referred to as a genre, other times the term graphic novel is labelled a genre. In comics studies, great emphasis is often put on separating the medium of comics from the genres it can encompass, since many scholars note that the low status of comics as an art form originates in a conflation of medium and genre. This means that historically, comics have been thought of only as superhero stories, humorous strips or horror stories, limiting the perception of what kinds of stories can be told in the medium. Part of the reason for this confusion of genre and medium stems from the fact that, from its inception, comics as an art form relied on a few very popular genres that have shaped the history of comics; it is often emphasized how this conflation of the medium of comics with specific genres has made the medium appear more simplified and thus open to criticism. It has been stressed that comics as a medium is not limited to specific genres, but the issue of genre still looms large in comics scholarship and certain genres have received great attention.[1] In many of the studies discussed here, however, it becomes apparent that very clear distinctions between genres are hard to come by and that, most often, comics include characteristics from several genres. For example, a sci-fi comic will include elements of the romance and horror genres, or a superhero comic will have elements of sci-fi and humour, so the genres often supplement one another, and an analysis of comics based on genre will have to acknowledge that multiple genres might be on display. This section is dedicated to scholarship which addresses what might now be called 'the comics pendant to genre fiction' but which in comics remains a very central part of mainstream comics: popular genres that have shaped how comics are viewed and have developed as a medium.

The need for a system of classification or a set of boxes to sort different types of comics has been heavily influenced by other media and their genres. One of the first comprehensive presentations of comics in German, Reinhold Reitberger and Wolfgang Fuchs's extensively illustrated *Comics: Anatomie eines Massenmediums* (1971) [trans. as *Comics: Anatomy of a Mass Medium* (1972)], uses genres as one way of sorting the material. The authors note how comics at that point did not contain serious topics. Fuchs and Reitberger follow a brief introduction to formal characteristics of comics with a slew of examples of various genres. The main ones are humour and everyday life, adventure and melodrama, and superheroes; the first two especially are subdivided into other genres often thought of as comics genres. The different types of humour include 'fall guy' humour, a specific kind of humour which arises from the misfortunes of the humble, anonymous man of the masses; family humour; 'kid' humour; and funny animal humour. The adventure genres are categorized under 'Back to nature' (e.g. Tarzan); science fiction; 'The old tales of chivalry'; melodrama (romance); detection; war; and Western. Discussing censorship and the Comics Code, the book describes the horror genre and later comments on sex and satire as genres.

Comics: Anatomy of a Mass Medium mainly uses American comics examples in the first part but is notable because of its section on the European comics scene which describes a European comics tradition and provides examples from French, Belgian, German and British comics. This book is an early attempt at describing what comics are and uses genres as an important way of distinguishing between different types of comics.

Superheroes

The superhero originated in comics and is still an important genre in the medium, but it has also always been a transmedial phenomenon which has experienced great success, especially recently, with many superhero movies becoming Hollywood blockbusters. The dominance of superheroes as genre in American comics has led many scholars to address the genre, although its supposedly inferior status has meant this scholarship has sometimes struggled to be taken seriously. Charles Hatfield, Jeet Heer and Kent Worcester's *The Superhero Reader* (2013) points to the way comics scholarship is currently separating the form of comics from its many genres (xi). In insisting that the superhero genre merits attention, they also examine the conflict between superheroes and the graphic novel within the field of comics studies, indicating the critics of superhero comics who have often warmly promoted the graphic novel as an especially literary form of comics. The close and sometimes overlapping neighbourhoods of superhero comics scholars and fans have contributed to the disrespect towards scholarship on superheroes, since the enthusiasm of superhero fans is seen as a lack of professionalism and an uncritical practice. Hatfield, Heer and Worcester note that not all genres have been elevated evenly in the development of comics being perceived as an artform and that, although cultural studies approaches might find ideological aspects of the superheroes a valid area of research (see Chapter 2), the idea that superhero comics merit an aesthetic analysis is less common. The authors insist that a scholarly approach needs to take this two-sided problem into account and recognize that the superhero genre has developed as part of very specific historical, ideological and commercial contexts that cannot be ignored in serious debates involving superheroes. The scepticism from the Academy has also meant that superhero scholarship has historically been lacking. Recently, however, works on superheroes are pouring out of academic and independent publishers.

Richard Reynold's *Superheroes – A Modern Mythology* (1994), an early study of the superhero, offers an analysis of the superhero through a tentative definition, looking at different types of continuity and the relationship between myth and superhero. As our discussion of 'what is comics' showed (see Chapter 2), the definition of what superheroes are is at the centre of early superhero studies and, just like with the central definition discussion, this serves to delimit what *is* and what *is not* a superhero as well as offering examples of predecessors in an effort to name the first superhero. Definition criteria are reciprocally connected with how to determine who is the first superhero. Reynolds offers a list of features that can define the superhero, using the first Superman story as a standard mould:

1. Lost parents
2. The man-god
3. Justice
4. The normal and the superpowered
5. Secret identity
6. Superpowers and politics
7. Science as magic (1994: 10–16).

From this, Reynolds draws out a set of qualities that characterize the superhero as marked out from society, dedicated to justice, extraordinary compared to his/her surroundings (the qualities of their superheroic persona are contrasted with their mundane alter-egos) and using science as a kind of magic. Reynolds moves on to discuss continuity by addressing the superhero costume as a key element because the costume is one of the things separating superheroes from non-costumed heroes and it introduces one aspect of continuity by being stable despite different people donning the mask/costume. Finally, Reynolds considers the connection between myth and superhero, noting how the superhero is based on older myths (Greek, Roman, Norse) that have superheroic main characters. While the link is clear with a figure like Thor, Reynolds argues that modern superheroes work as myths that can be used to understand the society they appear in.

Definitional questions characterize genre studies and are also explored in Peter Coogan's *Superhero: The Secret Origin of a Genre* (2006). Coogan's definition is often quoted and stipulates that superheroes are defined by having a mission, powers, a split identity and a costume. Coogan bases his discussion of superheroes heavily on Thomas Schatz' *Hollywood Genres*

(1981) and, like Reynolds, looks for predecessors for superheroes in earlier pulp and mystery novels just as he looks for inspiration for 'the first superhero', Superman, in earlier characters such as The Phantom and Popeye.

Roz Kaveney's *Superheroes! Caped Crusaders in Comics and Film* (2008) explores the mainstream DC and Marvel multiverses, arguing for their significance as the largest narrative constructions in human culture (even exceeding the body of myth and legend that underlies Latin and Greek literature). Kaveney's critical readings consider various storylines, characters and collected editions as examples of epic narrative that challenge and explore concepts such as heroism, power and conflict. Her detailed discussion highlights the nuance of the concepts using her notion of the 'thick text', one that is valued for its allusive qualities. The analysis remains almost entirely, however, at the level of plot and narrative – little attention is paid to the visuals of these comics. The book is aimed at those with little experience of superhero comics who want to acquire insights into their value. To readers more familiar with the genre's themes and scholarship, the book offers detailed plot summaries into the backstories of various characters with brief reflections on their ideological significance.

As the scholarship on superheroes matured, it also developed away from general discussions of genre into more specialized analyses and interdisciplinary approaches which adopted theoretical perspectives from other fields and started focusing on emergent themes such as gender, the body and identity. For example, the superheroic body emerges as a key theme in Scott Bukatman's *Matters of Gravity: Special Effects and Supermen in the 20th Century* (2003). Bukatman considers superheroes on a transmedial scale that is original in its scope since it covers comics and films but also amusement parks and musicals. Bukatman investigates how superheroes absorb and rework many of modernity's concerns and shocks, such as technological developments, masquerading and wearing masks, and the impact of city life. All this is investigated through the centrality of the body.

The analysis of intersectional identities relating to the body is also the basis of José Alaniz' study *Death, Disability and the Superhero* (2014) which studies American silver age superhero comics building on theory from death and disability studies. As a way of framing his study, Alaniz points to previous studies of the superhero genre and notes how superheroes have been considered an American monomyth and discussed as an inherently fascist genre because physical dominance is a key component of the genre and a master–slave relationship is built into its origins. In focusing on the silver age superheroes, Alaniz picks a period where the superhero's powers begin to be questioned and we start to encounter disabled and dying heroes as part of the mainstream genres. He sees the development of the superhero genre in these years as a reaction against a crisis in American masculinity that starts appearing in the post-war years and further understands the silver age comics as deeply involved in attempting a discussion of death in America that has proven difficult throughout the years.

Looking at superhero stories through the lens of disability studies, Alaniz finds fault with the depiction of disability in many of the stories. Disability is sometimes shown as an illness that the patient just has to cure or shrouded in a language of 'overcoming' where the disabled person has to mentally overcome the challenge of being disabled, which is seen as a problem to be fixed. The notion that disability can and should be conquered by motivation is prevalent in many superhero narratives and has been criticized by modern disability studies. In a comparison between the *X-Men* series and the *Doom Patrol* series, Alaniz notes their many similarities but underlines how they differ in their depiction of disability. Whereas Professor Xavier is often portrayed as weak, not having any luck with women, being thrown out of his wheelchair and unable to fight his enemies without help, Caulder in *Doom Patrol* (who also uses a wheelchair) shows agency, has romantic relationships and employs his chair to charge at his enemies. Similarly, supervillains are often disfigured or disabled in a depiction that equates an inner with an outer which helps position the disabled characters as the radical 'Other' of society. In superhero stories, disabled characters are rarely depicted as people who are whole and complete and can live fulfilling lives where their disability is an accepted part of their being.

In the last part of the book, Alaniz uses a theoretical framework from death studies to analyse representations of death in superhero stories and to discuss how they reflect on discussion of death in society. He references Umberto Eco's famous essay (discussed in Chapters 2 and 4) to note how the superhero cannot die both for commercial and narrative reasons. The superhero serial has to continue, but still there have been several cases of dead superheroes that have for the most part turned out to be 'what if' deaths, in parallel universes or alternate realities, so the death could be undone and the superhero continue to star in comics and help sell them. Alaniz concludes by emphasizing that the perspective of death and disability studies helps expose central anxieties within the genre of superhero comics and affirms that the depiction of disabled characters and nuanced treatments of their lives are important both to the disabled community and to able-bodied readers.

Although the superhero genre is one of the most distinctly American genres, it has made it to other places on the globe, very often in a form that both honours its American origins and reflects the local traditions and culture. In his historical survey *The British Superhero* (2017), Chris Murray compares the American original with the ways in which British superheroes have manifested themselves throughout the decades and the ways British authors have influenced the American superhero tradition. As Murray notes, the idea of a British superhero seems like a paradox because the superhero genre revolves around 'truth, justice and the *American* way' (2017: 3), but the British superhero does have a history, albeit with certain detours that make it differ from its American origins. Murray begins by charting the predecessors of the genre in Britain through an overview of different types of popular magazines, adventure papers and schoolboy stories, mostly in text-only form, which set the scene for the superhero later. Notably, British magazines sported stories about 'mystery flying men' and were influenced by other genres such as the horror and gothic of the 'penny dreadfuls'. Often these protagonists were the villains or at least not the clean-cut heroes known from American magazines; according to Murray, this indicates some early differences between British and American superheroes: the British superhero often parodies or subverts the American superhero genre model, in particular by detaching itself from the straitlaced heroics and overt patriotism of its American counterpart. Murray connects these differences to the different cultural and historical contexts of the heroes, commenting for instance that the spectacular heroics of Spider-Man swinging in his webs across Manhattan in the post-Second World War USA do not translate to the dreary reality of a Britain that had severe economic difficulties following the war. Perhaps the biggest importance of British superheroes comes from the deconstruction of the genre in the 1980s with the so-called 'British invasion' when British writers started writing superheroes published by American companies in ways that challenged the idea of the superhero. Alan Moore spearheaded the invasion when he was asked to write *Swamp Thing* for DC Comics, but it was his later work *Watchmen*, drawn by fellow Briton Dave Gibbons, that challenged the core foundations of the superhero for good, opening the doors for writers and artists like Neil Gaiman, Grant Morrison, Frank Quitely and Garth Ennis to work on American superhero titles. These creators had a huge influence on the genre with what was considered darker and more subversive comics that also represented political and philosophical content that departed from a predictably patriotic superhero.

Horror

Horror has long been a central genre in comics, but American horror comics definitively caught the attention of readers, parents, teachers, politicians and researchers in the 1950s (see Chapter 3). Michael Walton's 2019 book *The Horror Comic Never Dies* offers a good history of the development of the genre in the United States, with descriptions of early publications, the moral panic of the 1950s and the Comics Code, and more recent instances of horror comics from both mainstream publishers like Marvel and smaller comics publishers like Dark Horse Comics, Image and Fantagraphics. This book serves as a comprehensive general introduction to the genre and the main events in its history in the United States.

Critical approaches to American horror comics generally focus on the genre's use of tropes such as monstrosity with relevance to cultural context (specifically war and politics), moral messages, or intersectionality. Martin Barker has paid special attention to the political backdrop to the horror comics debate and his *A Haunt of Fears: The Strange History of the British Horror Comics Campaign* (1992) dissects the motives underlying the discussion of horror comics in Britain. Barker criticizes the campaign against horror comics for not theorizing thoroughly enough about the comics and for not actually reading the comics themselves. He then proceeds to map out the many parties involved in this campaign and their various motives for agitating against comics (and very often specifically horror comics). Barker tests their arguments against his analysis of selected comics, using as his case studies the most notorious stories cited in the press and in court ('The Orphan', 'The Way to a Man's Heart' and 'You, Murderer') which he also reprints in full. He questions some of the problematic assumptions in the accusations against the horror comics. He argues that it is difficult to know precisely what the child readers are taking from the stories. Not understanding the basics of how the horror genre works leads the critics to wrong conclusions about how the children interact with the stories. For instance, Barker argues that the fear of the impact on readers relies on a potentially wrong assumption that children are inspired by what they read and want to mimic the actions of the characters in the stories. Assuming this means not crediting the reader with the understanding that horror comics are fiction and often act as parody. Barker argues that horror comics allow the reader to worry and think about difficult and less wholesome concepts and ideas and that this is in fact not a bad thing. He demonstrates that the strategies of shock logic, social commentary, parody and self-awareness are consistently employed in the service of moral lessons, and are all ignored by the critics. He concludes that the campaigners against the comics somehow completely misread these books: finding in them the opposite of what is actually there, based on their own political and ideological assumptions. The book ends with an appendix that flags up an overlooked type of comic that should have been a real cause of concern: the Korean War comic, whose use of 'horrifying normality' in violent wartime scenes naturalizes its overt and jingoistic messages of anti-communism.

Other critical articles about horror comics also focus on war and its political impact, such as Smith and Goodrum's 'Corpses … Coast to Coast! Trauma, Gender and Race in 1950s Horror Comics' (2017). This explores the presence of nuclear war as both backdrop and theme in the 1950s horror comics, and the ways in which these titles explored issues of PTSD and the veteran and refugee experience, and the victimization of women. Smith and Goodrum conclude that the genre had a complex relationship to contemporary sociopolitical conditions and offered many unpalatable truths in its articulation of the Cold War fears and trauma. Goodrum's current work extends this focus to consider the political import of horror, for example noting the role of imperialism in zombie comics of the 1950s ('The Past That Will Not Die', 2020), and his book *Printing Terror* explores the relationship between American horror comics and the Cold War.

Publishers EC Comics were at the centre of the American discussion of horror comics, specifically because owner William Gaines gave a now-famous witness statement at the Kefauver hearings. Qiana Whitted's book *EC Comics: Race, Shock & Social Protest* (2019) examines EC Comics' intentional use of genre and the way it used its reputation as a publisher of shock and entertainment to address contemporary social issues. Whitted argues that the constraints of well-known genres at EC and the publisher's relationship with its readers made it possible to create stories which challenged social norms and called out racial prejudice, religious intolerance and anti-communist debates. 'The Preachies', as the stories were called, used the popular format of suspense stories in comics to relay a moral message. Whitted argues that the genre conventions helped EC convey their political messages and that the positive interactions with readers through the letters pages (most reactions were positive) made it possible for EC comics to put controversial issues on the agenda. The story 'Judgement Day' is an example of how EC uses the genre of science fiction to discuss racial segregation, and the use of a Black man as its protagonist resulted in it not being approved by the Comics Code, but EC published it anyway. By insisting on a non-caricatured Black man as its main figure and by showing him addressing the segregation of blue and orange robots on a planet far from Earth as less civilized, EC Comics made important advances in civil rights part of their entertaining comics series. *EC Comics* concludes that EC Comics was an important player in the civil rights movement because it brought the idea of social engagement through art into the public sphere and found a space within the genres of horror and sci-fi for stories that engaged the audience and exposed them to a general civil rights fight. These intersectional identity issues also inform Smith and Goodrum's work discussed above. EC Comics' role in developing comic-book horror and its impact on American society is also the focus of other scholars.

David Hajdu's work (see Chapter 3) considers the early creation of this industry and its impact on American culture. Terrence Wandtke's *The Comics Scare Returns: The Contemporary Resurgence of Horror Comics* (2018) returns to Bill Gaines' witness statement and uses it to structure its analysis of the re-emergence of contemporary horror and to trace a line from early incarnations to some of the most popular American comics of today. Wandtke argues that horror has resonated in comics from the 1950s boom to the present day, where it figures strongly in works from star creators like Moore, Gaiman, Mignola and Kirkman (see Chapter 6). He explores the origins of horror (oral folktales) and examines the genre's early presence in dime novels, penny dreadfuls, pulp fiction magazines and cinema, drawing attention to the dominance of monster characters and sensationalism, and contrasting this with the most popular American horror comics, which were 'realistic and sophisticated' (18) – more about inhumanity and cultural anxiety than established archetypes. Wandtke reflects particularly on EC's continued fame (despite their small market share) and considers the post-Code market and the work of publishers like Warren who negated the Code by producing black-and-white 'magazines', also noting the less accomplished texts from publishers such as Skywald and Eerie. Wandtke follows this with a closer look at DC and Marvel, noting particularly the way that host characters and story events blur the 'real' world and (layers of) fiction.

Wandtke's remaining chapters explore the work of Alan Moore (*Swamp Thing, From Hell*), Neil Gaiman (*Sandman*), Mike Mignola (*Hellboy*), Eric Powell (*The Goon*) and Robert Kirkman (*The Walking Dead*), tying analysis of each writer's work to one aspect of Gaines' testimony. He argues that

Moore and Gaines share the view that comics are an art form that works by new rules, with the power to reach a vast audience in a meaningful and entertaining way, and that Moore's work on *Swamp Thing* not only engages with key horror tropes such as abjection (through both sex and violence), but also evidences the way that horror continually exists beneath the surface of society as it absorbs older characters and story arcs. This is cemented further as Wandtke argues that *From Hell* reflects the commodification and embedded nature of horror and (s)exploitation in our culture. His following analysis of Gaiman's *Sandman* is structured around Gaines and Gaiman's arguments about the pleasures of horror; the work of Mignola and Powell is considered against the much-debated relationship between good/bad taste, absurdity and horror; and the concluding analysis of Kirkman's *Walking Dead* franchise is based around Gaines' claim (and EC Comics' common theme) that moral messages can exist within distasteful material. Wandtke argues that each of these mainstream horror comics has reconfigured the industry and its publishing practices in unique ways, and that the comics medium continues to share affinities with the dynamism and critical capability of folktale horror.

As the American horror comics gained global notoriety, many lavish collections emerged, including numerous volumes of the EC Archives, collections dedicated to the work of high-profile artists such as Richard Corben, and others with a more general scope, such as *The Horror! The Horror!* (Trombetta, 2010) and *Four Color Fear* (Sadowski, 2010). Some of these, such as Sadowski and Trombetta, contain useful commentary on the stories and their creators and reprint some lesser-known stories. Alongside this, many other reference books on American horror comics exist, such as William Schoell's *The Horror Comics: Fiends, Freaks and Fantastic Creatures, 1940s–1980s* (2014). Schoell proceeds chronologically through the gold, silver and bronze ages of American comics history and dedicates each chapter to one publisher (or a group linked by competition or status) and describes the different comics they released. These sections are entirely made up of summaries of the stories and although Schoell notes the artists who worked on these titles where known, there is no visual analysis or commentary. The book is, however, a helpful reference source for those wanting to know more about the comics published by early companies like American Comics Group and Prize Comics, or smaller publishers like Ace, Avon, Quality, and more, and the story summaries are a useful record as many of these comics have not yet been collected and reprinted.

Romance

Romance comics have at different times and in various international contexts been a very popular and significant genre, but popularity does not automatically attract academic attention. Although romance comics were a significant part of comics in the Anglophone world, there is very little scholarship in this field. Existing studies cohere around five main areas. Survey-type books describe the breadth and range of titles published, often giving story summaries, or noting the varied aesthetic of the titles, which ranged from cheap and flimsy to glossy magazines. Audience-based analyses explore the wide readership (from schoolgirls to married women) and how they were catered for. There are several ideological readings that flag up moral messages or sexist content, and finally a selection of cultural critiques that relate the comics to contextual shifts within teen culture, social norms or political movements such as equal rights. These often focus on a particular aspect of these anthology comics, such as the problem page, the fictionalized host/editor figures, or the story content. Finally, some work also points to the international connections between titles, arguing that the relationship between them is perhaps closer than has been realized.

In her descriptive overview of American romance comics, *Love on the Racks* (2008), Michelle Nolan works from the perspective of the comics collector and makes a comprehensive survey of the many titles and publishers that populated the field of comics in a period of thirty years from 1947 to 1977. She estimates nearly 6000 titles made their way to the shelves and meticulously lists the multiplicity of titles grouped chronologically. Nolan posits that much of the material for this history of romance comics has been saved by eager fans and comics collectors and highlights the importance of comics collectors in accumulating valuable sources for comics historians. She argues that unlike the popular superheroes, romance comics were primarily aimed at a female audience, which in turn might explain the lack of academic interest afforded them (Gibson [2015] and Round [2019] also make this argument). Nolan predominantly writes summaries of individual stories and tracks themes and the chaotic rise and demise of publishers of romance comics but refrains from close readings or any overarching analyses of the comics. From the very simply described pulp predecessors or romance comics to the heroines depicted throughout most of this period, women were rarely given agency in these stories and historical contexts were often used as pretext for a romantic encounter, preferably with a bit of scandal involved. As the underground comics movements developed and women were given more nuanced portrayals as well as entering fandom and the creator side more prominently, the era of romance comics was over in American mainstream comics and love stories found different forms and outlets in the comics medium.

An equivalent book exploring British publications is Susan Brewer's *A History of Girls' Comics* (2010). The British romance comics began in the mid-1950s and dominated the following decade through titles such as *Marilyn* (Amalgamated, 1955–65), *Valentine* (Amalgamated, 1957–74), *Roxy* (Amalgamated, 1958–63), *Mirabelle* (Pearson, 1956–77), *Romeo* (DC Thomson, 1957–74) and *Jackie* (DC Thomson, 1964–93) – an exceptional comic that by the early 1970s was selling over a million copies per issue (Sabin, 1996: 84). Brewer dedicates a chapter to this genre that gives short descriptive summaries of each title, sometimes noting key stories and themes. Paul Gravett and Peter Stanbury's *Great British Comics* (2006), Roger Sabin's *Comics, Comix and Graphic Novels* (1996) and James Chapman's *British Comics* (2011) all have brief accounts of the British romance titles; these are predominantly summaries of the main titles with some analysis of their key themes (see further below). *Jackie* in particular is a point of focus; Joan Ormrod's 'Reading Production and Culture' (2018) argues, however, that comics scholarship's predominant focus on this blockbuster comic has prevented exploration of the origins and build-up of this comics genre, as *Jackie* began in 1964.

Scholars such as Penny Tinkler (1995, 2014), Joan Ormrod, Alan Kidd and Melanie Tebbutt have investigated the way in which (British) romance comics and other women's magazines catered for a varied readership. Tinkler's article 'Are You Really Living?' (2014: 600) surveys young women's magazines in the 1960s and suggests that there is a 'noticeable shift around 1963 towards a more youthful and dynamic image'. Joan Ormrod's 'The Case of the Curious Speech Bubbles' (2016) also notes a wide readership, using analysis of the story content to argue that *Mirabelle* was initially aimed at older women, as story protagonists were often married and themes included subjects like miscarriage, but that subsequent mergers with titles such as *Glamour* (1958) created a younger target audience. Other critics such as Alan Kidd and Melanie Tebbutt focus on a particular aspect of these comics (such as the problem page) to identify changes to the audience of a single comic. Kidd and Tebbutt's chapter 'From "Marriage Bureau" to "Points of View"' (2017) analyses the changing tone and nature of the guidance given in *Mirabelle* across two decades, noting a consistently strong moral tone alongside a decreasing emphasis on passivity. They compare their results to the work of scholars such as Angela McRobbie (see below) and against the advice pages of other British periodicals. This chapter includes a survey of different romance titles and their average audience age, alongside changes in sales figures that characterized the 1960s.

Early ideological readings of romance comics often form part of a bigger project focusing on magazines or girlhood. Pioneering examples include the works of Alderson (1968), Sharpe (1976) and Walkerdine (1984), all of whom argue that these publications offer undesirable stereotypes and oppressive role models based around escapism, simplicity and passivity. Later critics like Chapman (2010: 111) echo this angle, with claims that girls' comics construct a 'socially approved model of adolescent femininity'. Perhaps the most famous ideological critique of the romance comics genre is that of Angela McRobbie (1978a, 1987b, 1981, 1991), who uses analysis of *Jackie* to argue that these titles convey a clear message of conformity. McRobbie's parsing identifies four codes (romance, fashion and beauty, pop, and personal and domestic life) within the romance comics, which transmit clear criteria of acceptability in these fields. She acknowledges readers' agency in negotiating readings but focuses on the messages of conformity conveyed, particularly by the problem pages. As noted in Chapter 3, however, Martin Barker has disputed this work and argued that these comics are less unified than McRobbie's analysis suggests.

More recent ideological and cultural critiques of the romance genre in comics include the work of Sydney Heifler. Her 'Teen Age Temptations: How Romance Comic Books Condemned Precocity' (2015) explores the ideological links between American romance comics and the war effort, and gives close readings of stories that reflect the changing context of dating and courtship pre- and post-Second World War (which saw a movement from multiple dates that were treated as light-hearted commodities towards 'going steady' and parental fears of increased sexual intimacy). Heifler focuses on the educational tone and interpellation within the stories around the theme of anti-precocity. Her work also includes several blog posts (2018a, 2018b) that highlight the anti-feminist messages of these comics, which often supported ideas of 'women's lib' within the workplace, but not within romantic relationships. This angle is also seen in the work of other critics, such as Jeanne Emerson Gardner's 'She Got Her Man, but Could She Keep Him? Love and Marriage in American Romance Comics, 1947–1954' (2013). Gardner focuses on the way these romance comics portray female experience and set the boundaries for women's love life in this period. She notes that the stories are about and aimed at white middle-class young women and offer a very narrow concept of both dating and married life that places the responsibility of acting properly entirely upon the women. Gardner emphasizes that the stories often take the women's feelings and frustrations very seriously, but that they nonetheless conclude by confirming how a proper woman and wife 'should' behave. Continuing this analysis into later decades, Kidd and Tebbutt (2017) note that British romance comics continued to change to follow trends in the 1970s as social norms affected girls' own views of appropriate feminine behaviour (e.g. regarding women's lib). The comics foregrounded these questions, as readers' own experiences began to replace fictional photo stories, and men became increasingly objectified.

Cultural readings of the relationship between the romance genre and pop music in Britain are also of interest: Alderson (1968) notes that by 1966, 50 per cent of the comics' content was devoted to pop, and Ormrod's 'Reading Production and Culture' (2018) notes a steady increase of pop content throughout the decades. Ormrod argues that the British romance comics provided a vital access point to pop music in the 1950s and 1960s, which was wildly popular but largely unavailable via UK mass media. She demonstrates that British pop stars saturated the pages of British comics (advice columns, text and graphic stories, features, editorials, free gifts), mimicking aspects of American culture, but via much more accessible figures. Ormrod explores the religious treatment and 'sacred discourse' around stars and how this appears in the story structures of these comics (the quest and the magical donor), as well as through free gifts that directly address the fan and invite them into the star's world/presence. This work is developed further in Ormrod's online essay 'Promoting Tommy Steele through 1950s UK Comics' (2019), which examines *Marilyn*'s construction of this British pop star.

While this section has focused on the American and British industries, some recent work flags the international influences on these comics. David Roach's *Masters of Spanish Comic Art* (2017) notes the dominance of Spanish artists within the British industry and reflects on their impact. In her study of readers and memory, Mel Gibson's *Remembered Reading* (2015) notes a relationship of imitation between the British and the American romance titles, claiming that the British industry developed its titles in response to the popularity of the American comics, while also developing romance content from pre-war British story papers. Joan Ormrod investigates the genre's origins further in her analysis of the speech balloons in *Mirabelle*, noting that this title was modelled on the Italian magazine *Grand Hotel*, and that sharing material transnationally was common: for example other British titles, such as *Romeo*, published American material from Timely comics (Marvel after 1960) and *The Chicago Tribune*. Kidd and Tebbutt (2017) also expose links between the countries, arguing that the British comics adopted their dynamism and forcefulness from US comics in the 1960s.

Conclusion

Comics and genre exist together in an uneasy relationship that has influenced the way studies about genre comics have been pursued. The fusion of the comics medium with certain genres which have been considered low culture has affected the quest for legitimization that comics scholarship has suffered from. Some of the most popular genres in comics are not the ones getting the most attention from scholars, which suggests that these genres still bear a stigma of low culture. The scholarship around genres in comics shows, however, a great diversity and mixing of genres. Comics draw heavily on genres established in other media as well as developing ones created in the medium, although the limits of genre conventions sometimes become a straitjacket and prevent narratives from being truly subversive and breaking new ground.

Moving from the super popular genres to the supposed fringes of the comics medium, our next chapter takes us outside the mainstream where superheroes, horror and romance are not the centre of discussion.

Note

1. See for instance McCloud, Scott (1993) *Understanding Comics: The Invisible Art*. Northampton, MA: Kitchen Sink Press, 6; Wolk, Douglas (2007) *Reading Comics: How Graphic Novels Work and What They Mean*. Cambridge, MA: Da Capo Press: 12.

Works cited

Abell, Catherine. 'Comics and Genre'. In Aaron Meskin and Roy T. Cook (eds), *The Art of Comics: A Philosophical Approach*. Chichester: Blackwell Publishing, 2012, pp. 68–84.
Alaniz, José. *Death, Disability, and the Superhero: The Silver Age and Beyond*. Jackson, MS: University Press of Mississippi, 2014.

Alderson, Connie. *Magazines Teenagers Read with Special Reference to* Trend, Jackie, *and* Valentine. London: Pergamon Press, 1968.

Barker, Martin. *A Haunt of Fears: The Strange History of the British Horror Comics Campaign.* London: Pluto Press, 1984.

Brewer, Susan. *A History of Girls' Comics.* Barnsley: Pen & Sword Books Ltd, 2010.

Chapman, James. *British Comics: A Cultural History.* London: Reaktion Books, 2011.

Coogan, Peter M. and O'Neil, Dennis. *Superhero: The Secret Origin of a Genre.* Austin, TX: MonkeyBrain Books, 2006.

Gardner, Jeanne Emerson. 'She Got Her Man, but Could She Keep Him? Love and Marriage in American Romance Comics, 1947–1954'. *Journal of American Culture* 36:1, March 2013: 16–24.

Gibson, Mel. *Remembered Reading: Memory, Comics and Post-War Constructions of British Girlhood.* Leuven: Leuven University Press, 2015.

Goodrum, Michael. 'The Past That Will Not Die: Trauma, Race and Zombie Empire in Horror Comics of the 1950s'. In Dominic Davies and Candida Rifkind (eds), *Documenting Trauma in Comics: Traumatic Pasts, Embodied Histories, and Graphic Reportage.* London: Palgrave Macmillan, 2020, pp. 69–84.

Goodrum, Michael. *Printing Terror: American Horror Comics as Cold War Commentary and Critique.* Manchester: University of Manchester Press, 2021.

Gravett, Paul and Stanbury, Peter. *Great British Comics.* London: Aurum Press, 2006.

Hatfield, Charles, Heer, Jeet and Worcester, Kent (eds). *The Superhero Reader.* Jackson, MS: University Press of Mississippi, 2013.

Heifler, Sydney. 'TeenAge Temptations: How Romance Comic Books Condemned Precocity'. *Prized Writing*, 2015–16: 97–111. https://prizedwriting.ucdavis. edu/sites/prizedwriting.ucdavis.edu/files/users/mtrujil3/97PW%20Heifler.pdf. Accessed 21 January 2020.

Heifler, Sydney. 'Comic books v. "Women's Lib"'. *Re-reading the Second Wave*, March 2018a. https://hyenainpetticoatsblog.wordpress.com/2018/03/10/comic-books-v-womens-lib/. Accessed 21 January 2020.

Heifler, Sydney. 'Romance Comic Books, the Cold War, and Teaching Women Their Place. Ex Aula: Research From the Hall', March 2018b. http://mcr.seh.ox.ac. uk/romance-comic-books-the-cold-war-and-teaching-women-their-place/. Accessed 21 January 2020.

Kaveney, Roz. *Superheroes!: Capes and Crusaders in Comics and Films.* London: I.B. Tauris, 2008.

Kidd, Alan and Tebbutt, Melanie. 'From "Marriage Bureau" to "Points of View". Changing Patterns of Advice in Teenage Magazines: *Mirabelle*, 1956–1977'. In Alan Kidd and Tebbutt Melanie (eds), *People, Places and Identities.* Manchester: Manchester University Press, 2017, pp. 180–201.

McRobbie, Angela. '*Jackie*: An Ideology of Adolescent Femininity'. Occasional paper. Centre for Cultural Studies. University of Birmingham, 1978a.

McRobbie, Angela. 'Working Class Girls and the Culture of Femininity'. In Women's Studies Group, Centre for Contemporary Cultural Studies (ed.), *Women Take Issue: Aspects of Women's Subordination.* London: Hutchinson, 1978b, pp. 96–108.

McRobbie, Angela. *Feminism and Youth Culture: From* Jackie *to* Just Seventeen. London: Macmillan, 1991.

McRobbie, Angela. 'Just like a *Jackie* Story' [1981]. In McRobbie Angela and Trisha McCabe (eds), *Feminism for Girls: An Adventure Story*. London: Routledge, 2013, pp. 113–128.

McCloud, Scott. *Understanding Comics: The Invisible Art*. Northampton, MA: Kitchen Sink Press, 1993.

Murray, Chris. *The British Superhero*. Jackson: University Press of Mississippi, 2017.

Nolan, Michelle. *Love on the Racks: A History of American Romance Comics*. Jefferson, NC: McFarland, 2008.

Ormrod, Joan. 'The Case of the Curious Speech Bubbles'. Unpublished Conference Paper. Femorabilia. Liverpool: Liverpool John Moore's University, 2016.

Ormrod, Joan. 'Reading Production and Culture'. *Girlhood Studies* 11:3, 2016: 18–33. https://www.berghahnjournals.com/view/journals/girlhood-studies/11/3/ghs110304.xml. Accessed 20 January 2020.

Ormrod, Joan. 'Promoting Tommy Steele through 1950s UK Comics'. Confessions of an Aca-Fan. http://henryjenkins.org/blog/2019/11/10/promoting-tommy-steele-through-1950s-uk-comics-part-i-by-joan-ormrod. Accessed 20 January 2020.

Reitberger, Reinhold and Fuchs, Wolfgang J. *Comics: Anatomy of a Mass Medium*. Boston, MA: Little Brown, 1972.

Reynolds, Richard. *Super Heroes: A Modern Mythology*. Jackson, MS: University Press of Mississippi, 1994.

Roach, David. *Masters of Spanish Comic Book Art*. Mt. Laurel, NJ: Dynamite, 2017.

Round, Julia. *Gothic for Girls:* Misty *and British Comics*. Jackson, MS: University Press of Mississippi, 2019.

Sadowski, Greg. *Four Color Fear: Forgotten Horror Comics of the 1950s*. Seattle, WA: Fantagraphics, 2010.

Schatz, Thomas. *Hollywood Genres: Formulas, Filmmaking, and the Studio System*. New York: Random House, 1981.

Schoell, William. *The Horror Comics: Fiends, Freaks and Fantastic Creatures 1940s–1980s*. Jefferson, NC: McFarland, 2014.

Sharpe, Sue. *Just like a Girl: How Girls Learn to Be Women*. Harmondsworth: Penguin, 1976.

Smith, Philip and Goodrum, Michael. '"Corpses…Coast to Coast!" Trauma, Gender, and Race in 1950s Horror Comics'. *Literature Compass* 14:9, 2017: 1–15.

Tinkler, Penny. *Constructing Girlhood: Popular Magazines for Girls: Growing Up in England, 1920–1950*. London: Taylor and Francis, 1995.

Tinkler, Penny. '"Are You Really Living?" If Not, "Get With It!": The Teenage Self and Lifestyle in Young Women's Magazines, Britain 1957–70'. *Cultural and Social History: The Journal of the Social History Society* 11:4, 2014: 597–619. https://doi.org/10.2752/147800414X14056862572186. Accessed 29 July 2018.

Trombetta, Jim. *The Horror! The Horror! Comic Books the Government Didn't Want You to Read*. New York: Abrams, 2010.

Walkerdine, Valerie. 'Some Day My Prince Will Come: Young Girls and the Preparation for Adolescent Sexuality'. In Angela McRobbie and Mica Nava (eds), *Gender and Generation*. London: Macmillan, 1984, pp. 162–184.

Walton, Michael. *The Horror Comic Never Dies: A Grisly History*. Jefferson, NC: McFarland and Company, 2019.

Wandtke, Terrence R. *The Comics Scare Returns: The Contemporary Resurgence of Horror Comics*. Rochester, NY: RIT Press, 2018.

Whitted, Qiana J. *EC Comics: Race, Shock, and Social Protest*. New Brunswick, NJ: Rutgers University Press, 2019.

Wolk, Douglas. *Reading Comics: How Graphic Novels Work and What They Mean*. Cambridge, MA: Da Capo Press, 2007.

CHAPTER 10
OUTSIDE THE MAINSTREAM

This chapter discusses critics who have addressed titles or genres that exist outside the mainstream of comics publishing. It is notable that, due to Anglocentricity in scholarship, publishing and franchising, whole cultures of comics could in fact be considered 'outside the mainstream', as Marco Farrajota (2015) suggests in his discussion of Portuguese comics. This chapter incorporates this awareness although its focus primarily alternates between Europe and America. It opens by exploring research into the underground in the UK and the United States after the introduction of the Comics Code in 1954 and extends this into a closer look at the scholarship surrounding 'autobiographix' (autobiographical comics), as an increasingly dominant presence in independent comics, zines and graphic novels. In so doing, it touches upon marginalized voices from female and minority creators and demonstrates that comics' treatment of life writing has enabled the medium to critically engage with the key issues of authenticity and representation that characterize the genre. The second half of this chapter covers sources on the establishment and significance of alternative publishers in France and Belgium with a focus on artists collectives such as L'Association and Fremok. Given the close connections of such alternative presses to fan practices, the section also includes a brief discussion of sources on fanzines and the small press in Francophone contexts.

Underground comix in North America and the UK

While small press and underground comics are often ignored by the popular press, who claim comics 'grew up' in the 1980s with the emergence of mainstream graphic novels, several scholars have researched these publications. When critics speak about American and British underground 'comix' they generally refer to the 1960s, when these small press titles gained in popularity due to the decade's counterculture. However, independent comics date back much further and evolved alongside the more mainstream books and strips – for example, the small eight-page pamphlets published in America from the 1920s onwards: most commonly remembered are the 'Tijuana Bibles' and fetish pamphlets which depicted sexual scenarios, but also included parody and more political books.

The most prominent scholarship in this field often draws on personal interviews and anecdotes and puts different genres and cultures in dialogue with each other (as many notorious titles were exported and shared). Roger Sabin's *Adult Comics* (1993) has three parts, which discuss, respectively, Britain, America and the rest of the world. Sabin traces the existence of comics for adults in England back to satirical illustrated literature (Hogarth, Rowlandson, Gillray, Cruikshank et al.), which was well established by the early nineteenth century, but gave way to a predominantly children's market of weekly titles by the early twentieth century. He proceeds to explore the emergence of titles and markets, up until the 'graphic novel' boom of the 1980s. Part 2 gives an overview of the rise of the 1960s American underground in response to the Comics Code. The third part of his book examines the development of the industry in Europe and Japan. Each section tells a now-familiar story of how comics' popularity gave way to attacks that (to a greater or lesser degree) led to their main audience being more narrowly defined as children, alongside a popular (but often critically ignored) underground or alternative market. Sabin also discusses the relationship between comics and other media and genres (movies, television, science fiction and fantasy) and the emergence of female creators, and ends by contextualizing the 1980s graphic novel (and the new wave of superstar creators) against this history. Overall, Sabin's argument is retrospective, demonstrating that adult comics have always been around, just largely ignored; he supports this with numerous examples woven into a linear narrative. Each chapter also contains useful suggestions for further reading (many referenced below).

Many of the other books exploring the underground have a narrower, but more immediate, focus. For example, Mark Estren's *A History of Underground Comics* (1974) is a snapshot of the medium that also appears immersed in it. Published just seven years after the generally accepted start of the American underground (R. Crumb's *Zap* #1, 1967), it gives a close-up and detailed picture of the ideas and assumptions of the industry and its participants, conveyed in the present tense and in an anecdotal style. Nonetheless, it is full of information about the development of the underground movement and the creators, publishers, distributors and readers that enabled it. After surveying the inspirations and forerunners to the underground, and detailing how it developed, Estren summarizes its pioneers and main themes, before looking more closely at their depictions of sex, violence, politics and drugs. He also explores censorship and suppression and the migration of these creators and their work into the mainstream. His focus is solely on the US industry and the book draws heavily on the words of the creators themselves, rather than any analysis of their work, although it is crammed with black-and-white reprinted extracts from the comics. As such, and also due to its time of publication, it is a useful primary resource for those studying this period.

Les Daniels' *Comix: A History of Comic Books in America* (1973) is a general history (discussed in more depth in Chapter 5), but contains a section dedicated to underground comics. Like Estren's book, it was written while the comics themselves were being published and with no awareness of the place they would hold in history. Because of this it looks back to the underground's predecessors, noting the overlooked political content of some of the early eight-pagers, and reprinting extracts from both the 1920s and 1960s comics.

Dez Skinn's well-illustrated small-format book *Comix: The Underground Revolution* (2004), introduced by small-press pioneer Denis Kitchen, traces the development of underground comics, acknowledging their accepted beginnings in Haight-Ashbury, San Francisco with R. Crumb's *Zap* #1 (1967), alongside ample additional detail. He explains the importance of forerunners such as Tijuana Bibles (1930s–1950s), EC Comics publications (particularly editor Harvey Kurtzman and *Mad* magazine, 1952) and other early comix and magazines such as *Help!* (1960). Skinn provides biographical summaries of the major players at various times and places, including the original movement in the United States (R. Crumb, Gilbert Shelton, Rick Griffin, Denis Kitchen, Vaughn Bode, S. Clay Wilson, Spain Rodriguez and Art Spiegelman) and the UK (Hunt Emerson and Bryan Talbot), and the later emergence of Wimmen's Comix (Nancy Kalish, Trina Robbins, Willy Mendes). He considers taboo themes such as sex (bestiality, incest, violence) and drugs (noting a changing message as availability and perceptions of drugs changed). The accessibility of underground artwork is explored through analysis of festivals and music albums, and discussion of the printing and distribution processes used by companies such as Rip Off Press, Kitchen Sink (who were instrumental in forming the Comic Book Legal Defence Fund) and Last Gasp. Skinn also notes strategies of censorship including police raids and obscenity trials, arguing that it was the political content of these comics which made them targets and examines the subsequent development of the industry through title such as *Brainstorm*, *Near Myths*, *Viz* (which never saw such attacks), and *Escape*. He concludes by summarizing the subsequent fate of this first wave of underground artists, many of whom have passed on, and examines their legacy and the emergence of a new generation in the 1980s (publishers such as Fantagraphics and Drawn & Quarterly, and creators like the Hernandez brothers, Daniel Clowes, Dave Sim, Chris Ware and Joe Sacco). Finally, Skinn points towards the redefinition of these comics as art house objects and offers a checklist of nearly one thousand key underground titles, a most useful resource.

David Huxley's *Nasty Tales: Sex, Drugs, Rock 'n' Roll and Violence in the British Underground* (2001) focuses on UK comics from 1966 to 1982, situated against the backdrop of the American publications. Like the other books noted, Huxley first discusses the origins and cultural context of these titles, then explores the key themes listed in his title. He ends by reflecting on the problems of creating a canon of such an unstable and oppositional moment and repositioning the British titles in the context of Europe, where experimental comics have moved towards respectability. He concludes that whereas the British underground was heavily inspired by and initially reprinted many of the American pioneers, it also gave access and experience to many key creators who went on to shape the industry and expand the boundaries of comics' possibilities, and produced some titles of genuine quality. The book also includes a chronological list of underground and alternative titles published in Britain 1966–82.

Autobiographix

Although the underground comics tended towards excess and taboo-breaking, autobiography (whether real or fictionalized) informed many of their depictions and themes, as creators often drew themselves into strips or engaged with questions of identity and sexuality. Comics' visual representations have meant that the medium has long seen autobiographical incursions, dating back to the early 1900s.[1] The more general revaluation of literary autobiography in the 1960s and 1970s led to this subject being redefined more inclusively and as a genre with a complicated relationship with fictionality. Relabelled as life writing (or, in comics studies, autobiographix), a trend towards autobiographical comics is now apparent in many cultures; for example Lim (2014) explores the rise of this genre in the Singaporean market.

Witek argues that the disappearance of a coherent underground movement in the late 1970s left several creators adrift who then turned to autobiographix. His *Comic Books as History* (1989) is among the earliest examples of Anglo-American comics scholarship that considers the genre and contains chapters on Art Spiegelman and Harvey Pekar. In these, Witek argues that *Maus* represents Spiegelman's attempt to control the legacy of the Holocaust in his own life, comparing the contrasting artistic styles of his various attempts at the story and his use of the conventions of animal comics. He also explores the way in which *Maus* blends public and private history, and foregrounds the 'ineluctable fictionality' of any narrative, even autobiography, through its constantly shifting identification between author and character. Witek also analyses the construction and distribution of Pekar's *American Splendor*, whose diversity of narrative technique and style sits at odds with its single-minded autobiographical focus. He contrasts Pekar's approach (which is deliberately off-beat and undercuts conventions such as plot and narrative structure) with that of contemporaries such as Justin Green and R. Crumb.

Many later general works on comics discuss autobiographix. For example, the same creators are revisited in two chapters of Hatfield's *Alternative Comics* (2005), which explores 'The Problem of Authenticity', arguing that underground comics have established a new, working-class type of confessional autobiography that creates serial selves and problematizes simple notions of 'truth' through ironic authentication. Hatfield also analyses 'Irony and Self-Reflexivity', demonstrating that these comics use personal trauma to address sociopolitical issues, exploiting the tension between artifice and authenticity. Versaci's *This Book Contains Graphic Language* (2007), Wolk's *Reading Comics* (2007) and Miller's *Reading Bande Dessinée* (2007) also contain chapters on and case studies of various autobiographical comics. Beaty's *Unpopular Culture* (2007) (discussed further below) contains a chapter on autobiography in French-language publications, focusing on three key works: David B.'s *Epileptic*, Philippe Dupuy and Charles Beriberian's *Journal d'un album* (1994) and Fabrice Neaud's *Journal* (1996–2002) and arguing that these artists depict their creative process as a positive and affirmative action that contributes to their sense of personal identity.

It seems appropriate that some of the earliest scholarly pieces to focus exclusively on this marginalized genre also examine a format that remains outside mainstream comics publishing. Fredric Wertham's *The World of Fanzines* (1973) is the first serious attempt to survey the zine format. In counterpoint to his notorious *Seduction of the Innocent* (1954) (discussed in Chapter 4), Wertham finds much to admire about the fanzine format and particularly notes the zines' intensely personal qualities and communicative aims. Stephen Duncombe's *Notes from the Underground: Zines and the Politics of American Culture* (1997) also explores the history of self-published zines and the communities that built up around them, reprinting numerous examples and drawing on extensive interviews with creators. His especially interesting second chapter explores the ways the zines enabled a particular type of oppositional identity construction. Finally, Anna Poletti's *Intimate Ephemera* (2008) looks explicitly at the zine format in Australia, a region where comics scholarship itself remains quite marginal. This empirical study of the depiction of youth experience in Australian 'perzines' (personal zines) argues that this medium and community allows young people, whom the dominant public sphere often excludes, a rare voice. Poletti's introduction defines the zine format and notes the challenges of approaching and analysing these ephemeral, subcultural and highly personal texts. She reviews the various critical approaches taken to date (feminist, fan-based, resistive), from which she proceeds to set her critical focus on the concept of the 'audit self' and the DIY ethic. She then considers the ways in which the 'cut and paste' aesthetic and narrative problematizes notions of speech that affect the makers and readers of these zines. Subsequent chapters discuss the narration of motifs such as the bedroom or themes of depression, networks of distribution and consumption, and issues of style and materiality. Overall Poletti argues that perzines resituate life writing, removing hegemonic qualities, and thus require new analytical methodologies. These include an understanding of authorship as filtered through a series of material and narrative strategies, and an approach to reading that is collaged and contextualized.

More general critical works acknowledge the increasing popularity of autobiography in comics; for example Gillian Whitlock's *Soft Weapons* (2007) closes its discussion of multimedia life narratives of the Middle East with a detailed critical reading of Marjane Satrapi's *Persepolis*, which notes its sophisticated use of the medium and its affective power. Several journals and other collections also pick up the theme, such as *Belphégor* (4[1], 2004), *Biography* (31[1], 2008), and *Studies in Comics* (1[2], 2010). These special issues examine diverse examples of the genre. *Belphégor* contains a mixture of French and English articles, focused primarily on Europe, and ranging from Laurence Grove's or Julien Rosemberg's examinations of early bande dessinée, to those analysing more modern works such as Annabelle Martin's discussion of Edmond Baudoin's *Le portrait*, or Valerio Rota's consideration of the Italian translation of David B.'s *Epileptic*. The special issue of *Biography* contains pieces on the development of 'autography', and key texts such as Bechdel's *Fun Home,* Matt's *Peepshow,* and Solomon's *Leben? oder Theatre?* [*Life or Theatre?*]. There are also articles on the art of José Legaspi, and the development of zines. Finally *Studies in Comics* contains articles on Alison Bechdel, Art Spiegelman, Aline Kominsky-Crumb, Dave Sim, David B. and David Small, from various perspectives. McDaniel explores the serial nature of experience in Spiegelman's *Portrait of the Artist as a Young %@&*!* (2000). Oksman examines Kominsky-Crumb's depiction of the Jewish body as implicitly gendered, arguing that her work destabilizes the boundaries between how we define ourselves and how others define us. Theisen examines Dave Sim's use of parody, and Mitchell employs autobiographical comics to explore the relationship of image fragments, advocating an approach that goes beyond the panel as the smallest signifying unit. El Refaie also examines the semiotic resources available to comics creators, using David B's *Epileptic,* and Vågnes explores the use of silence in David Small's *Stitches.* Two articles from Spiers and Schneider consider, respectively, the queer relationships and gothic tropes used in *Fun Home.* Interviews with scholar Thierry Groensteen and comics artist Gabrielle Bell, along with a creative section showcasing work from several artists, approach the questions surrounding comics and representation from further angles. Taken as a whole, these special issues consider a wide range of international case studies and explore the multiplicity of tools that the comics medium has available to convey and complicate lived experience.

A wave of critical interest in autobiographix rises around 2010–12, with the publication of three works in English: Hillary Chute's *Graphic Women* (2010), Michael Chaney's edited collection *Graphic Subjects* (2011) and Elisabeth El Refaie's *Autobiographical Comics* (2012). Chute argues that, as a hybrid and spatial medium, comics are especially suited to telling developmental life narratives, which convey a dual subjectivity as the creator/protagonist is both narrator and subject, and to feminist cultural production, as spatiality and the image are opposed to masculine systems of temporality and language (here citing William Blake and W.J.T. Mitchell). Her introduction gives a historical summary, and the following five chapters focus in turn on the heavyweights of this emergent genre: Aline Kominsky-Crumb, Phoebe Gloeckner, Lynda Barry, Marjane Satrapi and Alison Bechdel. Chute uses close analysis and extensive interview material to demonstrate the diverse ways that each creator employs the comics medium to testify to the ordinariness of trauma in female lived experience. For example, Kominsky-Crumb's 'ugly' excess of style is a specifically feminine aesthetic response to patriarchy and idealization; Gloeckner juxtaposes her meticulous, skilful style (reflecting her experience as a medical illustrator) with shocking content to create ambivalent narratives around images of erotic abuse or beautiful pain; and Barry uses incomplete images and gaps and blurs 'high' and 'low' art to express the subject of memory while simultaneously reproducing its effects.

Chaney's collection contains twenty-seven short chapters, in four sections. The first, dedicated to Art Spiegelman, has four chapters exploring Spiegelman's different formats (digital, material) and themes (mourning, memory, postmemory, revision, selfhood). Part 2 is global in scope, considering works of bande dessinée, Japanese manga and a memoir of the African genocide in Rwanda. Part 3 focuses on women's life writing, examining feminist creators such as Bechdel, Satrapi, Sedgwick and Leonard and including an artist's perspective from Phoebe Gloeckner on the tension between the label 'autobiography' and the creative process it requires. Part 4 explores 'Perspectives of the Self', considering creators like Justin Green, Chester Brown, Seth, Joe Matt and Lynda Barry, and examining some fictional pieces (*American Born Chinese* and *Watchmen*) through the lens of autobiography.

Finally, Elisabeth El Refaie's book draws widely on literary and cultural theory, social semiotics, linguistics, narratology, art history, philosophy, psychology, psychoanalysis, sociology and media studies. Rather than focus closely on a few key case studies, El Refaie aims to identify general trends within the genre by surveying a corpus of eighty-five European and American autobiographical comics. She enumerates four key properties of the genre based around the search for appropriate ways to:

1. represent the self;
2. convey past events and future dreams;
3. create authenticity;
4. engage the reader.

El Refaie offers a critical background to the genre (taking in both literature and comics), and her subsequent chapters are structured around these communicative goals. By identifying their formal properties and narrative techniques she provides the basis of a model for exploring autobiographix, arguing that comics' reinvigoration of the genre has allowed scholars to reconsider both the nature of life writing and how we read comics, and enabled diverse voices to reach a wide audience. This visual development of autobiographix has placed a clear emphasis on the body, grappled effectively with human perceptions of time, foregrounded the problems inherent in authenticity, and used multimodal methods to engage the reader cognitively and emotionally.

The collection *Drawing from Life: Memory and Subjectivity in Comic Art* (2013), edited by Jane Tolmie, explores the usual big names (Bechdel, Barry, Satrapi, Spiegelman, Ware) alongside more diverse case studies. Baetens examines Vaughn-James's *The Cage*, Chaney considers animal bodies, Bush discusses *Yokiko's Spinach* and the 'nouvelle manga' aesthetic, Chase explores female adolescence and feminist autobiography, O'Brien dissects graphic medicine, and Cates analyses various Gaiman-McKean collaborations that have engaged with 'fake memory' and interpretative uncertainty. Trauma (both public and private) is the subject of the latter chapters, which explore responses to 9/11, abuse and illness. Tolmie's introduction uses autobiographix's treatment of trauma as a lens for the whole book, arguing that, by departing from the 'buffer' of words, these comics can confront, liberate and emancipate both creator and reader. Along similar lines, *Canadian Graphic* (2016), edited by Candida Rifkind and Linda Warley, collects ten essays focused on life writing within the Francophone and Anglophone Canadian alternative comics scenes. These cover themes such as illness and identity, gender, toxic masculinity and female sexuality, and indigenous suffering and colonial narratives. The texts studied allow for some diversity of critical voices and the overall argument brings nuance to the question of the suitability of comics as a vehicle for autobiography.

Most recently, Frederik Bryn Køhlert's *Serial Selves* (2019) builds on the work done by the above scholars, with a particular emphasis on marginalized and diverse selves. He argues that autobiography is encouraged, enabled and enhanced by several key properties of the comics medium: the idiosyncrasy of the drawn line, the sequential nature of the artwork and the serial format. Comics' visual nature means that the self cannot be hidden behind an anonymous 'I' but must be visualized and placed on display, and choices made about representation thus carry political connotations. The use of sequential art and the multimodal nature of the narrative sustain multiple images of the narrating subject, creating a plural and unfixed self that is performed across space and time. The serial format reinforces this, providing multiple vantage points for both creator and reader to encounter characters, making the process of self-production transparent and further undermining notions of a singular, cohesive identity. Køhlert's five chapters explore the works of key creators Julie Doucet, Phoebe Gloeckner, Ariel Schrag, Al Davison and

Toufic El Rassi, using these case studies to explore the depiction of gender, trauma, queerness, maturation, agency and stereotyping. He shows how each creator uses different aspects of the medium to reinforce and intensify the emotional effects of their narrative. For example, Doucet's unruly style coheres with her challenging of reader conceptions of femininity, while Gloeckner's more traditionally beautiful artwork invites the reader to look on staged scenes of trauma and abuse that are more usually hidden. Schrag plays with the openness and serialization of the comics medium to create a narrative of maturation: increasingly experimenting with and 'queering' the medium in a similar manner to her own personal development. In counterpoint to his own reality (where he has been marginalized by the discourses surrounding his medical condition), Davison uses comics' visuality to assert himself as a masculine ideal and direct a 'counterstare' at the reader. Finally, El Rassi deconstructs the Arab stereotype through sustained use, forcing the reader to consider its historical and contemporary ubiquity. Køhlert argues that these artists use comics' multimodal codes to foreground issues surrounding representation and that the medium itself is a particularly apt space to work out the complex relationships between the self and the world.

French-language[2] alternative and small press publications

This section builds on the discussion of the autobiographical trend in comics and the rise of independent publishers in the English-speaking world. It discusses independent and alternative presses and the role of abstraction in experimental comics, and elaborates on the existing work on small presses and fanzines in Francophone contexts. It is noteworthy that both creative and fannish practices are closely interlinked and that recent comics artists have not shied away from highlighting the connections between a passion for comics, often developed in their youth, and their adult creative practices. The chapter ends by introducing Philippe Capart's chapter on 'store memory', or how one comics store in Brussels indulged in alternative practices to preserve comics and disseminate out-of-print ones. In lieu of a chronological overview of developments, this section tracks the rise of academic interest in experimental forms and discusses how fan practices contributed to comics criticism (building on the discussion in Chapter 4 on legitimation and early criticism in the Francophone sphere) and, more recently, comics making.

Artists' collectives

In her overview of bande dessinée publishing in *Reading Bande Dessinée* (2007: 3–69), Ann Miller considers the 1970s as the decade where the bande dessinée expanded its horizons and indulged in unprecedented experimentation (25–32), the 1980s as a period of 'recuperation by the mainstream' (33–48) and the 1990s as marking the return of independent bandes dessinées (49–57). This section will start with a discussion of the sources on the 1990s independent and alternative comics and trace its connections to bande dessinée publishing in the post-1968 countercultural context.

Bart Beaty's *Unpopular Culture* (2007), as noted above, examines the French small press scene and reflects on its role in reshaping cultural perceptions of comics. Beaty claims that comics exemplify the subjective and unstable nature of cultural value and that there is a tension in the term 'comic book' as it relates to works defined as popular culture, opposing them to those conceptualized as art. He draws on the work of Pierre Bourdieu (briefly introduced in Chapter 4 and discussed further in Chapter 7) to argue that the idea of the comic book has fundamentally altered over the previous fifteen years, and that the artist's book, rather than the novel, is now the main point of comparison and indicator of value. Beginning with the work of L'Association in the 1990s, Beaty's seven case studies demonstrate how shifts in production, format and aesthetic led by the small press have resulted in avant-garde art replacing literary pretensions as hallmarks of seriousness and quality in comic books at large.

The French artists collective L'Association was founded in May 1990 and remains a key alternative comics publisher. Many of the artists published by L'Association – David B., Marjane Satrapi, Edmond Baudoin, Lewis Trondheim – have acquired international fame. The collective gets its name from the 1901 French law for non-profit organizations, which highlights its status as a publisher not seeking to make profit. Instead of imposing pre-decided formats, themes and styles, L'Association privileges the comics artists and their work, adjusting the form of its publications to the artist's preferences. Both Ann Miller in *Reading Bande Dessinée* (53–57) and Laurence Grove in *Comics in French* (161–162) provide concise overviews of the formation and significance of L'Association. Grove describes how alternative bande dessinée becomes a marketable entity in its own right (2010: 220–228). A thorough and richly illustrated source on the publishing house is *L'Association: Une Utopie éditoriale et esthétique* [*L'Association: An Editorial and Aesthetic Utopia*] (2011), edited by Erwin Dejasse, Tanguy Habrand and Gert Meesters. Acknowledging L'Association's important role in marking the contemporary bande dessinée scene, the editors are also careful to contextualize its appearance. Habrand, for instance, recalls Edmond Baudoin's remark in an interview that L'Association artists are in many ways Futuropolis' 'enfants spirituels' (11). Founded in 1974 by comics artist Florence Cestac and comics editor and publisher Étienne Robial, Futuropolis belongs to young adult and adult comics pioneers, along with magazines such as *Pilote*, *Charlie Hebdo* and *Fluide Glacial*, and publishers such as the Humanoïdes associés (12). Here too the aim was to reject commercializing practices and assure authorial autonomy in the production process. Futuropolis was also a bookstore visited by the founders of L'Association, most notably Menu. This highlights the relevance of comics makers' memories and nostalgia and the role of bookstores in fostering and channelling comics reading. Furthermore, it shows how experimentation in comics did not emerge from a void but remains anchored in comics history and practices that are not always obvious at first glance (and often overlooked by critics).

Jean-Christophe Menu's extensive thesis, *La bande dessinée et son double* [*Comics and Its Double*] (2011) provides background information about and insights into L'Association's origins and workings. His memoir *Krollebitches* is a more concise, personalized and often emotional pendant to the theoretical reflections in his thesis and sheds light on Menu's early interest in comics. It ends with a brief account of his first fanzine at the age of seventeen and his later exposure to experimental American comics artists such as Chris Ware and Charles Burns, alternative artists such as Renée French, and older masters such as Frank King. As we will see below, these different non-mainstream practices – underground, independent, alternative, self-publishing – have mutually influenced each other and have travelled across cultures.

The richly illustrated volume on L'Association assembles a multidisciplinary set of chapters that interrogate autobiographical and reportage comics published by the group. It also provides critical reflections on the collective's editorial logic and development and chapters exemplifying stylistic and semiotic analyses of major artists such as Joann Sfar and François Ayroles.

L'Association has published magazines such as *Lapin* (sporadically since 1992), which includes contributions by the collective's founding members and showcases a variety of styles and themes. The collective was also the impetus behind the OuBaPo [Ouvroir de la bande dessinée potentielle (workshop for potential comics)], founded in 1992, which includes many artists affiliated with L'Association. As Ann Miller reminds us, the landmark Cerisy conference on comics, *Bande dessinée et modernité* organized by Thierry Groensteen, was the occasion when Menu and Trondheim first met and the possibility of a comics version of OuLiPo was broached (2007b: 117). Similar to the experimentations characterizing Ou-X-Po's such as OuLiPo (which included many *nouveau roman* novelists), the OuBaPo worked with the specific constraints in their comics listed by Thierry Groensteen in the first *OuBaPo* volume, *OuPus* (*OuPus*, 13–59). Miller groups these constraints under four categories:

1. 'restriction [...] of motifs within the diegesis (like faces), graphic elements (like colour), or enunciative resources (like framing)' (2007b: 118–119).

2. 'iteration, complete or partial' (119).

3. 'plurilecturability [or pluri-readability] a set of constraints that reorder the panels to enable new readings' [Guide author's insertion in square brackets].

4. 'predetermined distribution of either motifs or of graphic or enunciative elements' (ibid.).

In reviewing the first volume of *OuPus*, Jan Baetens (1998) extols its usefulness for theoretical reflections on word–image relationships and semiotic practices, despite its short length and tendency towards nonseriousness. Meesters' brief chapter on *OuBaPo* (Dejasse, Habrand, Meesters: 132–129) provides a useful, well-illustrated overview of the main participants in its earlier years.

Groensteen's *plurilecturabilité* [pluri-readability] can also be translated as pluri-narration to emphasize the visual dimension of the transposition of the OuLiPo concept to OuBaPo. Côme Martin has highlighted the impact of the pluri-narration constraint on comics artists such as Jason Shiga and Leif Tande who experimented with it in long-form comics, in contrast to the brief ones the Francophone artists made (Martin, 2012: 7). Similarly, Martha Kuhlman has demonstrated the impact of the OuBaPo constraints on Chris Ware's comics, emphasizing the ironic element of these constraints and characterizing 'Ware's work as a factory for comics experiments' that test and expand the limits of comics (2010: 86).

Although the European Francophone – Belgian, French, Swiss – sphere is home to many alternative publishers, including La Cinquième Couche, L'Emploi du Moi, Ego Comme X and Cornélius, and many of the works are regularly the subject of scholarship, scholars have yet to turn their attention to the specificities and practices of the publishers themselves. The French-Belgian publisher FRMK is one of the few exceptions to this.

Beginning as a merger between the French Amok and the Belgian Fréon, Fremok, now known as FRMK, describes itself as a platform for publishing graphic literature ranging from comics to visual poetry. It does not limit itself to publishing but also includes performances and even training. Before discussing Fréon in his 2008 article 'Of Graphic Novels and Minor Cultures', Baetens elaborates on two possible movements of intermediality: one is the convergence into a kind of *Gesamtkunstwerk* or whole whereas the other involves 'the mutual questioning of conflicted media' (97). Using the graphic novel interchangeably with bande dessinée, he also discusses the rise of the former as a means of comics legitimation before elaborating on the particularities of the Belgian collective Fréon, which was also formed in the 1990s and, like L'Association and similar independent publishers, 'represents a typical avant-garde stance within the field of the graphic novel, combining technical and formal experiments, a hands-on, do-it-yourself approach and a clear political commitment' (98). Fréon's political commitment is resolutely multilingual (which is particularly significant for the Belgian context of politicized linguistic communities) and even 'infralingual' in its tendency to offer readings carried through images alone. Miller points out that, in contrast to many independent comics publishers, FRMK emphasizes comics' connections to the visual arts instead of book publishing (Miller, 2007: 55). This reinforces Baetens' claim that Fréon constitutes a minor culture in Deleuze and Guattari's sense of the term and broaches aspects of deterritorialization and politicization (2008: 99). According to Baetens, this politicization unfolds primarily on the level of image-making practices which break away from conventional comics to highlight the materiality and objecthood of each work: this breaking away is political since it blurs the assumed limits between popular, more constrained arts and the more experimental, 'higher' arts (113).

The two-volume *Abstraction and Comics/Bande dessinée et abstraction*, edited by the ACME group, assembles interventions by comics artists and scholars on the different rapprochements between comics and abstraction, including both abstract comics and the possibilities of reading abstraction in comics. Transcending the traditional disciplinary, generic, artistic and canonical boundaries, it proposes reconsidering the scholarly and artistic assumptions surrounding comics. *Abstraction and Comics* intervenes in these diverse aspects through nine major sections. 'Archaeologies' looks at nineteenth- and early twentieth-century comics by artists such as Cham, Nadar, Doré (Jacques Dürrenmatt) and Cliff Sterret (Katherine Roeder). The last contribution in this section by Jean-Charles Andrieu de Levis focuses on the abstract comics of Ibn Al Rabin and Andrei Molotiu, highlighting and contextualizing the contrasting approaches of these two artists: the former uses abstract elements to create narration whereas the latter avoids narration and combines figurative and abstract elements. De Levis argues for a broad understanding of abstract comics that is not restricted by definitions and appreciates the diversity of abstraction and its experimental capacity.

'Practices' incorporates practitioner insights into the use of sequential art, while 'Narration', the third and longest section, contains chapters by Jan Baetens, Kai Mikkonen, Barbara Postema, Pascal Lefèvre and Hugo Frey on the possibilities of narrative in abstract comics. Like most of the volume, this section also contains a comic ('Tangram' by Berliac) that complements the chapters. 'Significations' broaches the issue of meaning-making in abstract comics. Jakob F. Dittmar suggests that 'non-sequitur' relationships between panels are non-existent. Fred Andersson considers abstraction from a semiotic point of view and suggests that some narrative element persists in even the most abstract of comics. Jean-Louis Tilleuil highlights the connection between the abstraction of comics images and increasing literariness of dialogue in contemporary comics.

The second volume of *Abstraction and Comics* contains a broader variety of original and innovative readings and analyses of abstract comics that are grouped under 'Epistemologies', 'Opacities', 'Brut' (a comics-only section), 'Variations' and 'Parallels'. It also contains a range of comics art, including Richard Kraft's 'Here Comes Kitty: A Comic Opera', Pascal Matthey's '4365' and Cátio Serrão's untitled abstract comics. The kinds of comics this volume covers include graphic novels by Ephameron and Olivier Schrauwen (Benoît Crucifix and Gert Meeters), Alberto Breccia (Laura Caraballo) and Jack Kirby (Roberto Bartual's and Amadeo Gandolfo's respective chapters). In one of the volume's final chapters, Erin La Cour broaches the issue of exhibiting comics in a manner that accounts for their affective qualities while breaking away from the restrictions of both the spaces of the museum and the confines of the book.

Fanzines and alternative practices

Connections between fanzines, identity, comics and autobiography are
already drawn out above with a focus on English-language production.
This section turns to French-language fanzines to trace the influences on
alternative comics practices.

As Gavin Parkinson suggests in 'Pogo, Pop and Politics: Robert Benayoun
on Comics and Roy Lichtenstein' (2016), comics infiltrated the arts in
several ways, including via alternative art movements such as surrealism.
Younger surrealists like Benayoun (active during the 1950s and 1960s) had
a keen interest in comics, much like Éric Losfeld, a writer and publisher of
erotic work who was extremely popular among the surrealists. Parkinson
shows how, in addition to Benayoun's texts praising American comics such
as Walt Kelly's *Pogo*, comics elements had a strong impact on Benayoun's art.
Benayoun also published on comics, including *Vroom, tchac, zowie: le ballon
dans la bande dessinée* [*The Word Balloon in Comics*] (1968), which provides
a history of the word balloon. Parkinson's edited volume, *Surrealism, Science
Fiction and Comics* (2015), goes into further detail on the connections and
mutual influences between different surrealist artists and comics in France,
the UK and the United States.

Franquin et les fanzines [*Franquin and the Fanzines*] (2013), edited
by Elisa Renouil, collects André Franquin's numerous interviews and
communications with fanzines and other underground publications from
the 1970s and the 1980s. It reveals two relatively overlooked aspects of
comics culture: the relationship between the artist and his fans and, in
particular, between a relatively mainstream artist and the underground,
alternative press. The latter highlights the close ties that can exist between
mainstream and alternative publications.

La Fabrique de Fanzines par ses ouvriers même [*The Fanzine Factory by
Its Own Workers*] (2011) combines comic strips narrating how each of the
contributors, or 'workers' to use the book's term, began making fanzines.
The 'factory' [*fabrique*] began in 2003. Despite the different drawing styles
and potentially autobiographical accounts, each comic ends with the same
collective signature; none of the brief comics is openly attributed to a specific
artist. The book also includes a brief history of fanzine-making told, like
the rest of the book, in comics form. One of the first fanzines, titled 'The
Comet' was self-published by Walter Denis and Raymond A. Palmer of the
Science Correspondence Club in Chicago in May 1930. It was formed of
readers of the science fiction magazines, particularly *Amazing Stories*, which

had started a letters column in 1926. At the time 'The Comet' was only a 'letterzine' or 'fanmag'. The term fanzine appeared in 1940 (Al Rabin et al.). It forms part of the constellation of comics and comics criticism that exists alongside the more established channels of mainstream comics publication.

Benoît Crucifix and Pedro Moura's 'Bertoyas dans la jungle. Bande dessinée et edition sauvage' ['Bertoyas in the Jungle. Comics and Wild Publishing'] (2016) takes a close look at fanzine publishing through Jean-Marie Bertoyas' works and emphasizes its anti-institutional approach. Although this French comics artist has been published by more established alternative publishers such as L'Association, fanzines and other informal means of 'micro-publishing' remain his preferred means of publication. The authors elaborate on the ephemeral, often unarchived and unarchivable supports of micro-publishing, considering it a form of 'wild literature' (*littérature sauvage*), a term coined by literary scholar Jacques Dubois. Tanguy Habrand used this concept in the *Comics in Dissent* anthology (2014) to denote independent publishers hovering between institutionalized and wild practices. Finally, Crucifix and Moura invoke Sara Ahmed's concept of stickiness to discuss the affective driving force behind the small and micro presses.

Comics in Dissent explores the different kinds of non-mainstream comics publishing practices – alternative, 'avant-garde', independent, self-publishing and underground – in Europe (France, Belgium and the Netherlands) and North America and traces their interaction with each other and with mainstream publishers. Covering the previous forty years of comics publishing, the volume successfully challenges the supposed dichotomy between independent and alternative publications and mainstream ones and highlights their overlaps and grey areas, especially in Tanguy Habrand's, Christopher Dony's and Thierry Groensteen's respective essays. In 'Les Independants de la bande dessinée: entre édition établie et édition sauvage' ['The Independents of Comics: Between Established and Wild Publishing'], Habrand suggests that 'independent' functions both as a category designating publishers affiliated to a particular network (such as the French alliance of independent publishers) or institution and as a way of understanding alternative publishing practices; using DC Comics' Vertigo imprint as an example, Dony delineates the grey zone between mainstream and alternative publishing; and Groensteen describes his own experience of establishing L'An 2, a publishing venue for experimental, non-mainstream comics artists which, due to financial constraints, eventually became an imprint of the established literary publisher, Actes Sud.

The exhibition catalogue, 'Lire (sur) la small press' (published in A5 format and with a photocopied aesthetic) accompanied the 'Indie Americans' exhibition in Brussels in September 2018. It includes several useful texts on the complex world of the small press, an important publishing avenue for fanzines, but also a broader underground, alternative cultural phenomenon. Notably the form and printing of the catalogue echo small-press practices. Jean-Paul Jannequin's essay (reprinted from the October 2004 issue of the fanzine, *Comix Club*) provides a useful, concise history of the small press, which sidesteps the trap of oversimplification and generalization by constructing the narrative around key tensions between the notions of small press and independent publishing (8–21). Small-press comics usually have an A6 (digest) or A5 (mini-comic) format and a limited number of photocopied issues (10, 13). A comic published in the typical comic book format (17 × 23cm) is categorized under independent or even alternative comics, whereby 'alternative comics' is often used for publications from the 1970s and 1980s. In addition to changing market dynamics, the late 1970s and early 1980s were also periods of increased availability of photocopy machines. Jannequin traces the blurred lines between small press publications and the rise of zine culture, which produced comics fanzines but also zines on a broad range of topics, especially music (17). In the same catalogue, Jean-Matthieu Méon unpacks the overlaps and differences between independent, alternative and small press (28–37). While independent comics often subscribe, or at least retain close connections, to mainstream genres such as superhero, science fiction and fantasy, alternative comics engage with the themes of countercultural, underground comics, such as social critique and autobiography (30–31).

While some scholarship is available on these alternative and independent practices surrounding comics making and criticism, less is known about the roles of communities – of readers, fans, collectors and stores – in facilitating the circulation and appreciation of comics (Benjamin Woo's work, a rare exception, is discussed in Chapter 7). In this respect it is worth considering Philippe Capart's essay on 'store memory', in which he recalls how Michel Deligne, a Brussels-based aficionado of comics and popular culture, salvaged comics heritage by circulating and reprinting old comics. Deligne was in many ways enabled by the increasing organization of comics readers and fans in the late 1960s (Capart, 2018: 277). He founded the Curiosity House in Brussels in 1972, which was soon accompanied by the *Curiosity Magazine*. Although influenced by early fanzines such as *Ran Tan Plan* and *Schtroumpf*, the *Curiosity Magazine* traded analysis for a focus on adventure strips of the 1930s and 1940s and their new incarnations (279). This shows how comics fandom and comics scholarship have favoured different historical periods and genres guided by individual and group inclinations. Furthermore, it captures the trajectories of influences on the valorization of comics that comics scholarship is only gradually beginning to understand: stores offer comics to comics fans, but the relationship is not entirely one-sided since comics fans also influence the offerings in their favourite stores. Memories of (conventional) comics and comics fandom in turn leave their traces in many experimental productions such as those of L'Association. The production and consumption of comics unfolds in a complex ecosystem, moulded by creators' and readers' experiences, for which scholarship does not always account.

Conclusion

Despite wider perceptions of comics often revolving around big publishers and established genres, marginal genres and publishing practices exist alongside these. The above scholarship explores the ways in which the comics medium has developed around alternative formats, genres and themes in Europe and America. It demonstrates the significant impact of changes wrought in the small press and the underground and argues that these comics have evolved in an inclusive manner, which foregrounds wider issues of representation, fictionality, subjectivity and identity. It also highlights the role of alternative and small presses in innovating and introducing new styles and techniques. These are sometimes incorporated into the mainstream (as in the case of some 'artistic' and 'literary' tendencies such as painterly or non-comicsy drawing styles and the interest in subjectivities and identities), while other formats and practices (such as fanzines, the small press and the more obscure abstract comics) resist such assimilation.

Notes

1. Although Wikipedia is not generally considered a good scholarly source, the page https://en.wikipedia.org/wiki/Autobiographical_comics is a clear and not-too-Anglocentric list of autobiographical events in comics dating back to the 1880s.

2. It is important to note that numerous works examining autobiography exist outside French and English scholarship, such as Nina Ernst's *Att Teckna Sitt Jag* [*To Draw Your I*], published in Swedish (2017).

Works cited

Al Rabin, Ibn, Baladi, Alex, Kündig, Andréas, Lavasseur, Yves and Novello, Benjamin. *La fabrique des fanzines*. Geneva: Atrabile, 2011.

Baetens, Jan. 'Une déclaration d'indépendance: Oulipo et Oubapo'. *9e Art: Cahiers du Musée de la Bande Dessinée* 3, 1998: 124–125.

Baetens, Jan. 'Of Graphic Novels and Minor Cultures. The Fréon Collective'. *Yale French Studies* 114, 2008: 95–115.

Beaty, Bart. *Unpopular Culture: Transforming the European Comic Book in the 1990s*. Toronto: University of Toronto Press, 2007.

Capart, Philippe. 'Store Memory'. In Maaheen Ahmed and Benoît Crucifix (eds), *Comics Memory: Archives and Styles*. Cham: Palgrave Macmillan, 2018, pp. 277–280.

Chaney, Michael A. (ed.) *Graphic Subjects: Critical Essays on Autobiography and Graphic Novels*. Madison: University of Wisconsin Press, 2011.

Chute, Hillary. *Graphic Women: Life Narrative and Contemporary Comics*. New York: Columbia University Press, 2010.

Collective. *Indie Americans: Lire (sur) la Small Press*. Brussels: Les éditions ça et là, L'employé du Moi and Cultures Maison, 2018.

Crucifix, Benoît and Moura, Pedro. 'Bertoyas dans la jungle. Bande dessinée et édition sauvage'. *Mémoires du livre* 8:1, 2016: https://www.erudit.org/fr/revues/memoires/2016-v8-n1-memoires02805/1038027ar/

Daniels, Les. *Comix: A History of Comic Books in America*. London: Wildwood House, 1973.

Dejasse, Erwin, Habrand, Tanguy and Meesters, Gert (eds). *L'Association: une utopie éditoriale et esthétique*. Brussels: Les Impressions Nouvelles, 2011.

Dony, Christophe, Habrand, Tanguy and Meesters, Gert (eds). *La bande dessinée en dissidence: alternative, indépéndance, auto-edition/Comics in Dissent: Alternative, Independence, Self-Publishing*. Liège: Presses universitaires de Liège, 2014.

Duncombe, Stephen. *Notes from Underground: Zines and the Politics of American Culture*. London: Verso, 1997.

El Refaie, Elisabeth. *Autobiographical Comics: Life Writing in Pictures*. Jackson, MS: University Press of Mississippi, 2012.

Ernst, Nina. *Att Teckna Sitt Jag* [*To Draw Your I*]. Svenska: Dankst Band, 2017.

Estren, Mark James. *A History of Underground Comics*. Berkeley, CA: Ronin Publishing, [1974] 1993.

Farrajota, Marcos. 'Disquiet'. *Desassossego* 20, 2015. http://kushkomikss.blogspot.com/2015/02/desassossego.html. Accessed 3 March 2019.

Huxley, David. *Nasty Tales: Sex, Drugs, Rock'n'Roll and Violence in the British Underground.* Manchester: Critical Vision, 2001.

Køhlert, Frederik Byrn. *Serial Selves: Identity and Representation in Autobiographical Comics.* New Brunswick, NJ: Rutgers University Press, 2019.

Kuhlman, Martha B. 'In the Comics Workshop: Chris Ware and OuBaPo'. In David. M. Ball and Martha B. Kuhlman (eds), *The Comics of Chris Ware: Drawing Is a Way of Thinking.* Jackson, MS: University Press of Mississippi, 2010, pp. 78–89.

Martin, Côme. 'OuBaPo et la pluri-narrativité'. *Formules* 16, 2012: 301–310.

Miller, Ann. *Reading Bande Dessinée: Critical Approaches to French-Language Comic Strip.* Bristol and Chicago, IL: Intellect, 2007a.

Miller, Ann. 'Oubapo'. *A Verbal/Visual Medium Is Subjected to Constraints: Word and Image* 23:2, 2007b: 117–137.

Ouvroir de la Bande Dessinée Pontentielle, OuPus 1. Paris: L'Association, 1997.

Parkinson, Gavin. 'Pogo, Pop and Politics: Robert Benayoun on Comics and Roy Lichtenstein'. *European Comic Art* 9:2, 2016: 27–58.

Poletti, Anna. *Intimate Ephemera: Reading Young Lives in Australian Zine Culture.* Victoria: Melbourne University Press, 2008.

Renouil, Elisa (ed.) *Franquin et les fanzines. Entretiens avec la presse souterraine 1971–1996.* Brussels: Dupuis, 2013.

Rifkind, Candida and Warley, Linda (eds). *Canadian Graphic: Picturing Life Narratives.* Waterloo, ON: Wilfred Laurier University Press, 2016.

Robbins, Trina. *From Girls to Grrrlz.* San Francisco, CA: Chronicle Books, 1999.

Rommens, Arrnoud, Crucifix, Benoît, Dozo, Björn-Olav, Dejasse, Erwin and Turnes, Pablo. *Comics and Abstraction = Abstraction et Bande Dessinée. Vol. 4 La cinquième couche.* Liège/Brussels: Presses universitaires de Liège, 2019.

Round, Julia and Murray, Chris (eds). *Studies in Comics* 1: 2. Bristol: Intellect Books, 2010.

Sabin, Roger. *Adult Comics: An Introduction.* London: Routledge, 1993.

Skinn, Dez. *Comix: The Underground Revolution.* London: Collins & Brown, 2004.

Tolmie, Jane (ed.) *Drawing from Life: Memory and Subjectivity in Comic Art.* Jackson, MS: University of Mississippi Press, 2013.

Tju, Lim Cheng. 'Current Trends in Singapore Comics: When Autobiography Is Mainstream'. *Kyoto Review of Southeast Asia*, 16 September 2014. https://kyotoreview.org/issue-16/current-trends-in-singapore-comics-when-autobiography-is-mainstream/. Accessed 19 June 2019.

Versaci, Rocco. *This Book Contains Graphic Language: Comics as Literature.* New York and London: Continuum, 2007.

Wertham, Fredric. *The World of Fanzines: A Special Form of Communication.* Carbondale, IL: Southern Illinois University Press, 1973.

Whitlock, Gillian. *Soft Weapons: Autobiography in Transit.* Chicago, IL: University of Chicago Press, 2007.

Witek, Joseph. *Comic Books as History: The Narrative Art of Jack Jackson, Art Spiegelman, and Harvey Pekar.* Jackson, MS: University of Mississippi Press, 1989.

Wolk, Douglas. *Reading Comics: How Graphic Novels Work and What They Mean.* Cambridge, MA: Da Capo Press, 2007.

CHAPTER 11
GENERAL REFERENCE GUIDES AND TEXTBOOKS

This chapter introduces guides for teaching comics studies and comics-making, general reference works on comics for a broad audience, introductions to critical approaches to comics studies for students, and more in-depth anthologies for comics scholars.

Teaching comics

Given the newness and interdisciplinary nature of comics studies – especially the combination of words and images, which are rarely studied together in traditional academic disciplines – teaching guides make a crucial contribution to the field. One of the earliest is Stephen Tabachnick 2009 MLA Handbook, *Teaching the Graphic Novel.* It assembles thirty-four essays on the form (definitions of comics, kinds of page layouts, reading time and word-image interactions), historical and social issues (Auschwitz, 9/11, comics by and about African Americans and women), and key artists (Chris Ware, Alan Moore, Frank Miller, Ben Katchor, Lynda Barry). Jesse Cohn's and Brian Tucker's essays offer useful introductions to, respectively, the page layout in comics and the hybrid, word-image nature of comics, for which Tucker convincingly turns to Lessing's *Laocoön* (see Chapter 2). Many of the chapters broach issues of life writing, memory and adaptation. The book covers canonical graphic novels, contemporary superhero comics and underground comics. The concise, insightful essays also offer pragmatic tips on how to teach graphic novels in different kinds of courses. The penultimate section of the book contains eleven chapters providing individual, international and interdisciplinary perspectives on teaching comics that cover history and art history classrooms, culturally specific studies (Hispanic, Franco-Belgian, Flemish, manga) and interdisciplinary overlaps with film and animation. The book ends with a seven-page bibliography listing books and articles in English and in French dealing with graphic novels on a general level (333–340).

Karin Kukkonen's *Studying Graphic Novels and Comics* (2016) offers a practical, easy-to-use guide to teaching and studying comics for both teachers and students, especially at the undergraduate level. Addressed to students, the book also offers suggestions for teaching comics, especially through its class activities, brief writing assignments, and longer essay questions. Major concepts and ideas are illustrated through different kinds of comics. The guide begins by introducing the key elements and functioning of the comics page through a cognitive lens. The second chapter turns to narrative aspects and emphasizes the balance between 'showing' and 'telling' in comics stories. After elaborating on autobiography and adaptation in graphic novels, Kukkonen offers a very concise overview of comics history that focuses on comics censorship and the rise of underground and alternative comics. Towards the end of the book, Kukkonen also offers useful tips for writing critical essays on comics, adding a playful edge by likening it to a detective case (139–147): after collecting evidence relating to a particular issue, potential connections with elements are investigated and used to develop an argument that is then presented in the form of an essay. In addition to the activities and several 'boxes' expanding on useful elements for comics reading and criticism, each chapter ends with a short, annotated recommended reading list. The book also offers a glossary of key terms and a list of canonical graphic novels with a strong focus on works in English.

Perhaps the only drawback of Kukkonen's book is its focus on graphic novels rather than comics at large, including comic strips. This, however, is a recurrent concern in textbooks on teaching comics that mirrors the legitimation trends discussed earlier (see Chapter 4). A wider set of critical perspectives and disciplinary varieties – ranging from narratology to cultural studies – features in Ann Miller's *Reading Bande Dessinée: Critical Approaches to the French-language Comic Strip* (2007). Although Miller focuses on Francophone works, many of the approaches she describes can easily be extended to different forms and genres of comics in other languages. Miller introduces tools for formal analysis, beginning with comics codes and narrative theory and ending with a discussion of comics as a postmodern art form. She divides additional analytical approaches into cultural studies approaches (national identity, postcolonial identity, social class and masculinity) and subjectivity (autobiography, psychoanalysis and gender).

For readers of German, Julia Abel and Christian Klein's introduction to comics and graphic novels, *Comics und Graphic Novels: Eine Einführung* [*Comics and Graphic Novels: An Introduction*] (2016), is a compact guide co-written by several leading comics scholars. It combines comics history (in the United States; Europe and, from the 1920s, in Japan) with an elaboration of key genres and formats and a brief guide to comics analysis which builds on the visual, stylistic and technical elements of comics. A second volume in the same series, *Comicanalyse: Eine Einführung* [*Comics Analysis: An Introduction*] (Packard et al. 2019), offers further detail about the diverse possibilities of comics analysis, covering semiotics, narratology, multimodality, genre theory and the less classic, relatively new intersectional and intercultural perspectives.

Teaching the Graphic Novel in the English Classroom: Pedagogical Possibilities of Multimodal Entertainment edited by Alissa Burger (2018) emphasizes, like most guidebooks on teaching comics, the possibilities of teaching on an interdisciplinary scale, by using and analysing comics' multimodal and imagetext essence. That said, Burger's volume is centred on teaching English and covers the uses of comics for teaching language skills, literary analysis, rhetoric, composition and gothic literature. Examples cover the use of comics in high-school and college settings. In addition, Riki Thompson's chapter 'Writing Through Comics' describes the design and uses of a creative writing course that involved making mini-comics (43–65). Craig Hill's anthology *Teaching Comics through Multiple Lenses* offers a broader set of chapters broaching topics that other teaching guides rarely cover. These include Johnson and Darragh's chapter on studying representations of class and poverty, and Eckert's chapter on teaching Native American comics. Other sections cover teaching representations of the mind and mental illness, young and LGTBQ bodies, and multimodality.

Also emphasizing multimodal approaches to teaching comics, Leah Misemer's and Aaron Kashtan's articles on course design in a special *Composition Studies* issue on Comics, Multimodality and Composition (2015) offer two useful examples of how comics can be productively integrated into general courses on composition writing, seeking to create awareness of typographical variations (Kashtan) and multimodal criticism and writing through comics and eventually film (Misemer).

The possibility of using comics to teach English and other languages is broached by Stephen Cary's *Going Graphic: Comics in the Multilingual Classroom* (2004). Cary, an ESL teacher and researcher, offers a list of twenty-five activities geared to fine-tune students' English language abilities through studying and making comics. The activities are flexible enough to be applicable for different grades and ESL classrooms. Cary also provides an overview of the kinds of comics that can be used in the classroom. Comics have often facilitated the teaching of foreign languages, as confirmed by several articles dating as far back as the late 1970s. Referring to pioneering comics theoretician Fresnault-Deruelle, James W. Brown (1977) points out how comics convey valuable cultural information through both visual and linguistic modes. Brown proposes several simple and effective exercises for using comics to improve students' oral and written expression and reading comprehension. Using a variety of American and French-language comics, such as *Peanuts, Mickey* and *Lucky Luke,* Rufus K. Marsh (1978) also advocates the use of comics for teaching contemporary expressions, grammar, conversation skills and cultural codes. He adds that comics such as *Astérix*, which are rich in references to French culture and satire, are suitable for advanced students. Jean-Pierre Berwald's article on the uses of humour for teaching French and Francophone cultures reinforces Brown's and Marsh's claims regarding the pedagogical uses of bande dessinée for teaching linguistic and cultural specificity. This contrasts with American comics which, as Berwald points out, are often culturally neutral and therefore more useful for teaching basic grammar and semantics.

Tying in with this notion of going beyond grammar and semantics in language learning, the volume *Films, Graphic Novels and Visuals*, edited by Elsner, Helff and Viebrock (2013), emphasizes the idea of multiliteracies in language learning in a way that centres on visual, multimodal, digital and transcultural competence and critical-reflection. The anthology includes general chapters on theories of multiliteracy and three chapters focusing on the use of graphic novels and comics in the foreign language classroom.

With Great Power Comes Great Pedagogy: Teaching, Learning and Comic Books (2020), edited by Susan Kirtley, Antero Garcia and Peter E. Carlson, is a new guide that stands out in its combination of insights on teaching how to make comics and how to read and analyse them (as suggested by Fredrik Byrn Køhlert and Nick Sousanis' chapter). Comics creators and academics such as Ebony Flowers and Nick Sousanis, in their respective chapters, 'On Copying' and 'Thinking in Comics: All Hands-On in the Classroom', highlight the importance of engaging with comics and image-making practices for a more holistic understanding of comics. Jonathan Flowers' chapter, 'Misunderstanding Comics', argues for the continued relevance of critically engaging with McCloud's landmark book, *Understanding Comics.*

For online resources, the essays on the *Comic Book Legal Defense Fund* page (cbldf.org) under the tag 'graphic novels in education' offer a generous set of case studies as well as resources for convincing libraries and institutions to include comics and graphic novels.

In addition to these sources, the journal *SANE* (*Sequential Art Narrative in Education*) offers articles on how to teach comics and rationales for individual comics that can be used by teachers needing to convince institutions to teach comics at different ages.

Making comics

This brief section turns to two books by comics artists that offer practical instructions on the art of cartooning and making comics. Both Ivan Brunetti's *Cartooning* (2011) and Lynda Barry's *Syllabus* (2014) can easily be transposed onto the weekly rhythms of course work.

Ivan Brunetti, known for the award-winning *Schizo* strips, offers a fifteen-week lesson plan in his *Cartooning*. Combining concise, easy-to-follow exercises with homework assignments, Brunetti walks budding artists through the technical basics of comic strips. Beginning with a lesson on 'spontaneous drawing', Brunetti works his way through single panel cartoons to full-page strips and, ultimately, a four-page story. He complements this by explanations of two kinds of grids – the democratic grid where all panels are of the same size and the hierarchical grid where the panels are sized according to their narrative function – and by exercises in different drawing techniques and styles.

Lynda Barry's *What It Is* (2008) interweaves reflections on the basic constituents of comics – the image, imagination, the past, thinking – with memories of her childhood and adolescence, and the anxieties still plaguing her as a comics artist. Barry also provides an 'activity book' of more than fifty pages to encourage creating comics. Her unique genre of graphic memoir/how-to books also includes *Picture This: The Near-Sighted Monkey Book* (2010) and *Syllabus*. All three contain exercises and playful-philosophical questioning that encourage drawing and storytelling. *Syllabus*, for instance, transposes the courses Barry gave over three years at the University of Wisconsin-Madison's art department. These books are therefore useful tools for both teachers and students.

Exemplifying the growing trend of combining the study and making of comics, the young online journal *Sequentials* offers brief essays in comics form that provide useful, accessible information on diverse themes (queer, postmodernism, materiality).

General and critical reference works

The *French Comics Theory Reader*, already mentioned in previous chapters, collects influential texts originally published in French. *A Comics Studies Reader* (2008), edited by Jeet Heer and Kent Worcester, does similar work for predominantly – but not exclusively – English-language scholarship. With its temporal, geographical and generic scope, *A Comics Studies Reader* offers a quick introduction to the main concerns of comics studies.

Jan Baetens and Hugo Frey's *The Graphic Novel: An Introduction* (already discussed in Chapter 3) is a useful starting point for acquiring an in-depth understanding of the graphic novel. The issues and characteristics associated with the graphic novel introduced by this book are further diversified and nuanced in *The Cambridge History of the Graphic Novel* (2019), edited by Jan Baetens, Hugo Frey and Stephen E. Tabachnick. This critical anthology 'provides a new literary history of the formation and development of the graphic novel' (1). While the focus is on Anglophone works, some of the volume's thirty-five chapters turn to Francophone comics and Japanese manga. The introduction highlights the complexity of the graphic novel, due to the contested nature of the term, its connections to comics legitimization, and changes in distribution and valorization practices. The literary history has three parts: Part 1 covers the years 1799–1978; Part 2 surveys 1978 to 2000; and Part 3 considers graphic novels in the new millennium. The volume contains a broad variety of chapters connected through their concerns with the origins of the graphic novel and its relationship to other cultural productions (mainstream comics and genres, novels, cinema). Stephen Tabachnick's *The Cambridge Companion to the Graphic Novel* (2017) is an additional resource on (older) debates surrounding its topic. *The Cambridge Companion* includes chapters on autobiography and biography, revisionist superheroes, historical fiction, the international scope of the graphic novel, non-fictional or journalistic graphic works and intermedial connections with film and the novel. Notable chapters include Bart Beaty's apt summation and interrogation of comics research around three 'classics': Lynda Barry's memoirs-art instruction manuals mentioned above, David B's *Epileptic* (1996–2003) and Jiro Taniguchi's *The Walking Man* (1992) (175–191). As Beaty points out, much of the study of comics is informed by biases inherited from university disciplines, which both strengthens the scope of the graphic novels considered and contributes to the marginalization of comics at large. James Bucky Carter's chapter, which closes this volume, offers suggestions for designing and teaching a (literature) course on comics.

The Routledge Companion to Comics (2016), edited by Frank Bramlett, Roy T. Cook and Aaron Meskin, combines numerous brief essays on pertinent broad themes. Divided into four sections – history and traditions, comics genres, issues and concepts, other media and other disciplines – *The Routledge Companion* provides comprehensive overviews of a fairly international set of comics contexts, including Central European and East European, Latin American and Indian comics, even though the focus remains on American ones. The issues and genres covered are even broader and more diverse and offer accessible introductions that should be useful to both students and scholars embarking on a new field of research.

More in-depth chapters are collected in *The Oxford Handbook of Comic Book Studies* (2020) edited by Frederick Aldama, which stands out in its inclusion of several chapters on cartooning (Pizzino, Shwed, Chaney and Chaney, Abate, Serrano). In addition to chapters on key themes and genres such as autobiography and memoir (Smith and Watson, Schell), complex issues surrounding the basic constituents of comics such as page layout (Kelp-Stebbins), the speech bubble (Kwa) and drawing (Crucifix), the handbook has several chapters on feminist (Miller, Hassler-Forest, Kirtley), racial and intersectional issues (Kunka, Brown, Hassler-Forest, Ghosal). It also includes chapters interrogating comics studies as a discipline (Bramlett, Gordon, Woo, Duncan and Smith). While focusing on comics in English, *The Oxford Handbook* does incorporate some chapters on comics from other contexts such as Columbia, Czechoslovakia, Australia and Hong Kong (Serrano, Patrick, Chu).

Departing from narratology and, more broadly speaking, narrative studies, Daniel Stein and Jan-Noël Thon's critical anthology, *From Comic Strips to Graphic Novels: Contributions to the Theory and History of Graphic Narrative* (2015), offers a diverse and useful set of perspectives and case studies for considering comics and graphic novels. The first section examines comics from a narratological perspective, covering issues of space and temporality (Kukkonen), subjectivity (Mikkonen), narrators (Thon) and world-building (Horstkotte). The second part covers issues of intermediality (Rippl and Etter), memoir (Pedri), authorship in superhero comics (Stein) and a historical contextualization of the role of windows, frames and panels in the arts from the renaissance until today (Smith). The third part explores the notion of the graphic novel (Meyer), offers a history of narration via comic strips (Gardner) and examines the role of early comics in Spiegelman's *In the Shadow of No Towers* (Jenkins) and the crossover genre of humoristic adventures in the Flemish context (Lefèvre). The volume ends with transcultural perspectives on the graphic novel, covering the British and American (Round), European (Baetens and Surdiacourt) and Japanese contexts (Berndt) and examining the possibility of considering graphic novels as world literature (Schmitz-Emans).

Most critical anthologies combine a variety of historical and critical approaches. Robin Varnum and Christina Gibbons' *The Language of Comics: Word and Image* (2007) includes chapters on nineteenth-century comics and cartoons in Europe (Kunzle) and Jan Baetens' essay on Philippe Marion's concept of 'graphiation', the first text in English to introduce and critically build on the concept from Marion's doctoral thesis *Traces en cases: travail graphique, figuration narrative et participation du lecteur* [*Traces in Panels: Graphic Work, Narrative Figuration and Reader Participation*]. Graphiation accounts for the hybridity of graphic, narrative and textual elements of comics. Joyce Goggin and Dan Hassler-Forest's *The Rise and Reason of Comics and Graphic Literature: Essays on the Form* (2010) contains a similarly diverse and insightful range of essays.

Three anthologies edited by Matthew Smith and Randy Duncan, *The Power of Comics: History, Form & Culture* (2009, with Paul Levitz), *Critical Approaches to Comics: Theories and Methods* (2011) and *More Critical Approaches to Comics* (2019, both co-edited with Matthew J. Brown), form a useful introduction to the possibilities of reading comics. *Power of Comics* tackles basic issues such as the problem of defining comics, the history of comics and key comics genres. It also serves as a class handbook offering a list of activities and discussion questions. *Critical Approaches to Comics* is an anthology bringing together chapters by key comics scholars. Divided into sections on form, content, production and context, each chapter introduces a particular theory, selects a test case, explains the selection and applies the theory. It offers a practical guide that can be useful to both students and scholars by covering theories on diverse aspects of comics including wordless books, narrative tools (*mise-en-scène* and framing, temporality), image functions and modes, propaganda, ideology, feminism, intertextuality and even ethnography. *More Critical Approaches to Comics* augments the more traditional critical approaches explored in the preceding volume with chapters on, among others, postcolonial theory, critical race theory, disability studies, historiography and autographics. Its final section covers adaptation, transmedia storytelling and parasocial relationships (relationships between fans and comics). The chapters follow the same format as *Critical Approaches to Comics* by introducing and then applying a particular theory.

In considering comics as part of a broader media environment [*médiaculture*], Maigret and Stefanelli's *La bande dessinée: une médiaculture* (2012) assembles chapters by leading comics scholars to consider comics from a relatively international perspective, combining insights on English- and French-language comics and Japanese manga, and to offer guidelines for a holistic consideration of comics. It begins with Stefanelli's summary of comics research, followed by Maigret's overview of the different kinds of theories used to analyse comics: comics as a language, text-image relations, comics flux (evoking Raymond Williams' analysis of television), sociohistorical aspects of comics and the contextualization of comics in the light of changing concepts of the images and techniques of visualization. Thierry Smolderen offers a historical discussion of comics styles and introduces his concept of 'polygraphy' to consider them. The final chapters consider comics' cinematic connections (Stefanelli; Gordon) and the rise of the graphic novel (Baetens). Philippe Marion proposes his concepts of *séries culturelles* (cultural series, developed with film scholar André Gaudreault), *médiagenie* (media genius) and 'graphiation' to offer a preliminary poetic framework for understanding comics. The volume has a forward-looking conclusion that provides the foundations of a cultural theory of comics through emphasizing the strategic marginality of comics, the immersiveness of comics, its affordances and liminal modernity, since it combines both pre-modern and modern elements.

Alexander Dunst, Jochen Laubrock and Janina Wildfeuer's *Empirical Comics Research* (2018, Routledge Advances in Comics Studies series) introduces quantitative methods ranging from digital tools for corpus selection (Beaty and Woo) and analysis to linguistic and cognitive perspectives. The latter include models for quantitatively analysing images, such as Dunst and Hartel's 'visual stylometry' (43–61) and Rigaud and Burie's chapter on coding images through combining different degrees of visual complexity (from 'high level' to 'low level'). Other chapters discuss aspects as diverse as the analysis of fan mail in *Amazing Spider-Man* from 1963–95 (Walsh, Martin and St. Germain) and drawn lines (Lefèvre and Meesters). Bateman, Beckmann and Varela analyse reader response to page layouts, while three other chapters combine eye-tracking and questionnaires to study character developments (Tseng et al.), degrees of information conveyed by comics (Bucher and Boy) and the stimuli steering eye movements (Kirtley et al.). The volume ends with linguist and comics scholar Neil Cohn's discussion of his visual language theory as a means of quantitatively studying comics. Another useful source for broaching the digital analysis of comics is John A. Walsh's online article explaining the development of a comic book markup language (2012).

Tackling the rarely broached issue of the (primarily) visual style in comics, each chapter of *Style(s) de (la) bande dessinée* (2019), edited by Benoît Berthou and Jacques Dürrenmatt, is co-written by several comics scholars. In focusing on comics style, the book exemplifies the move away from literary modes of analysis to a focus on the visual. It opens with a chapter on collaboration and its potential imprint (or lack thereof) on style and then covers the notions of inheriting and imitating, the creation of individualistic styles, intermedial connections, manipulation of formal elements of comics, the role of genre and the discursive use of style, highlighting its ambivalence in the processes of both legitimation and contestation.

Exemplifying studies oriented around key works, Thierry Groensteen's *The Expanding Art of Comics: Ten Modern Masterpieces* (2017; trans. Ann Miller) combines comics history with close reading of 'masterpieces', or game-changing comics from both sides of the Atlantic, beginning with Hugo Pratt's *The Ballad of the Salty Sea* (1967) and ending with Jens Harder's *Alpha* (2015) and *Beta* (2019). Notably most of the works considered are graphic novels rather than mainstream comics, and many of them are canonical and widely acclaimed (*Watchmen, Building Stories, Fun Home, L'Ascension du Haut Mal* [*Epileptic*], and Dominique Goblet's *Faire semblant c'est mentir* [*Pretending Is Lying*] [2007]).

Expanding the scope to discuss several thematic elements oriented around key works, Hillary Chute's *Why Comics? From Underground to Everywhere* (2019) aims at a broad audience. It discusses comics through ten angles, arguing for the medium's distinctive connection with each of them: disaster, superheroes, sex, suburbs, cities, punk, illness and disability, girls, war, queer. Chute ends with a coda on fans which includes an overview of comics conventions and cosplay. This book was recently the subject of a *PMLA* special issue in which articles further develop the premise in Chute's title – why comics? – and engage critically with the book.

This chapter has offered an overview of the rich body of comics studies textbooks, especially critical reference works with a broad scope. Testifying to a rapidly growing field, the works mentioned above reflect the interdisciplinary inclinations of comics studies. Even though literary scholars still dominate the field, cultural studies, history and art history are gradually acquiring greater prominence. Furthermore, there is a diverse body of literature offering suggestions on how to incorporate comics into a variety of courses and study programmes.

Works cited

Abel, Julia and Klein, Christian. *Comics und Graphic Novels: Eine Einführung.* Stuttgart: J. B. Metzler, 2016.

Aldama, Frederick L. *The Oxford Handbook of Comic Book Studies.* Oxford: Oxford University Press, 2019.

Baetens, Jan and Frey, Hugo. *The Graphic Novel: An Introduction.* Cambridge: Cambridge University Press, 2014.

Baetens, Jan, Frey, Hugo and Tabachnick, Stephen E. (eds). *The Cambridge History of the Graphic Novel.* Cambridge: Cambridge University Press, 2018.

Barry, Lynda. *What It Is.* Montreal: Drawn & Quarterly, 2008.

Barry, Lynda. *Picture This: The Near-Sighted Monkey Book.* Montreal: Drawn & Quarterly, 2010.

Barry, Lynda. *Syllabus: Notes from an Accidental Professor.* Montreal: Drawn & Quarterly, 2014.

Berwald, Jean-Pierre. 'Teaching French Language and Culture by Means of Humor'. *The French Review* 66:2, 1992: 189–200.

Bramlett, Frank, Cook, Roy T. and Meskin, Aaron (eds). *The Routledge Companion to Comics.* New York: Routledge, 2016.

Brown, James W. 'Comics in the Foreign Language Classroom: Pedagogical Perspectives'. *Foreign Language Annals* 10:1, 1977: 18–25.

Brown, Matthew J., Duncan, Randy and Smith, Michael J. (eds). *More Critical Approaches to Comics: Theories and Methods.* New York: Routledge, 2019.

Brunetti, Ivan. *Cartooning: Philosophy and Practice.* New Haven, CT: Yale University Press, 2011.

Burger, Alissa (ed.) *Teaching the Graphic Novel in the English Classroom: Pedagogical Possibilities of Multimodal Literacy Engagement.* New York: Palgrave Macmillan, 2018.

Cary, Stephen. *Going Graphic: Comics at Work in the Multilingual Classroom.* Portsmouth, NH: Heinemann, 2004.

Chute, Hillary. *Why Comics? From Underground to Everywhere.* New York: Harper, 2017.

Duncan, Randy, Smith, Matthew J. and Levitz, Paul. *The Power of Comics: History, Form and Culture.* London: Bloomsbury, 2009.

Dunst, Alexander, Laubrock, Jochen and Wildfeuer, Janina (eds). *Empirical Comics Research: Digital, Multimodal and Cognitive Methods.* London: Routledge, 2018.

Elsner, Daniela, Helff, Sissy and Viebrock, Britta. *Films, Graphic Novels and Visuals – Developing Multiliteracies in Foreign Language Education – An Interdisciplinary Approach.* Vienna: LIT Verlag, 2012.

Goggin, Joyce and Hassler-Forest, Dan (eds). *The Rise and Reason of Comics and Graphic Literature: Essays on the Form.* Jefferson, NC: McFarland and Company, 2010.

Groensteen, Thierry. *The Expanding Art of Comics: Ten Modern Masterpieces.* Ann Miller (trans.). Jackson, MS: University Press of Mississippi, 2017.

Heer, Jeet and Worcester, Kent (eds). *A Comics Studies Reader.* Jackson, MS: University Press of Mississippi, 2008.

Hill, Crag (ed.) *Teaching Comics through Multiple Lenses: Critical Perspectives.* New York: Routledge, 2017.

Kashtan, Aaron. 'ENGL 1102: Literature and Composition, Handwriting and Typography'. *Composition Studies* 43:3, 2015. https://www.uc.edu/content/dam/uc/journals/composition-studies/docs/backissues/43-1/43.1%20Kashtan.pdf

Kirtley, Susan E., Garcia, Antero and Carlson, Peter E. (eds). *With Great Power Comes Great Pedagogy: Teaching, Learning, and Comic Books.* Jackson, MS: University Press of Mississippi, 2020.

Kukkonen, Karin. *Studying Comics and Graphic Novels.* Hoboken, NJ: Wiley-Blackwell, 2013.

Marsh, Rufus K. 'Teaching French with the Comics'. *The French Review* 51:6, 1978: 777–785.

Maigret, Éric and Stefanelli, Matteo (eds). *La bande dessinée: une médiaculture.* Paris: Arman Colin, 2012.

Miller, Ann. *Reading Bande Dessinée: Critical Approaches to the French-language Comic Strip.* Bristol: Intellect, 2007.

Misemer, Leah. 'English 177: Literature and Popular Culture: The Graphic Novel'. *Composition Studies* 43:3, 2015. https://www.uc.edu/content/dam/uc/journals/composition-studies/docs/backissues/43-1/43.1%20Misemer.pdf.

Packard, Stephan, Rauscher, Andreas, Sina, Véronique, Thon, Jan-Noël, Wilde, Lukas R. A. and Wildfeuer, Janina. *Comicanalyse: Eine Einführung.* Stuttgart: J. B. Metzler, 2019.

'On Hillary Chute's Why Comics'. *PMLA* 134:3, 2019: 569–637.

Smith, Matthew J. and Duncan, Randy (eds). *Critical Approaches to Comics: Theories and Methods.* New York: Routledge, 2011.

Stein, Daniel and Thon, Jan-Noël (eds). *From Comic Strips to Graphic Novels: Contributions to the Theory and History of Graphic Narrative.* Berlin: De Gruyter, 2013.

Tabachnick, Stephen E. (ed.) *Teaching the Graphic Novel.* New York: MLA, 2009.

Tabachnick, Stephen E. (ed.) *The Cambridge Companion to the Graphic Novel.* Cambridge: Cambridge University Press, 2017.

Varnum, Robin and Gibbons, Christina T. (eds). *The Language of Comics: Word and Image.* Jackson, MS: University Press of Mississippi, 2007.

Walsh, John A. 'Comic Book Markup Language: An Introduction and Rationale'. *Digital Humanities Quarterly* 6:1, 2012. http://www.digitalhumanities.org/dhq/vol/6/1/000117/000117.html.

Yang, Gene Luen. 'Comics in Education', 2003. http://www.geneyang.com/comicsedu/index.html

Yang, Gene Luen. 'Graphic Novels in the Classroom. Language'. *Arts* 85:3, 2003. https://www.ncte.org/library/NCTEFiles/Resources/Journals/LA/0853-jan08/LA0853Graphic.pdf

CHAPTER 12
CONCLUSION

In this Guide we have aimed to condense and structure the rapidly growing, and still diversifying, scholarship on comics. This has not been easy, and in selecting areas for consideration we remain conscious of what has had to be omitted. Nonetheless, we hope that the summaries contained here offer students and new academics an entry point to some of the main research areas of comics studies. For those already working in the field, it is hoped that the arrangement of this book and the dialogue created between texts will reveal new points of synergy and key debates. While many of the works discussed relate to more than one of our chapter headings, we have tried to group criticism productively to identify emergent trends and recurring questions. In the process we have also aimed to go back in time as far as possible to uncover early exemplars of comics criticism. Along with the international scope we have strived for, this highlights the importance of historically and culturally contextualizing criticism and the necessity to create a dialogue across contexts.

Surveying the work that has been done, it seems that some debates have played out more than others. Attempts to identify the first comic, or to arrive at a universal working definition of comics, seem doomed to circularity. Such touchstones have been the backbone of many major works with a historical focus, although progress has been made recently by giving attention and voice to more marginalized genres or through a tighter focus on overlooked periods. Other prominent recent trends include an interest in the global history of comics that stretches back as far as the eighteenth century and includes comic strips and comics magazines of the type that are often omitted from the archives. Similarly, there has been increased focus on diversity and the representation of minorities in comics across multiple genres and cultures and on the presence of minorities in comics making. Notably, but not unsurprisingly, these trends in scholarship are also reflected in the comics being published that are moving towards more diverse characters. Comics are also being increasingly considered within a transmedial context (with a focus on adaptation theory, remediation and so forth).

As well as identifying trends shared across themes and cultures, surveying the field has also revealed much about the research methods of comics scholars. It could be claimed that a methodological shift has taken place, with an increased focus on visual, cultural studies or even sociologically oriented criticism. Comics studies' interdisciplinary background has led to a combination of diverse critical traditions in some respects (as comics may be read using literary critical theory, communication theory, psychoanalytically and so forth). Comics studies has, however, historically made its home in literary and cultural studies departments, leading to a dominant set of research methods based primarily on qualitative textual analysis. New research methods have been informed by a deeper awareness of the creative industries, which has placed an increased focus on the negotiated and collaborative processes by which a comic is produced, and the numerous invisible workers involved in this. Leading on from the thematic focus on diversity noted above, an increased emphasis has been placed on ethnographic research methods and sociological perspectives. This has resulted in some larger-scale studies and approaches, for example drawing on quantitative analysis, although there is great scope for further work in this area.

The process of writing this Guide also exposed some surprising gaps in what is being studied. For example, while critical work on children's comics is expanding, Young Adult comics to date seem to have attracted very little scholarly attention. Voices and genres outside the mainstream are also increasing in visibility, but this seems largely dependent on the availability and accessibility of the corpus under study. Unwieldy or hard-to-find series are largely omitted from published scholarship and large areas of the globe are ignored. While an increased focus on graphic novels has led to greater critical engagement with new genres and more serious themes, surveying this scholarship also indicates that we must proceed with caution and be wary of establishing a narrow canon of texts within a medium of such great flexibility and potential.

Compiling this Guide also revealed a pressing need for more translation of critical work and greater dialogue across linguistic and cultural spheres. While our critical discussion has touched on some French-language publications, we have effectively limited ourselves to works published in English for this Guide to be workable. Translation of scholarship should be a priority as the field develops further, and we must also look to our international conferences and other events, journals and blogs, as well as technological communications, to seek out a greater exchange of ideas.

Just over a decade ago, comics studies was a nascent field with just a couple of academic journals and a handful of university courses. Since then many fully peer-reviewed journals have emerged, alongside dedicated imprints within mainstream publishers' catalogues, and numerous institutions worldwide now offer comics studies courses at both an undergraduate and postgraduate level. Like the comic book itself, legitimation has been a battle (which continues in some spaces), but the process of legitimation itself is far from flawless and contextually revealing.

The rapidly changing and diversifying landscape of comics scholarship means that this work is perhaps best characterized, like a comic book panel, as a particular moment in time and space, viewed from a particular angle. Like practised comics readers, then, we must interpret what is here, fill in the gaps as best we can, and take this knowledge forward as we read on – for who knows what the next panel will bring?

INDEX

Index

Index

Index

Index

Index

Index

Tintin
Age of Bronze
Maus
Persepolis